Social Economy in Asia

Social Economy in Asia

Realities and Perspectives

Edited by
Euiyoung Kim
Hiroki Miura

LEXINGTON BOOKS
Lanham • Boulder • New York • London

Published by Lexington Books
An imprint of The Rowman & Littlefield Publishing Group, Inc.
4501 Forbes Boulevard, Suite 200, Lanham, Maryland 20706
www.rowman.com

6 Tinworth Street, London SE11 5AL, United Kingdom

British Library Cataloguing in Publication Information Available

Library of Congress Cataloging-in-Publication Data

Names: Kim, Euiyoung, 1962- editor. | Miura, Hiroki, editor.
Title: Social economy in Asia : realities and perspectives / edited by Euiyoung Kim,
  Hiroki Miura.
Description: Lanham : Lexington Books, 2021. | Includes bibliographical references
  and index. | Summary: "In Social Economy in Asia: Realities and Perspectives,
  thirteen specialists discuss the multi-dimensional characteristics and challenges
  of the social economy in Asia, arguing for its unique effectiveness as a political
  economic system in the twenty-first century"—Provided by publisher.
Identifiers: LCCN 2020050340 (print) | LCCN 2020050341 (ebook) |
  ISBN 9781498598941 (cloth) | ISBN 9781498598965 (pbk)
  ISBN 9781498598958 (epub)
Subjects: LCSH: Economics—Asia—Sociological aspects. | Sustainable
  Development—Asia—Social aspects. | Asia—Social policy—21st century. |
  Social entrepreneurship—Asia. | Nonprofit organizations—Asia.
Classification: LCC HM548 .S6133 2021 (print) | LCC HM548 (ebook) |
  DDC 330.95—dc23
LC record available at https://lccn.loc.gov/2020050340
LC ebook record available at https://lccn.loc.gov/2020050341

Contents

Preface

The social economy generally refers to a specific form of economic activity, public policy system, or political economic culture, the primary objectives of which are the creation of social and human-centric values rather than profit seeking and accumulation of materialistic wealth. The social economy has been understood as a major part of the third sector in a triangular structure of the welfare state, in which the government (first sector) and market (second sector) were recognized as traditional service providers or problem solvers. The paradigm has emerged in response to the growing social needs and problems of various kinds, which the traditional government or market alone cannot effectively manage or solve.

Based on the classical and philosophical debate and thought on the original meaning of economy, ideals and problems of the contemporary state, and perspectives on modern humanity, the mainstream discourse of social economy emerged and quickly spread in the 1980s and 1990s. In this initial stage, the discussions tended to focus on its organizational activity and institutional forms and design, including cooperatives, mutual benefit societies, civic associations, and foundations. However, the scope of discussion has continued to be enlarged and transformed by embracing newly emerged organizational forms and various issues such as social cooperatives, hybrid organizations, social finance, community capital flow, work integration, civic energy projects, corporate citizenship, as well as public-private partnership (PPP). Recent discourse relating to social economy has also manifested a deep interest in innovative public policies, systems, and a normative culture that are expected to promote such economic activities effectively from broad, strategic, and long-term perspectives. In particular, the policy and system-level discussion has been searching for more effective operating principles or goals associated with the relationship among citizens, state, and the market.

Some influential ideas or concepts include active citizenship and human empowerment, cocreation of services and values, community resilience and ecosystems, democratic innovation and plural coevolution, and inclusive and sustainable development. It is the dynamic synergy of these human-centric norms, systems, organizations, issues, and activities that create the social economy—a unique, practical, and alternative model of a political economic system in the twenty-first century.

A growing number of studies have examined the dynamic and complex nature of social economy, paying attention to the various characteristics and conditions that are embedded in each region and country in the world. While many books and reports have been published on Europe, North and South Americas, and OECD member countries, Asia has been relatively neglected and has received scarce attention thus far. In this book, thirteen researchers from different academic disciplines analyze the reality and perspectives of the social economy in Asia.

Drafts were first presented at the InterAsia Connection meeting cohosted by the Social Science Research Council of the United States and Seoul National University Asia Center of South Korea in April 2016. Based on a series of meetings and workshops during 2017–2019, all drafts were revised and some chapters were added in order to make the book structure more systematic and inclusive. By shedding new light on a region that has been insufficiently studied so far, we hope that our interdisciplinary approach and detailed case studies in this book will help readers better understand the multidimensional characteristics of the social economy in Asia, provide theoretical and policy-relevant implications for scholars and practitioners in the region, and enrich both comparative and global discussion on the social economy.

Chapters in this book are divided into two parts. The first part includes four chapters, introducing theoretical arguments, fundamental controversies and tensions, and comparative perspectives regarding the present social economy in Asia. The second part consists of country-specific case studies on China, Japan, South Korea, and India. Each chapter provides a detailed description on specific cases or practices of social economy, together with the overall environment, conditions, or institutional arrangements in each country. The following are brief introductions of each chapter.

Chapter 1 explores the political environment in which the social economy is developing in Asia and evaluates whether it is instrumentalized by a pre-dominantly market-driven economic development strategy that has characterized the region for many years or whether and to what extent the social economy is an innovative and disruptive force that challenges this strategy. The authors articulate two competing perspectives of the social economy in Asia as developmentalism-functionalism and substantivism, and they conclude that these two tendencies are in tension but the balance is shifting to the latter. Regarding the substantive social economy, chapter 1 elaborates Karl Polanyi's thought on the economy and the good life and its possible applications.

Chapter 2 identifies two interesting phenomena in development discourse and practices in Asia over the recent decades: the expansion of social protection, mainly through various forms of tax-financed or subsidized contribution-based noncontributory schemes; and the emergence of various forms of the Social and Solidarity Economy (SSE). The authors argue that these two expansion processes in the context of "social turn" have created three interfaces where social policy and the SSE interact with each other: development strategy, participation, and partnership. This chapter explains actors, institutions, and processes involved in the interactions between social policy and the SSE in Asia and identifies opportunities and challenges created by specific tensions in each interface, and strategies to scale up both social policy and the SSE in a synergistic way.

Chapter 3 presents a comparative view of mapping social economy organizations (SEOs) in China, Japan, and South Korea, based on the detailed analysis of more than sixty legal institutions and major policies governing social organizations of the three countries. From a unique and systematic perspective, the authors categorize the social organizations of the three Asian countries into four groups according to their relevance to an ideal governing structure of social economy organizations in terms of their democratic, economic, and social realms. The authors emphasize that we need to pay more attention to the quasi-social economy organizations (e.g., commercialized producer cooperatives, noninstitutionalized community service organizations, corporate social responsibility of for-profit enterprises) in addition to the major social economy organizations (e.g., certified social enterprises and grassroot consumer cooperatives) in order to realize a more inclusive, complementary, and effective organizational ecosystem and enable more effective social service provision.

Chapter 4 is a comparative study of three Southeast Asian cases of SSE. By utilizing the United Nations' Sustainable Development Goals (SDGs) framework, the author explores the goals, targets, critical indicators, and common challenges of the three cases. The first case is HomeNet in Thailand, an organization working with the informal sector. The second case is OA Organics in Malaysia, an organization working for the indigenous forest-based communities who are making the transition from nomadic life to organic farms. The third case is Dompet Dhuafa in Indonesia, an Islamic philanthropy and investment entity seeking to empower rural communities through microfinance and community development. These alternative stories are innovative initiatives of human empowerment, seeking local solutions in addressing their challenges through mutual cooperation and self-determination.

Chapter 5 explores the relationship between the state, the market, and social service organizations in China through a case study of Happy Living, a social service organization that provides senior and youth services in Hangzhou. Its funding largely comes from government contracts, even though efforts have been made to transform the youth services sector of the organization into a de facto social enterprise in order to diversify its sources of revenue. Because of the budgetary restrictions in government-funded projects, the organization has devised multiple ways, including creative accounting, to get around the restrictions and sustain its operations. The authors suggest that, for social service organizations like Happy Living to provide real alternatives to provisions by the state and the capitalist market in China, it will require more participation in the organization's operation and decision-making process by multiple stakeholders including staff members and beneficiary groups, bringing back their agency. In addition, more meaningful collaboration with other social service organizations will be needed to integrate and coordinate the entire sector and develop solidarity in China.

Chapter 6 focuses on Japanese nonprofit organizations (NPOs). The status of the Japanese social economy has drastically changed since the late 1990s and the Law to Promote Specified Nonprofit Activities was enacted in 1998 which introduced the free establishment of NPOs by citizens. The author summarizes the background, basic institution, and the current state of NPOs as new social economic organizations in Japan. Through the statistical and comparative analysis of prefectures in Japan, the author also discusses the multiple factors including the government, market, and civil society which have specific influence in their respective realms growth and area expansion.

Chapter 7 explains how social economy institutions have evolved in South Korea. Despite the traditional argument that the growth of social enterprises is attributed to the country's characteristically strong leadership role undertaken by the central government, the author tries to provide an alternate explanation by highlighting the role of the third sector as the "policy entrepreneur." Traditionally, the role of civil society in South Korea has been focused on participation in the "politics of protest" during the 1980s and 1990s. However, its main concern and awareness have begun to be transformed. As a result, coproduction and cocreation of social value has received more attention since the early 2000s. This chapter showcases successful development of social enterprises despite the absence of a welfare state or a well-developed third sector at this early development stage and argues that the South Korean experience should hold numerous policy implications for other Asian countries.

Chapter 8 discusses the SSE as a means of implementation of the SDGs at the local level. The author carries out a network analysis of 249 social economy organizations and enterprises (SEOEs) in Seoul, South Korea. The analysis found out that they have strong potential to contribute to achieving all targets established in Seoul city's SDGs. Particularly, the analysis provides evidence of their meaningful contribution to the following targets: reduce all forms of inequality; end poverty in all its forms; inclusive, safe, and sustainable cities for all citizens; inclusive and sustainable economic growth and decent work; quality education and lifelong learning; sustainable consumption and production; good health and well-being; and infrastructure and industrialization. The chapter also emphasizes that there is considerable scope to adopt further innovations to achieve the SDGs at the local level. In particular, SEOEs prioritizing economic and social objectives need to pay more attention to environmental SDGs to ensure that they themselves are genuinely integrated and balanced at the local level.

Chapter 9 analyzes a case of social innovation in India, which can be also interpreted as part of the entrepreneurial dimension of the social economy. In order to understand the challenges and opportunities of employing social innovation to create social value and empower agency, the author conducted research on a hybrid public-private initiative called Women on Wheels, which trains and employs poor urban women as chauffeurs and taxi drivers in New Delhi. Preliminary findings provide evidence of the potential for social innovation to alleviate poverty and promote gender equality. Through the study of an innovative urban economic empowerment project that brings together state agencies, nongovernmental organizations, corporations, and social enterprises, the author argues for the emergence of a hybrid model of capitalism, multiple-stakeholder governance, and civil society participation that may provide a viable means for promoting social justice.

Co-editors
Euiyoung Kim
Hiroki Miura

Acknowledgment

This research was supported by the Research Grants for Asian Studies funded by Seoul National University Asia Center.

Part I

THEORETICAL AND
COMPARATIVE PERSPECTIVES

Chapter 1

A Polanyian View of the Social and Solidarity Economy

Against Developmentalism-Functionalism

Marguerite Mendell and Gibin Hong

INTRODUCTION

The development of the Social and Solidarity Economy (SSE) throughout Asia is the subject of a great deal of attention today. This is not surprising given the recognition of the role of the SSE in the social and economic development of many countries throughout the region, the rapid growth of SSE initiatives internationally, the adoption of numerous enabling public policy measures throughout the world, and the recent recognition of the potential role of the SSE in achieving the 2030 Sustainable Development Goal (SDGs) of the United Nations (Utting 2015).

In this chapter, we will explore the political environment in which the SSE is developing in Asia and evaluate whether it is being instrumentalized by a predominantly market-driven economic development strategy that has characterized the region for many years or whether and to what extent the SSE is an innovative and disruptive force that challenges this strategy. It is well known that, despite the economic performance of many countries in Asia and the perceived image of the region as the "engine" of the growth in the world economy, the dramatic expansion of the market economy has also generated much discontent and social instability throughout the region. The very high population density of the "Rimland" of the Pacific and Indian oceans has also increased the social costs brought about by rapid industrialization and economic growth and thus, the risk of social upheaval (cf. Sloan 1988). How do we understand the rise of the SSE in this context? We will present two competing perspectives that represent different realities and visions of the SSE in Asia.

Asia is a region where "developmentalism" has been applied over a long period of time, prioritizing rapid economic growth over any other objectives and values (Evans 1995). Moreover, this "developmentalist" approach reduces social relations and institutions to functionalist responses to accommodate the prevailing developmentalist agenda and to attenuate its social consequences.

Developmentalism-functionalism acts as the framework in which massive restructuring of social relations and institutions is conceived and executed. For example, it is clear that the emergence and growth of the SSE in many Asian countries increasingly requires legal and institutional forms both to define and distinguish its organizational structure and objectives and to "scale" its activities. Therefore, the question we ask is if the SSE in Asia is best understood within a framework of developmentalism-functionalism that circumscribes its role, its various subfields and organizations and, in the worst case, distorts its true nature and significance. Or is the reality of the SSE today and its increasing presence throughout the region, contesting the dominant paradigm and calling into question the underlying assumptions of a developmentalist-functionalist strategy?

Ours is a political economy approach, essential to situate the SSE in Asia within its political, institutional, and cultural context so as to better understand its constraints and its potential. The celebration of the SSE and its rapid growth urgently calls for such an analysis. Only then can we evaluate whether it is contesting the developmentalist-functionalist paradigm through its practice and in so doing, challenging the political forces to acknowledge and legitimate its actions. We hope to open a dialogue on the need for a different conception of the SSE in countries throughout Asia that acknowledges "agency" and "intentionality" as SSE initiatives multiply and gain support internationally, with important lessons for Asia and other parts of the world often caught in the tension between the instrumentalization of the SSE and the recognition of its transformative capacity. In other words, are SSE initiatives emerging in different sectors as autonomous actors challenging its appropriation and instrumentalization?

We need to explore SSE initiatives from the inside, from their self-identity, their objectives, the means created to achieve these goals, their practices of contestation through innovation, how they engage or reengage with the state and other private actors throughout society, and so on. Is the SSE contributing to a pluralization of the economy by assuming an increasing role as a market actor? If so, the development of the SSE in many Asian countries needs to also be understood as voluntary, autonomous, and deliberate actions by individuals within movements, associations, nonprofit organizations, social enterprises, cooperatives, and so on, as they respond to the undermining of security and equality caused by the ruthless pursuit of economic growth, and as they manifest a growing desire to meet societal goals through organizational innovation and collaboration.

Clearly, the inability of both the state and the market to adequately address social instability and inequality is an important factor that motivates people to look to the SSE for alternative solutions. In this sense, the SSE should be seen as an antithesis to the predominance of developmentalism-functionalism. Therefore, to define and institutionalize the SSE within a developmentalist-functionalist framework denies its own logic and identity. Is this occurring? If this characterizes critical scholarship on the SSE, does it suggest a misrepresentation or even a distortion of its reality? Does it reinforce perception of the SSE as residual in a market/state duality? And so on. We wish to provoke an important debate that takes us to the work of Karl Polanyi.

THE RELEVANCE OF KARL POLANYI FOR THE SSE

For the dogma of organic continuity must, in the last resort, weaken man's power of shaping his own history. Discounting the role of deliberate change in human institutions must enfeeble his reliance on the forces of the mind and spirit just as a mystic belief in the wisdom of unconscious growth must sap his confidence in his powers to re-embody the ideals of justice, law, and the freedom in his changing institutions (Polanyi 1977, iiv).

The economic thought of Karl Polanyi offers an alternative perspective from which we may conceptualize the SSE. The "economic solipsism" prevalent in today's world and the developmentalist-functionalist perspective does not capture the true nature and potential of the SSE. Polanyi provides a methodology for our work that insists on the "interdependence of thought and experience." In other words, as we develop an analysis of the SSE, we must work simultaneously on the narrative documenting the diversity of the SSE and conceptually to design the theoretical parameters that bring coherence to this diversity.

Extensive documentation, mapping, sharing of experiences internationally, has provided a rich canvas of democratic, self-organized initiatives in all sectors of society. These are often considered as fragmented and diverse experiences embedded in the dominant neoliberal paradigm and thus politically contained. In fact, the SSE is increasingly becoming a destabilizing force as it institutes a reconfiguration of market/state/civil society relations in many parts of the world, imposing incoherence on existing arrangements. The coexistence of contesting paradigms describes the reality of the context in which the SSE exists in many countries and regions. In Polanyi's terms, the "place of the economy in society" (Polanyi et al. 1957) becomes more complex as SSE initiatives move from the margins to occupy a more vital role as economic actors and engage in processes of economic democratization. Moreover, it imposes the necessity to better understand the SSE within a "wider framework of systemic change," requiring reconceptualization of the economy itself. In a recent article, Marco Berlinguer writes that we need to "encompass a new ecology of forms of production and reproduction, both in its narrower economic meaning and in its broader sense of the production and reproduction of society," so as to place our analysis within a "wider framework of systemic change" (Berlinguer 2014, 103).

Polanyi challenges the basic hypotheses underlying neoclassical economic theory. In sharp contrast to the axiomatic and deductive reasoning of neoclassical theory, Polanyi's concept of a "substantivist economy" defines the economy as the "instituted process" of provisioning that applies to all economies, whether dominated by market, nonmarket, or nonmonetary principles (Polanyi 1957a). His patterns of integration—reciprocity, redistribution, and exchange, to which he added householding—describe forms of economic organization and priorities. Indeed, our contemporary society features each of these patterns of integration, but is dominated by market principles. The SSE, as it evolves today, is another form of provisioning that begins with societal goals and builds the institutional structures and relationships required to achieve them. These include relations of production, consumption, exchange, and distribution governed under a different logic that seeks the "good life" (*buen vivir*) for the human community (Gudynas 2011). To achieve this fully, land, labor, and money, Polanyi's "fictitious commodities," must be removed from the market; these are not produced for sale. The SSE is also a process of "decommodification" as collective forms of ownership of land, of worker cooperatives, of solidarity finance, abound in the SSE, with a reconceptualization of value, both monetary and nonmonetary.

The substantivist economy describes the workings of the SSE and the role of human agency. It is a relational economy, not based on individualism and self-interest. While collective forms of ownership include the same objectives of efficiency and profitability applied to the private economy, value creation is based on needs and desires. Polanyi's economy of provisioning, or the substantivist economy, is all the more relevant to the Asian context so as to challenge the fundamental principles, limitations, and constraints imposed by developmentalism-functionalism.

This chapter first identifies certain features of the developmentalist-functionalist perspective and analyzes how this often contains or limits the practices of SSE in some Asian countries. We then explore Polanyi's prefigurative economic theory as it provides the basis for critique of the dominant model and the outlines of a competing analysis of economy and society. We then introduce those features that distinguish the SSE from the developmentalist-functionalist perspective. Namely, the latter denies the reality of an "intentional" SSE and its socioeconomic strategies of transformation that mobilize all social actors, including the state and the private sector.

TWO REALITIES: TWO COMPETING PARADIGMS—DEVELOPMENTALISM-FUNCTIONALISM VERSUS SUBSTANTIVISM

Developmentalism-functionalism dominated by market ideology has been the prevailing economic development strategy adopted within most of the Asian region. Despite the stark contradictions of a heavily interventionist state, the priority of economic growth associates market-led development with overall societal well-being defined in material terms. This approach identifies the Asian economy today notwithstanding countervailing trends including the SSE throughout the region, or the extensive economic power of large business conglomerates in Japan and South Korea, for example, violating free market principles and actively engaging the state. It is also true that in some cases, such as Japan, sectoral innovations in the SSE have existed for some time, but contained within the dominant preoccupation with growth and an adherence to market principles.

The summary that follows presents two conceptual approaches to the economy, one grounded in neoclassical economic theory, the other drawn from economic anthropology in a debate inspired by Karl Polanyi in the 1960s. This opposition has been called the formalist-substantivist debate and has great value today as we construct a theoretical framework for the SSE as it evolves throughout Asia and internationally.

DEVELOPMENTALISM-FUNCTIONALISM

Developmentalism-functionalism has been the prevailing worldview of twentieth-century capitalism and has exerted an especially powerful influence on Asian countries with a strong commitment to rapid industrialization and economic growth. The following summarizes some of its main features.

The exclusive commitment to economic growth as measured by GDP/GNP.

Enhancing economic power has been the predominant objective of all nation-states since the beginning of the modern era, and, in this sense, Asian countries are not unique in their pursuit of economic growth. However, we may say that they are certainly unique in that economic growth, as measured by GDP/GNP performance, has been and remains the supreme purpose of the state. The increase in the rate of economic growth became the imperative of the nation as a whole in these countries.

In contrast with Asia, this exclusive obsession with economic growth does not characterize the economies of late development. For example, Germany was born as a unified nation in the late nineteenth century and also intensively pursued a state-led strategy of industrialization in order to rival the global hegemony of the British Empire. However, the powerful state of Bismarck and Wilhelm II did not restrict its purpose to the expansion of productive power and national income measured by monetary value. Many economists belonging to the German Historical School with a strong influence on economic policy-making made it their purpose to assure the highest level of moral and cultural life in the civilized world for all and to build the material conditions as well as the cultural environment to achieve this. Many of these economists were actively involved in the Association for Social Policy (*Verein für Socialpolitik*) and became known as "podium socialists." State purpose was closely associated with societal well-being (Shinoya 2001).

For the Keynesian welfare states in postwar Europe, "state purpose" was greater than promoting economic growth. Economic well-being required designing a state architecture guaranteeing economic security for all. The legacy of "social Europe" remains, despite a widespread adoption of neoliberalism across the continent and the source of social and political instability in many countries. Unlike Europe and the resistance to a full-out neoliberal strategy in the past four decades, however, Asia did not share the history and experience of welfare state capitalism that characterized the postwar economy of western Europe.

Society is mobilized to achieve economic growth.

A developmental state takes it for granted that society will conform with the objective of enhancing economic growth. It is the essence of the developmental state that economic backwardness is overcome through the legal force of the state that restructures the whole of society for the purpose of enhancing economic performance.

As A. James Gregor argues, the Fascist regime of Mussolini in Italy was the very first developmental state (Gregor 1995). Chalmers Jones also traced the origin of the Japanese developmental state back to fascist governments in 1930s (Johnson 1982). There are some studies suggesting that the authoritarian form of the developmental state under the Park Jung-Hee regime in South Korea was also modeled upon the fascist Manchu-quo in the 1930s which Park Jung-Hee personally experienced as a military officer in the Japanese army (Han 2007). The nature and objectives of social relations and institutions transformed considerably to correspond with the principle of maximizing the speed of industrialization by means of the most efficient mobilization of human and material resources.

It was in the 1960s that countries such as Japan and South Korea identified "state purpose" with the increase in the rate of economic growth. We need to bear in mind the role of the geopolitics of the Cold War at the time. A group of conservative politicians surrounding Prime Minister Kishi Nobusuke, with the support of the United States, tried to transform Japan into a nation with military autonomy by revising the Constitution. After the massive popular resistance of 1960 (*Anpo* Struggle) thwarted their attempt, the ruling Conservative Party had to shift to an alternative policy line in order to regain its legitimacy among the population. The Ikeda cabinet, which replaced the Kishi administration, identified "doubling national income" as the new state purpose.

A parallel commitment was to be found in South Korea. The Park Jung-Hee administration, which took power with a coup d'état in 1961, focused on the threat posed by Communist North Korea, adopting "Modernizing Fatherland" as the rationale for its iron fist control. Thus, the acceleration of economic growth became the key or even the sole "state purpose" from then on. In the 1980s, post-Maoist China also adopted a new party line prioritizing economic growth even at the cost of contradicting its official ideology. Therefore, the so-called developmental state spread over Asia in the latter half of the twentieth century. This tendency became more pronounced and spilled over into other Asian countries swept up in the tide of neoliberal globalization, since the 1990s. Today, the ability to envision and realize a strategy prioritizing rapid economic growth is the most important pillar of political power in many Asian countries. This is illustrative of how developmentalism-functionalism shapes social reality.

As Cornelius Castoriadis once pointed out, it is a logical absurdity to reduce the reason of existence and concrete forms of a diversity of social relations and institutions to an instrumentalized function (Castoriadis 1987). Human society did not come into being and does not exist for the purpose of performing a set of functions determined and limited by the priorities set by governing institutions. Society is made up of men and women whose lives unfold in relation to others and to the natural environment. And their constant effort to achieve a "good life" both individually and collectively gives rise to the development of various institutions and practices. The key point here is that these do not necessarily (and ought not to) correspond with relationships constructed for the purpose of increasing economic growth. Therefore, the mobilization of society by the developmental state to achieve this goal, necessarily transforms existing social institutions, relations, and practices. This may even include institutions or "movements" representing social organizations. For example, labor unions in Japan and South Korea frequently take the form of separate "company unions" rather than constituting sectoral and/or national confederations. This type of labor union is more oriented toward consolidating the interests of the company than in representing and protecting the interests of working people vis-à-vis capital. This was also true during the Park Jung-Hee regime. In South Korea, the largest cooperative of farmers was transformed into a quasi-government branch delivering state policies to farmers and eventually became one of the largest financial holding companies in Korea. This type of co-optation of social institutions and practices by the developmental state has been widely practiced in numerous areas, such as family, education, even religion, as their nature and function are transformed to contribute to economic growth.

Over the long term, the accumulation of fatigue, discontent, and cynicism regarding the capacity and role of social institutions is inevitable. No doubt, how these institutions and organizations are perceived today is influenced by their legacy of accommodating the state. The hopes of men and women to achieve the "good life" frequently met with frustration, as the mobilization to develop alternative relations and institutions became deformed into apparatuses designed to meet the goals of the state. This total instrumentalization of society leads to the undermining of "social capital" and, in the long term, affects the potential of economic growth itself. This has been the experience of many countries within Asia and is the context in which the SSE exists today.

The SSE is likewise regarded and treated as a functional accessory that complements and enhances the working of the state and market.

If we consider these features of the developmental state, it is not unlikely that a similar type of co-optation of the SSE may occur in many Asian countries. The SSE with its various subfields and organizations might be redefined and institutionalized to correspond with the functions they are given to achieve more efficient economic growth. For example, South Korea is well known for the rapid development of the SSE, but it is embedded in a developmentalist-functionalist perspective that is very common among policy-makers, business people, and even academics. Very frequently, the SSE is seen as a functional accessory to the limits of the state and the market economy, filling the gaps, so to speak. As well, there is often a grotesquely distorted view, that new cooperatives and social enterprises are reserved for "losers," for those who cannot make their way in the competitive market economy, and that, therefore, they are an efficient (meaning inexpensive) means to create employment for those unable to access the labor market. They are also often perceived as efficient (less expensive) public service providers, minimizing the use of public resources to deal with the social fall-out brought about by the excesses of rapid capital accumulation and economic growth.

This perception of the SSE both denies its distinctiveness and its alleged complementarity to the state and market. Instead, it rips it apart into fragments, separating the SSE into different ministries or "silos" of government, for example. The case of South Korea presents a typical example. Different types of organizations in the SSE are under the jurisdiction of different government branches: social enterprise falls under the Ministry of Employment and Labor, the mandate for cooperatives is the Ministry of Strategy and Finance; rehabilitation community centers fall under the Ministry of Health and Welfare, community enterprise under the Ministry of the Interior. Recently there was an attempt to overcome this tendency and integrate the SSE into a coherent whole by enacting the Basic Law of Social Economy, but it was aborted due to opposition by those who argued that giving legal recognition to the SSE and establishing the support that would follow, would constitute a "socialist policy" and undermine the vitality of the market economy. There was a great turmoil in Korean politics between 2016 and 2017, and the newly elected government has adopted a much more proactive position toward the SSE, pressing for the adoption of a Basic Law of Social Value in the parliament. But the fragmented structure described above remains intact, and the Basic Law on Social Economy has yet to be passed.

SUBSTANTIVISM

In numerous writings before and after *The Great Transformation*, Karl Polanyi reflects on subjectivity, collective action, institution building, and economic provisioning. In the 1960s, his substantivist economics challenged the formalist neoclassical school in economic anthropology. As we noted above, substantivist economics describes the workings of all economies, the processes of wealth creation and distribution that, according to Polanyi, are always embedded in cultural and institutional contexts. The SSE institutes processes of economic provisioning, with its own logic embedded in social relations. Today, it is one of the many logics of a differentiated capitalism (Gibson-Graham 2006). Given the current global economic environment, this logic is gaining increasing significance as the dominant paradigm is discredited by its economic and moral failure. For mainstream economists, the SSE is evidence of market failure (Williamson 1981). Paradoxically, this argument has unexpected resonance today, though, of course, in a context of ubiquitous market failure and policy vacuum, this argument also becomes redundant. As an alternative to developmentalism-functionalism, Polanyi's substantivist economics describes the workings and the potentially transformative capacity of the SSE. In summary, the SSE as an economics of provisioning has the following features (Polanyi 1977).

The SSE provides the basis for a new epistemology, for new methodologies and approaches in the social sciences.

It challenges the orthodoxy through practice. As an economy of provisioning, the SSE is committed to societal well-being, to achieving the "good life." It is a relational and situated economy, based in communities. Polanyi's definition of the economy describes the provisioning of "livelihood." Today, theorists grapple with conceptualizing "a new ecology of forms of production and reproduction" (Berlinger, ibid.) arguing for a systemic approach to better comprehend the impact of the growing number of self-organized economic activities on political institutions and power relations. Today, movements, communities, networks, and associations have designed new institutional arrangements, often within the interstices of a developmentalist-fundamentalist ideology, but also increasingly destabilizing established and structured relations between the market, the state, and civil society. Is there evidence that this is occurring within Asia?

Society is not the object of mobilization but the subject that designs an economy of provisioning. In other words, society is an active subject that expresses its own values and organizes the production process to correspond with these values.

Drawing upon Polanyi, any type of group or organization that people voluntarily create in order to provide what is needed for the "good life" constitutes an autonomous subject. Moreover, civil society actors can design or codesign economic relationships embedded in an institutional context that reflects societal goals.

The SSE should be recognized as an undivided whole and granted an identity on a par with the state and market in a "plural" economy.

Within Asia today, the SSE should be recognized as an independent and integral part of a pluralist economy, with its distinct forms of organizing economic life, rather than as a functional accessory, an adjunct to the state and/or market.

In his writings in Vienna in the 1920s, Polanyi participated in debates rejecting both the free market economy and central planning. Inspired by the achievements of the socialist municipal government in Vienna, he sketched the framework for a "functional democracy" or what we may call an "associational economy" (Polanyi 1924a). In many ways, these early writings inform our own work, as we increasingly recognize that the transformative capacity of the SSE will only be realized within a systemic approach, within a new societal architecture. In some regions of the world, this is occurring in localities and regions and increasingly influencing national levels of government. This resonates with the institutional architecture of Polanyi's "functional democracy," its forms of economic organization and governance that codetermine the production and distribution of goods and services.

THE SUBSTANTIVIST ECONOMY
AND THE "GOOD LIFE"

It was not Karl Polanyi who first pointed out that the word "economy" actually contains two entirely different meanings. Ancient Athenians had two different words for each meaning. The Greek word *oikonomia*, the etymon of the English word "economy," literally meant the "governing of the household" and there was a different word, *chrēmatistikē*, for denoting "the art of acquisition." However, in the rapidly expanding market economy in Athens at the time, many Athenians seemed to frequently confuse the two as if they were synonymous. Aristotle began his *Politics* with a discussion of this difference and the relationship between the two meanings. He emphasized that *oikonomia* seeks the satisfaction of material needs of household members, while *chrēmatistikē* only makes sense as a means to achieve the ends of *oikonomia*. In other words, the former should be practiced only as instrumental to the purpose of the latter (Meikle 1997). The economic thought of Aristotle exerted a significant influence on the formation of Karl Polanyi's own thought of substantive economics (Polanyi 1957b).

With the emergence of modern market capitalism, a definition of the economy distinct from Aristotle's *oikonomia* took root: the economy was defined by choice under conditions of scarcity. Underlying this definition are the hypotheses that individuals are driven, above all, by self-interest, a desire to maximize satisfaction. As well, because the desire of human beings is limitless, this necessitates choice, under these conditions of scarcity. This definition of the word "economy" has prevailed since Lionel Robbins first articulated the scarcity principle in 1932 (Robbins 1932). However, some economic thinkers observed early on that this "scarcity" definition of the economy differs from the traditional "livelihood" definition and that the more limited definition of economics did not acknowledge this.

Awareness of this limitation appeared in the writings of economic thinkers in the early twentieth century. Especially noteworthy is the suppression of the publication's second edition of the neoclassical theorist Carl Menger's *Principles of Economics*, in which he distinguished between "technical direction" and "economizing direction" that rejected the scarcity principle and individual choice as the founding principles of economic theory (Menger 1923). Not permitting the publication of this important reformulation of Menger's economic principles limited the awareness of its existence until many years after its completion. Max Weber distinguished between "substantive rationality" and "formal rationality," the institutionalist theorist Thorstein Veblen distinguished between "serviceability" and "vendibility," and the Marxist economist Isaak Illich Rubin distinguished between "technical-material process" and "social form," to name a few.

Karl Polanyi was especially influenced by Carl Menger and Max Weber but, as stated earlier, developed his own "formal" versus "substantive" definitions of the economy.

> One simple recognition, from which all attempts at clarification of the place of the economy in society must start, is the fact that the term economic, as commonly used to describe a type of human activity, is a compound of two meanings. These have separate roots, independent of one another. It is not difficult to identify them, even though a number of broadly synonymous words are available for each. The first meaning the formal, springs from the logical character of the means-ends relationship, as in economizing or economical; from this meaning springs the scarcity definition of economic. The second, the substantive meaning, points to the elemental fact that human beings, like all other living things, cannot exist for any length of time without a physical environment that sustains them; this is the origin of the substantive definition of economic. The two meanings, the formal and the substantive, have nothing in common. (Polanyi 1977, 19)

While Polanyi's critique of the self-regulating market economy is increasingly cited today as the social, economic, and environmental crises brought about by neoliberalism revisit the failures of a self-regulating market economy he identified in *The Great Transformation* and in writings prior to and following its publication, few references are made to the misconception of human behavior, of what makes us human, that underlies his rejection of formal economics. Polanyi stressed that the formal definition was an artifact that denied the reality of human nature, of "societalized man." Methodological individualism denies our true nature as social beings. It has no relevance to a human economy. This point is clearly made in Polanyi's criticism of Max Weber, who adopted the formal definition of "rational choice" in his notion of "economic activity." For Weber, a worker performs "economic activity" only in the moment she decides which enterprise to work for, whereas he considers the actual work she performs each day a "sociological activity" of compliance with the authority of managers (Polanyi 1968, 138). This of course contradicts our common sense that it is the latter which constitutes "economic activity," transforming labor power into a commodity whose monetary value is determined in the labor market.

Moreover, for Polanyi, the formal definition of the economy does not represent our economic reality in a logically consistent way. The scarcity of resources does not automatically translate into the necessity of choice. When there is no competition among different ends, there can be no choice even if the means is extremely scarce. Indeed, this is the argument for responsible consumption in today's economy, as the scarcity of nonrenewable resources is transforming patterns of behavior. We can go further to refer to the growing literature on "abundance" that projects a world dominated by open knowledge rendering the scarcity principle obsolete.

Today, dismissing the relevance of the formal or neoclassical model is, in a sense, easy. It has no bearing on an increasingly complex economic landscape that is made up of a diversity of economic actors and nonmarket relationships that drive the global economy. At the root of this reality are power relations that determine and control the distribution of resources. Moreover, formal economics fully neglects collective needs and the collective means to fulfill them. Methodological individualism has no explanatory power to document and interpret the embeddedness of the SSE in a model founded upon collective commitment to the public good, to the "good life." And it has nothing to say about the growing number of needs and activities of individuals that are not mediated by the market which remain invisible in the formal definition. In Polanyi's words:

Of his wants and needs, only those mattered that money could satisfy through the purchase of things offered in markets; the wants and needs themselves were restricted to those of isolated individuals. Therefore, by definition, no wants and needs other than those supplied in the market were to be recognized, and no person other than individual in isolation was to be accepted as a human being. It is easy to see that what was being tested here was not the nature of human wants and needs but only the description of a market situation as a scarcity situation. In other words, since market situations do not, in principle, know wants and needs other than those expressed by individuals, and wants and needs are here restricted to things that can be supplied in a market, any discussion of the nature of human wants and needs in general was without substance. In terms of wants and needs, only utilitarian value scales of isolated individuals operating in markets were considered. (Polanyi 1977, 29)

The formal definition excludes individual and collective needs and activities that do not have monetary value in the SSE. For example, it was virtually impossible to purchase "organic food" in South Korea before the 1990s, simply because it did not exist in the market. Some groups of the urban middle class who expressed a desire for naturally grown vegetables and grain wanted to contact and directly transact with producers in the country, generating momentum for the burgeoning cooperative movement at the time. This recalls the history of Rochdale, the creation of consumer and producer cooperatives, Robert Owen's Equitable Labour Exchange in the mid-nineteenth century and the development of the international cooperative movement ever since. Today, the rapid growth of consumer, producer, and social or solidarity cooperatives in all sectors of the SSE is meeting various collective needs. These are both a new and unmet needs that neither the market nor the state can fulfill. But today, they are more than organizational forms complementary to the private and public sector. They reflect a growing desire for innovative forms of production to decommodify land, labor, and money by designing and establishing new institutions and collective modes of governance. This is distinct from the market-state duopoly in which "public consumption" as identified by Galbraith to meet a wide range of needs including material, moral, and cultural needs that are not provided by the market or the range of indivisible public goods in the public domain (Galbraith 1958). In order to respond to these needs, a new generation of SSE organizations has emerged including social enterprises and numerous and diverse associations. The social value they create greatly contributes to the "good life," regardless of its valuation in monetary terms.

SOCIETY AND SOLIDARITY

Polanyi adopts the Aristotelian conceptualization of the societalized individual. Influenced by Christian philosophy, Polanyi writes that each person is social in essence. Today, this resonates with Charles Taylor's view that it is our social and dialogical nature that governs our lives as individuals, that determines how we identify ourselves in relation to others as well as our participation in social organizations and groups. In a lengthy manuscript written by a former student of Karl Polanyi in Vienna, he summarizes this philosophy of man [*sic*] that influenced Polanyi at the time.

> Man [*sic*] is not a social being because he lives in society, but rather man can live in society because he is essentially social within his own consciousness. Thus "society" is not something between men, nor over them but within them, within each and every one of them, so that society as reality, not as concept is inherent within the consciousness of each individual. (Felix Shaffer manuscript, Polanyi archive, Shaffer referring to Max Adler's formulation of man in society. Quoted in Mendell and Polanyi Levitt 1987)

For Polanyi, social relations are not something to be reduced to their functions. Relationships are the 'key loci' of the self. Because society is an association of men and women, their solidarity is an end in and of itself, not a means to achieve other aims. As this solidarity develops, it needs to design those "organs" which enable its members to fully develop their potential in various activities. This is how society creates a complex of institutions and practices with their own defined logic and functions. In short, it is a society that actively creates and presides over its own functional branches.

Polanyi's concept of society and its institutions is expressed in his less well-known writings on functional democracy in the 1920s, referred to earlier in which he proposes an institutional architecture of associations of producers and consumers and an overarching "kommune," a citizen's assembly, to work in the collective interest. For it to succeed, it required commitment to the collective well-being (solidarity) as well as the "effective performance of each individual within his particular occupation and function." Polanyi underscored the role of transparent relations between associations, trade unions, civil society organizations, and so on, as vital for the creation of a functional democracy. He was also greatly influenced by the Guild Socialists at the time. In his words:

[Society] is essentially an organism whose individual organs carry out their functions in unity with each other. This is the starting point of the new functional social theory. . . . It derives the causes of social harmony . . . through the lives of the individuals who constitute society. The different functions of individuals are: production, consumption, neighbourly relations, intellectual life and their flourishing. These are the functions that encourage people to form associations: collective production, collective consumption, common neighbourhoods and intellectual associations. The contemporary incarnations of these natural associations are the trade unions, the co-operatives, community organizations, ideological and cultural groups, each of which expresses a function of individual life. (Polanyi quoted in Dale 2014. Polanyi's italic)

This explains why and how Polanyi held Robert Owen in such a high esteem in *The Great Transformation*. He credits Owen with "discovering society" in the throes of the industrial revolution at the turn of the nineteenth century. For Polanyi, Owen went beyond the important work of Henri de Saint-Simon in France, by refusing to accept the separation of society into political and economic functions and, alternatively, embracing a "social approach" that integrated the machine and industry into the society as a whole by reconstructing the latter (Polanyi 1944, 169–71). Owen's view of society was an important source of inspiration for Guild Socialism as well.

Polanyi's functional democracy provides the institutional architecture for the SSE today, a constellation of associations, networks, movements, organized horizontally in dialogic spaces and vertically in an overarching governing body. He was ahead of his times in insisting on our many intersecting identities, as consumers, producers, as members of community, family, social organizations, and so on. Economic activity flows from the interaction of all stakeholders in society. For Polanyi, the challenge was ultimately organizational. How to put in place and operationalize such institutions is today's challenge. This was taken very seriously in the 1920s in the heated debates on socialist accountancy in which Polanyi presented his model as an alternative to both the free market economy and central planning, insisting that a process of democratic negotiation, in which members of society share their knowledge about needs, preferences, as well as any dangers and sufferings inherent in the production processes, would effectively determine prices (Polanyi 1924b). For the SSE to achieve its goals, it requires an institutional architecture or "ecosystem" so that it becomes more than a collection of enterprises and associations that fills in the gaps continuously created by an unyielding adherence to developmentalism-functionalism, despite its mounting failures and urgency for solutions. Only then can the SSE realize its capacity for systemic change. Mobilizing those who are actively engaged in SSE activities beyond sectoral networks is critical to build the broader solidarity required.

THE "GOOD LIFE"

If we reject the formal meaning of the economy, that is, to accumulate as much as possible at the lowest cost, the *telos* of the economy in its substantive meaning cannot be anything other than the "good life." To return to Aristotle, the "good life" is the ultimate criterion in *oikonomia*, by which to determine the quality as well as the quantity of the material means to be acquired. There are two particular aspects of Aristotelian philosophy of the "good life" that we wish to raise. First, the notion of the "good life" in Aristotelian philosophy is closely bound up with that of the "common good" and fundamentally differs from "pleasure" in Benthamite utilitarianism. The latter refers to the pure quantity of satisfaction, regardless of its quality or ethical content, as is shown by Bentham's famous maxim that the poem and the pin are indifferent. In other words, it is entirely a psychological phenomenon within the mind of an individual, and there is no objective criterion by which to make any judgment on the pleasure of any other individual, or to be concerned or to recognize that one's pleasure is intimately linked to the pleasure of others. However, in Aristotelian philosophy, the essence of the "good life" is derived only from the collective life of a political community. For Aristotle, the human being is an "animal of political community." Political community is indispensable for human beings because discussion and a common life with others are the basis of a "good life."

Second, the Aristotelian notion of the "good life" includes *eudaimonia*. This Greek word literally means the condition in which one's divinity (*daimon*) is in a good (*eu*) state. When a person activates her own divinity, it will awaken her physical and spiritual capacity to become a fully developed human being, with many virtues and excellences (*arête*). This is why some translate this word as "human flourishing" (Yack 1993, 97–99).

Understood in this Aristotelian perspective, the notion of the "good life" has significant implications for both the theory and practice of the SSE as it embodies social and ethical values that have been undermined by the financialized market economy and the state that have subordinated these values to the market imperatives. The SSE may be compared to the ancient agora where discussion of social and ethical values and identifying the collective means to achieve the "good life" may flourish and increase the opportunities for its various participants to fully develop their potential.

SITUATING THE SSE IN THEORY AND PRACTICE

From our discussion above, we would suggest a description—not a definition—of the SSE from a Polanyian perspective: provisioning of what is needed for a "good life" through voluntary participation, self-organizing, and solidarity among people. And we would argue that the SSE should be recognized as an integral part of today's economy on a par with the state and market in a "plural" economy in Asia. Let us go one step further to state that this is occurring in some countries. We have only alluded to the diversity and rapid growth of the SSE within Asia and abroad. The international landscape is growing as is its political presence. Still, the conceptual work remains to be done. Working simultaneously on the SSE narrative and the construction of a theoretical framework that embeds the SSE within a systems theory of resource allocation must occur in tandem, as Polanyi astutely advises.

In this chapter, we have suggested that Polanyi inspires a broader reflection on the basic principles of economics that, in fact, undermines the validity of the basic hypotheses of the dominant paradigm and its misrepresentation of human behavior and values. In an article written in the 1920s, he writes:

Beyond the demand for justice in a classless society, the human race's true destiny only first opens up here. It is the realization of the highest social and personal freedom through the concrete conception of solidarity between man and man [*sic*]. The leap does not bring us to the end but only to the beginning of our task. (Polanyi 1927, 315)

The initiatives in the SSE are the work of numerous individuals in organizations, movements, and associations committed to social justice and economic democracy as they design socioeconomic initiatives and develop economic tools and relationships that challenge the limited repertoire of the market/state duopoly. But more fundamentally, as writers and activists in the SSE in Central and Latin America have recognized, achieving a "good life," *buen vivir*, is its ultimate goal. In the last chapter of *The Great Transformation* on "freedom in a complex society," Polanyi writes:

> After a century of blind "improvement" man is restoring his "habitation". If industrialism is not to extinguish the race, it must be subordinated to the requirements of man's nature. (Polanyi 1944, 249)

Polanyi did not live long enough to witness the return of unbridled market liberalism and the discrediting of the postwar compromise, the role of the state and organized labor in many parts of the world. We cannot attribute to Polanyi what we wish to assume, namely, that the SSE is, in his terms, a forceful countermovement that can be interpreted both as accommodating the dominant paradigm but also as the realization of another conception of a humanity committed to social justice, equity, living in harmony with nature, all of which is best achieved through working collectively. These two tendencies are in tension but we believe that the balance is shifting to the latter interpretation of the SSE. And so our chapter contributes to theorizing not only the new economic arrangements of the SSE but also to its capacity to restore a fundamental concept of humanity as a first principle upon which to construct a theoretical framework for the SSE.

REFERENCES

Berlinguer, Marco. 2014. "The Social Economy in Italy: Limits and Possibilities." In *The Solidarity Economy Alternative: Emerging Theory and Practice*, edited by Vishwas Satgar. Durban: University of KwaZulu-Natal Press.

Castoriadis, Cornelius. 1987. *The Imaginary Institution of Society*. London: Blackwell.

Dale, Gareth. 2014. "The Iron Law of Democratic Socialism: British and Austrian Influences on the Young Karl Polanyi." *Economy and Society* 43(4): 650–667.

Evans, Peter. 1995. *Embedded Autonomy States and Industrial Transformation*. Princeton: Princeton University Press.

Galbraith, John K. 1958. *The Affluent Society*. New York: Houghton Mifflin.

Gibson-Graham, J. K. 2006. *A Post-Capitalikst Politics*. Minneapolis: University of Minnesota Press.

Gregor, A. James. 1995. *Fascism and Developmental Dictatorship*. Princeton: Princeton University.

Gudynas, Eduardo. 2014. "Buen Vivir: Today's Tomorrow." *Development* 54(4): 441–447.

Han, Seok-jeong. 2007. *Manjukuk Keonkuk Ui Haeseok* (*The Reinterpretation of the Building of Manchu-kou*). Seoul: Dong-A University Press (in Korean).

Johnson, Chalmers. 1982. *MITI and the Japanese Miracle: The Growth of Industrial Policy*. Stanford: Stanford University Press.

Meikle, Scott. 1997. *Aristotle's Economic Thought*. London: Clarendon Press.

Menger, Carl. 1923. *Grundsätze der Volkswirtschaftslehre* 2. Aufl. mit einem Geleitwort von Richard Schüler, aus dem Nachlaßlerausgegeben von Karl MengerI, Wien und Leipzig.

Polanyi, Karl. 1924a. "The Functionalist Theory of Society and the Problem of Socialist Economic Accounting." In *Karl Polanyi. 2018. Economy and Society*, edited by M. Cangiani and C. Thomasberger. London: Polity Press.

Polanyi, Karl. 1924b. "New Reflections on Our Theory and Practice." In *Karl Polanyi. 2018. Economy and Society*, edited by M. Cangiani and C. Thomasberger. London: Polity Press.

Polanyi, Karl. 1927. "Über die freiheit." In *Karl Polanyi's Vision of a Socialist Transformation*. Montreal: Black Rose Books, 2018.

Polanyi, Karl. 1944. *The Great Transformation: The Political and Economic Origins of Our Time*. Boston: Beacon Press, 1957.

Polanyi, Karl. 1957a. "The Economy as Instituted Process." In *Trade and Markets in Early Empires*, edited by Karl Polanyi et al. Illinois, Glencoe: Free Press.

Polanyi, Karl. 1957b. "Aristotle Discovers the Economy." In *Trade and Markets in Early Empires*, edited by Karl Polanyi et al. Illinois, Glencoe: Free Press.

Polanyi, Karl. 1968. *Primitive, Archaic, and Modern Economies*, edited by G. Dalton. Boston: Beacon Press.

Polanyi, Karl. 1977. *The Livelihood of Man*, edited by H. Pearson. New York: Academic Press.

Polanyi, Karl, Conard Arsenberg, and Harry Pearson. 1957. "The Place of the Economics in Society." In *Trade and Markets in Early Empires*, edited by Karl Polanyi et al. Illinois, Glencoe: Free Press.

Polanyi-Levitt, K., and M. Mendell. 1987. "Karl Polanyi. His Life and His Times." *Studies in Political Economy* 22: 7–39.

Robbins, Lionel. 1932. *An Essay on the Nature and Significance of Economic Science*. London: Macmillan and Co.

Shinoya, Yuichi. 2001. *German Historical School: The Historical and Ethical Approach to Economics*. London: Routledge.

Sloan, Geoffrey R. 1988. *Geopolitics in United States Strategic Policy, 1890–1987*. Birmingham: Harvester Wheatsheaf.

Utting, Peter. 2015. "Realizing the 2030 Development Agenda Through Social and Solidarity Economy." Think paper commissioned by the United Nations Inter-Agency Task Force on Social and Solidarity Economy (UNTFSSE).

Williamson, Oliver. 1981. "The Economics of Organization: The Transaction Cost Approach." *American Journal of Sociology* 87(3): 548.

Yack, Bernard. 1993. *The Problems of a Political Animal*. Berkeley: California University Press.

Chapter 2

Synergistic Interactions between Social Policy and SSE in Developing Countries

Interfaces in Discourse and Practice

Ilcheong Yi, Hyuk-Sang Sohn, and Taekyoon Kim

INTRODUCTION

Facing[1] multiple[2] developmental challenges, an increasing number of governments in both developing and developed countries are paying attention to the importance of Social and Solidarity Economy (SSE) that creates jobs, combats poverty and inequality, and empowers workers. SSE, defined as economic activities and relations that prioritize social and often environmental considerations over private economic interests and profits, covers a diverse range of organizations and enterprises. They include but are not limited to cooperatives, mutual associations, grant-dependent and service-delivery nongovernmental organizations (NGOs), and communities and other forms of voluntary groups that produce goods and services, self-help groups, fair trade networks and other forms of solidarity purchasing, consumer groups involved in collective providing, associations of informal workers, and new forms of profit-making social enterprises and social entrepreneurs and NGOs that are having to shift from a dependence on donations and grants to sustaining themselves via income-generating activities. They involve forms of democratic management and governance which are often linked to active citizenship and democratic participation (Utting 2013).

Various contexts and factors have been combined to prompt SSE to expand, particularly in developing countries. Globalization, economic liberalization, and multiple crises in finance, food, and energy sectors often resulted in a heightened vulnerability, particularly among those living in developing countries. People, notably those affected heavily by these crises, began to organize themselves and engage in various forms of SSE organizations and enterprises to defend or improve their livelihoods. The expansion of SSE has also been accelerated by the increase of political and social forces organizing marginalized identities such as women and indigenous people. The search for alternatives to the norms and policies of market fundamentalism such as *Buen Vivir*, degrowth, and food sovereignty has provided normative underpinnings to SSE activists and practitioners (UNRISD 2016).

Laws, government's development policies, programmers, and institutions, particularly social policy programs and institutions, play a significant role in helping the SSE expand itself, exert its full potential for development, and be resilient and stable over time (UNRISD 2016). For instance, to implement social policy programs, governments in many developing countries, particularly those under fiscal constraints, have often sought partnerships with the private sector in delivering social services rather than expand the public sector. Public social service delivery by private sector institutions based on government contracts has resulted in various unintended negative impacts such as fragmented welfare infrastructure, low quality service, and adverse selection. SSE organizations and enterprises involved in delivering the contracted-out public services also run the risk of being coopted and instrumentalized by the government (UNRISD 2017).

Can SSE and social policy avoid these pitfalls? How can they create synergies in the sense that they are mutually reinforcing each other to deliver a high-quality social service in an inclusive manner and realize the mandated purposes, normative values, and organizational autonomy of SSE? To answer this question, we review the development discourses that offer an insight on interfaces between social policy and SSE and examine both discourses and policy practices with a focus on issues associated with participation and partnership which are considered key mechanisms of good, coherent, and synergistic governance (Brinkerhoff 2007; Waheduzzaman 2010). Given the exploratory nature of this research, the main purpose here is to draw insights on the synergies between SSE and social policy rather than undertake rigorous empirical analysis.

The chapter is structured as follows. The following section explains our approach to the interfaces between social policy and SSE within the broad context of state-society relations. Pointing to the limits of the past approaches to state, society, or state-society relations in explaining the interfaces between social policy and SSE, we suggest a new approach to social policy and SSE which can explain the distinctive forms and nature of social policy programs and SSE organizations and enterprises through its focus on relations between actors, institutions, and processes. It provides a conceptual and explanatory framework for the examination of empirical cases of interfaces between social policy and SSE in the context of state-society relations. The following empirical cases offer an opportunity to identify the exogenous conditions and endogenous factors including institutions, policies, and actors to facilitate participation and partnerships in the interfaces of social policy and SSE. In conclusion, the study draws lessons on making synergies between SSE and social policies, scaling up SSE, and creating enabling policy environments for SSE enhancement without weakening the institutional strength of the public sector. With these findings and lessons, the ultimate aim is to deepen the understanding of various pathways of SSE scaling-up in a sustainable way.

INTERFACES BETWEEN SSE AND SOCIAL POLICIES

All the major paradigms about the state, despite their different focuses on plural interest groups, elites, and classes, agree that the core function of the state is to regulate, coordinate, or govern multiple relations between social groups (Alford 1975). The interfaces between the voluntary sector including SSE and social policy constitute the state-society relation these major paradigms aimed to address. State-society relations have been a long-standing issue for academic debates (Migdal 1988), in particular in academic disciplines researching the issues associated with the voluntary sector to which most SSE enterprises and organizations belong. Various theories, premises, and concepts of state-society relations, however, have often revealed their limitations regarding their explanatory and analytical capacities. One of the major sources of these limitations is the biases or narrow understandings of the state and society themselves. For instance, the so-called statist or state-centered approach, placing primary focus on the state, highlights the regulatory role. The voluntary sector is explained mainly through the lens of the government such as in relation to government subsidies. Some variants of the state-centered approach show how state functions and wills are translated into NGOs by focusing on various institutional mechanisms other than regulation. However, approaches which emphasize concepts such as embeddedness mainly focus on capital rather than on civil society (Evans 1995, 2014). In this line of research, the autonomy of the state is assessed as against capital, thereby sidelining voluntary agencies (Wolch 1990).

The tendency to treat the state as a homogenous entity is also problematic in understanding various state-society relations. Modern states are comprised of institutionally distinctive policy sectors with highly diverse organizational structures. And the relations these policy sectors form with the society are also diverse. Even within the area of research which treats the subjects as homogeneous such as the welfare state or welfare regime, we can find vertical and programmatic diversity between national and local, and between income maintenance, housing, health, education, and care (Fine 2017). Neglecting the sectoral distinctiveness of welfare programs and policies constituting the welfare state significantly reduces the explanatory power of the theories or concepts which deal with the relations between the state and society. Scant attention to the distinctiveness of different aspects or parts of the state is also found in the case of national-level policy advice from donor agencies that impose undue homogeneity across different localities. This is problematic given that interactions between institutions, policies, and actors at the local level create different locality from one region to another (Sellers 2010).

Insensitivity to different social and geographical settings combined with Eurocentric concepts about civil society often excludes various hybrid forms of voluntary organizations which messy social construction processes in developing countries inevitably produce (Corry 2010). Although many studies indeed employ diverse terms and concepts to describe different agents of civil society in developing countries, since the meanings of these terms and concepts are in many cases similar to each other, it is fair to say that they have not been successful in capturing the distinctiveness of different forms of civil society organizations (Roginsky and Shortall 2009). As such, mainstream theories and concepts which fail to capture the diversity and distinctive nature of the state and civil society may not be helpful in deepening our understanding of the relations between social policy and SSE.

To deepen our understanding of SSE and social policies, in particular the distinctiveness of SSEs and social policies in different contexts, we establish several new approaches. First of all, we try to identify SSE both in terms of activities and organizations. On the one hand, SSE can be viewed as a particular form of communication between different systems, be it government or nongovernment, which facilitates economic activities prioritizing nonprofit values including but not limited to social and environmental values. On the other hand, SSE is also understood as a concept encompassing diverse organizations including both traditional social economy or third sector organizations and enterprise. The SSE concept, elaborated with activities and organizational entities, offers various analytical advantages, particularly in light of difficulties related to hybrid forms of SSE organizations and various interactions between SSE and public policies. Within this analytical approach, public policies, which have been normally treated as an exogenous variable or environment with unidirectional influence on SSE organizations, can be seen as an endogenous variable constituting a specific or distinctive SSE system, or what is often called the ecosystem of SSE.

Secondly, we also pay particular attention to different levels and sectors of SSE to identify their distinctive characteristics, particularly of SSE organizations and enterprises in developing countries. As a growing number of developing countries have adopted new policies, laws, and programs to promote

SSE or some aspects of it, many studies actively examine the variation of the so-called SSE turn at the national level (Corragio 2015). However, the fact that the existing literature mostly uses or borrows macro-level theories and concepts results in ignoring the contrasting details and differentiations shown by diverse actors involved in micro-level interfaces. Previous research focusing on local governments as a key player pays less attention to the sectoral differences, since it borrows the concept of the state as a homogeneous or monolithic entity from state-centered discourses such as the developmental state (Bateman 2015).

To explain the facilitators or inhibitors of synergy-making between social policies and SSE, while simultaneously reflecting the specific conditions for SSE in developing countries, we focused on both discursive and practice levels, in particular participation and partnerships which are considered the key elements of good governance for development. Explanations on these interfaces can offer an insight to those concerned with making synergies between policy sectors and institutions.

INTERFACES IN DISCOURSE:
DEVELOPMENT STRATEGIES

Since the late 1970s, the state-society relations of developing countries, particularly those dependent upon foreign assistance, have been profoundly influenced by the macroeconomic policies or policy frameworks imposed by international donors. For much of the 1980s and 1990s, neoliberal stabilization and market fundamentalism were advanced as the dominant norms and principles underpinning development strategies. Under these neoliberal prescriptions, redistributive social policies were treated as a source of market distortions. Government spending on social policy with a goal for redistribution in health, education, and pension was retrenched to conform to market principles and so as not to impose constraints on both the instruments and scale of macroeconomic policies.

This retrenchment was accompanied with a changed view on the state, particularly in developing countries: the state is a source of economic instability and inflation rather than a solution. The change of macroeconomic views and consequently development framework curtailed government's social expenditure and left a big gap in social service provision. Instead, the voluntary sector has been spotlighted as a good substitute to fill the gaps that governments otherwise should have taken actions for (Kendall 2003; Deakin 2001), and in some countries in Africa, Asia, and Latin America, up to one-third of health care services were provided by voluntary organizations in the 1990s (Hecht and Tanzi 1994). Not only prevailing views of the state as a source of the problem rather than a solution, but also growing pressure from NGOs for popular participation helped to create an interface between social policy and SSE, which was not integrated into macro-level government policies and mostly remained at project levels (Mkandawire 2004). The strategy of NGO-centered social service delivery did not make a great contribution to enhancing the capacity of local NGOs involved in service delivery, as the resources for the third sectors' delivery of service were mainly channeled into INGOS which became an increasingly important actor in the development policies of the 1980s (Agg 2006).

The 1990s witnessed increasing uncertainty and doubt about the development strategies based predominantly on the pursuit of market-friendly policies and stability. Social concerns such as poverty in multiple dimensions became prominently placed on the global and national development agendas at the turn of the millennium. The challenges to and tensions within the market principles and economic growth-centered development paradigm created a momentum for the turn of ideas and practices. They emphasized the social aspects of development, which have been often dubbed as "Post-Washington Consensus" (Stiglitz 2009), "quiet revolution" (Barrientos and Hulme 2009), or "social turn" (UNRISD 2016). Along with this ideational turn, new players such as emerging donors, charitable institutions, transnational corporations, and social movements emerged and entered into a "contested terrain of emerging global governance" (Deacon 2007; Ghimire 2005; Josselin and Wallace 2001). It is noteworthy that developing countries themselves also started establishing regional mechanisms to address transnational social problems in the region, creating a space of alternatives to the traditional donor-oriented social policy discourse and practice (Deacon 2007; O'Brien et al. 2000).

This social turn was strongly manifested in internationally agreed development initiatives and goals such as the UN's Millennium Development Goals, the International Labour Organisation (ILO)-UN's Social protection floors initiative, and the UN Resolution on Universal Health Coverage (UHC). They have played a significant role in shaping the discourse of social policy in developing countries at both national and global levels. In particular, these international frameworks and strategies for development, including internationally agreed development goals, played a significant role in bringing back the state as a problem solver and leading player in designing and implementing development policies again. Donors' policies, even in rhetoric, started to emphasize the need to work together with recipient governments to implement development projects, and new aid instruments such as budget support and sector-wide approaches were established to channel aid directly to recipient governments (Agg 2006).

International donor agencies such as the World Bank actively transfer and diffuse the ideas and policies of social protection programs including conditional cash transfers in developing countries where the state mainly implements them. Dominant trends in both low- and middle-income countries from the 1990s to the global crisis of 2008 had culminated in the expansion of social protection coverage, yet with wide variation across countries (Yi et al. 2015). Some emerging economies such as Brazil and China became the symbols of the "quiet revolution" or "social turn" in social policy fields. The expansion of social assistance programs—for instance, pensions for the elderly, cash transfer programs for children, and public employment programs involving direct employment creation by the government—has been a common phenomenon in developing countries, particularly middle-income countries. Also, social services—notably, education and health services—have continuously improved across developing countries, albeit to varying degrees (World Bank 2015).

In this process, the national governments and international donors actively searched for those who could work for service delivery with fewer costs but higher performance. Widespread norms and principles of new public management with a focus on efficiency, continuing trends of privatization, and fiscal constraints created an interface between social policy and non-governmental actors (Evers 1995; Kendal 2003; Kim 2008). In particular, civil society actors actively responded to this trend with their knowledge and experience in social service delivery accumulated over the past three decades (Ware 1989; Grindheim and Selle 1990; Salamon 1995).

Although SSE has a long history as a distinctive category of civil society groups, SSE emerged as a part of an alternative economic development agenda in development discourses and practices since the late 1990s.[3] A series of financial crises spanning different continents revealed the unsustainable nature of market fundamentalism, and global movements searching for social justice worked together to confront various neoliberal development projects (de Sousa Santos and Rodriguez-Garavito 2007; Scholte 2011; Smith et al. 2016). Various alternative economic agendas ranging from neo-Keynesian, progressive macroeconomic policies to micro-initiatives undertaken by marginalized and vulnerable people have been discussed in numerous international fora. International dialogues have never failed to put forward SSE as a viable alternative initiative. Many SSE organizations and enterprises started to create a relationship with the government. The nature of relationship established by SSE organizations and enterprise is different from that of NGOs which worked as operational arms of INGOs in the previous period. SSE not as a substitute for but as a complement to state provision of social services played a significant role in making sectoral services comprehensive by creating positive externalities such as consolidation of democracy through active participation, generation of jobs, and improved living standards at the community levels.

From the perspective of discourse and development strategies, the establishment of the UN Inter-Agency Task Force on Social and Solidarity Economy (UNTFSSE) in 2013 was particularly notable since it signaled the introduction of SSE into a public space of global development strategies and frameworks. The UNTFSSE was established as a follow-up action to the Conference on "Potentials and Limits of Social and Solidarity Economy," which was organized by the United Nations Research Institute for Social Development (UNRISD), bringing together UN agencies and intergovernmental organizations with a direct interest in SSE as well as umbrella associations of international SSE networks (UNRISD 2017). UNRISD, particularly its long tradition of a comprehensive approach to civil society, social movements, and social policy, played a significant role in forming the agenda of this global space for discussion, research, and advocacy for SSE within the UN system. The broad definition of social policy promoted by UNRISD emphasizes the multiple functions of social policy in economic and environmental dimensions (UNRISD 2016). This broad understanding of social policy, the often-called transformative social policy, has an elective affinity with the quintessential features of SSE, that is to say economic activities prioritizing social and often environmental objectives over profits.

Since 2013 the UNTFSSE has been making efforts to utilize the potential of SSE as a means of implementation of the SDGs. Moreover, one of the SDGs which UNTFSSE takes heed of is UHC, which has long been seen as a key social policy target (Yi and Kim 2015). To achieve UHC, UNTFSSE emphasizes the role of SSE organizations as an important partner in both health service delivery and health insurance. Indeed, various types of SSE organizations currently play a key role in providing accessible and affordable health care services. It is remarkable to note that they are particularly prominent in areas such as care for the elderly and persons with disabilities, HIV/AIDS infected persons, maternal care, mental health care, post-trauma care, and rehabilitation and prevention (UNTFSSE 2014).

INTERFACES IN PRACTICES: PARTICIPATION

Effective governance representing the voices and interests of all at local, national, regional, and global levels is a necessary condition for sustainable and inclusive development. It is fair to state that one of the essential tools which effective governance requires would be people's active participation, defined as "the involvement of citizens in a wide range of policy-making activities, including the determination of levels of service, budget priorities, and the acceptability of physical construction projects in order to orient government programmes toward community needs, build public support, and encourage a sense of cohesiveness within neighborhoods" (UN DPADM 2017).

In fact, participation has been one of the most important concepts and practices in development discourses and practices since official development assistance (ODA) began after World War II. In particular, since the 1980s when international agencies began to put a great emphasis on the role of civil society as a key development agent, participation has been an element integral to any development project. Greater participation has been considered necessary not only because it contributes to increasing project efficiency and effectiveness but also being central to increasing the self-reliance of people and increasing the numbers of beneficiaries of development. Ultimately, reinforcing participation in the field of development cooperation results in signifying the accountability of development projects, in that people's participation can hold the government to be more accountable (Kim 2017).

Although many development agencies hailed the virtues of participation, there has been a consistent concern about its reductionism to mere consultations with stakeholders, often chosen quite selectively by technocrats or other actors in positions of governmental power (Cernea 1985). In response to such reductionism, various interpretations of participation commonly indicate that it should be considered a continuum rather than an either-or practice (Arnstein 1969). Participation as a continuum includes beneficiaries or client groups' sharing the benefits of development programs; involvement of beneficiaries or client groups in decision-making, implementation, and evaluation processes; influences of beneficiaries or client groups on the direction and execution of a development project; and control of beneficiaries or client groups over resources and regulation of institution or full managerial power (Uphoff 1979; Paul 1987; Pearse and Stiefel 1980). The control or regulation by the groups and movements of those hitherto excluded from such controls is a particularly important part of participation and should be considered genuine participation (UNRISD 2003).

To examine the degree of organizational participation of SSE in policy-making and implementation processes, this study considers three mechanisms through which participating agents can have a different level of participation. The first is the incentive structure which materially rewards participation. In this case, organizations may make inputs or contributions into a project to enhance its chances of success or gaining economic benefits. The second mechanism is the formal participatory mechanisms of decision-making, implementation, and evaluation, all of which are widespread in many development projects led by governments and international agencies. The third mechanism is devolution, in which some forms of authority are delegated to participating agents. Although these mechanisms are not mutually exclusive in reality, the main thrust of participation practiced in development project process often assumes one or other of these mechanisms.

The Kudumbashree initiative in Kerala, India, "the community network of women and the Mission to support it" is a good example of how SSE ecosystems and the capacity of actors have been strengthened through participation.[4] Kudumbashree began as a municipal government's small pilot program to address poverty and women's empowerment through the organization of neighborhood groups, each of which has twenty women in the Alappuzha municipality, in the state of Kerala in 1992. As these groups proliferated, the Kerala local government registered them as an official organization (in Indian legal term, "society" under the Kerala state law) in 1998, and launched it as a state-wide program (Varier 2016). Currently, according to its website, there are 4,306,976 members organized by 277,175 Ayalkoottam (Neighbourhood Group).

For women to join the Kudumbashree program, they have to organize into an Ayalkoottam. This group is a basic unit of Kudumbashree providing a forum for members to plan and act with principles of democracy and solidarity and in many cases act as cooperatives or social enterprises (Kadiyala 2004; Mukherjee-Reed 2015; Rajan 2006). The Ayalkoottam sends elected representatives to the ward-level Area Development Societies, and then Area Development Societies send their representatives to the village or community-level Community Development Societies. Such a three-tier system facilitating the participation of Kudumbashree members into development planning and implementation is contiguous with the local self-governance system (the Panchayat Raj system) composed of three tiers. They include Gram Panchayat (Village Council, a village-level administrative body), Panchayat Samities (Block Council, an administrative body above villages such as Tehsil, Mandal, and Taluka, which include villages that are called "development blocks"), and the District Administration. The government has an office for administrating and supporting the Kudumbashree initiative in Panchayat, which is the government's focal point for street-level contact.

In a nutshell, the strongest feature embedded in this whole process of Kudumbashree comes from the essence of participation. First, Kudumbashree has been strongly influenced by the institutions and policies of the participatory planning processes which had been already firmly established in Kerala such as the "People's Planning Campaign" and Community Development Society (Isaac and Heller 2003; Kudumbashree 2017; Lakshmanan 2006; Mukherjee-Reed 2015). Second, the nature of the interaction between Mahatma Gandhi National Rural Employment Guarantee Scheme (MGNREGS) and Kudumbashree as an ecosystem of SSE has been also strongly influenced by this crucial value of participation firmly embedded in the institutions, actors, and processes of the government and Kudumbashree organizations.

Consequently, MGNREGS per se has an institutional mechanism to promote participation in the sense that MGNREGS, established in 2005, is a rights-based employment guarantee program in rural areas. The program provides a legal guarantee of at least 100 days of paid employment at minimum wages in local infrastructure development projects to every rural household. MGNREGS has a strong element of local autonomy since local government can decide the nature and forms of works the beneficiaries of MGNREGS undertake (Mukherjee-Reed 2015). In addition to government bodies at various levels, the Act of MGNREGS stipulates that CSOs, authorized by the Central Government or the State Government, are implementation agencies. The fourth edition of the MGNREGA Operational Guidelines includes CSOs as official stakeholders in enhancing awareness of the program and supporting and building the capacities of Gram Panchayat and State Governments in planning, implementation, and social audits of MGNREGS (Ehmke and Fakier 2016). However, depending on the institutional environment that governments provide and the extent of government efforts to involve CSOs as official partners at various stages of MGNREGS, the degree of civil society's involvement varies (Ehmke and Fakier 2016).

In Kerala, the government addressed two challenges in the process of implementations of MGNREGS: male workers' low interests in the works of MGNREGS whose wages were only a half of the workers' average wage; and the traditional exclusion of women—the potential workers of MGNREGS program—from the public space. To address these problems, firstly, the government appointed all the program supervisors of MGNREGS from the members of Kudumbashree affiliated to Area Development Societies. Such an action for the appointment resulted in creating interesting dynamics to strengthen MGNREGS and the ecosystem of the SSE. Most of all, Kudumbashree women appointed as supervisors actively participate in planning the work of MGNREGS and mobilize their Kudumbashree members to participate in the MGNREGS work. Regarding women's participation in MGNREGS, Kerala was ranked first according to surveys in 2011 and 2012. Second, the government trained these women program supervisors in order to enhance their capacities to manage the projects. The elements of training to increase their capacities are associated with their various responsibilities. The maxim of responsibilities includes: "identifying work opportunities, mobilising groups for work, preparing estimates in consultation with the overseer or engineer, supervising work, providing amenities at the worksite, preparing and submitting muster rolls, and handling emergencies" (Mukherjee-Reed 2015, 307).

With these active participations in the program as supervisors or workers, Kudumbashree women found the opportunity to utilize infrastructure development work in MGNREGS for various projects of the Kudumbashree programs. In particular, they could relate those rural infrastructure programs to farming such as Sangha Krishi (group farming) which is a part of the Kudumbashree program. Under Sangha Krishi, the government provides 10 million acres of land to more than 44,000 collectives with more than 250,000 women farmers for agriculture. Kudumbashree women linked the MGNREGS works such as the reclamation of fallow land and the improvement of infrastructure to enhance the productivity and consequently developed the group farming under Sangha Krishi into a new agricultural business (Mukherjee 2012; Mukherjee-Reed 2015; Varier 2016).

The strengthened capacity of Kudumbashree women, which is nurtured by well-designed institutional structure and policies, becomes a key factor to the successful establishment of the ecosystem of SSE. It is clearly confirmed by the increasing number of Kudumbashree women in electoral politics. In 2011, 11,000 Kudumbashree women ran for the Panchayat elections, and 5,404 won the election. The electoral rule of Kerala that reserves 50% of seats for women apparently played a significant role in this political empowerment of Kudumbashree women. All in all, political, social, and economic institutions for the participation of poor women contributed to making the ecosystem of the SSE successful, strengthening the social policy mandate of government to reduce poverty and enhance the capacity of SSE organizations and their members (Mukherjee-Reed 2015).

In Indonesia, a participatory community development initiative funded by the cash grant for the village—the National Community Empowerment Program Independent (Program Nasional Pemberdayaan Masyarakat, hereafter PNPM Mandiri)—demonstrates a different type of institutional configuration with various outcomes regarding the capacity of the government and SSE actors. During the democratization process after the Asian Financial Crisis in the late 1990s and the early 2000s, strong policy power and substantial financial resources devolved to district governments which are below provincial governments. It was part of President Habibie's strategy to pacify growing discontent among people in remote regions and to avoid the risk of separation from Indonesia of those provinces endowed with abundant natural resources following the example of East Timor. The devolution undertaken between 1999 and 2001 transformed Indonesia from one of the world's most centralized nations to one of its most decentralized. Beginning in January 2001, the central government handed over 90% of internal revenues and 100% of the responsibility for delivering most social services—including health care and education—to about 300 district governments. The role of coordination and supervision held by the provincial governments was conducted only on paper, simply because they had little resource to undertake this role (Pisani 2014). The combination of various political and economic factors created a perfect breeding ground for ineffective, short-term social protection schemes that favored the supporters of the local political elites. These factors included automatically transferred resources and the autonomy to spend, the weak capacity of district governments to govern, the strong legacy of clientelistic political relations, and regularly held local elections (Robison and Hadiz 2004). The deterioration of social services was not uncommon. The central government's social protection schemes, such as national-level cash transfers, were implemented in this context where organized coordination mechanisms between levels of government were weak—PNPM Mandiri was one of them.

PNPM Mandiri provides a block cash grant to selected small-scale local physical and economic infrastructure projects such as building roads, sanitation, hiring extra midwives for villages, improving health centers and schools, providing school uniforms and education materials, and so on. The selection of the projects is prepared by community organizations on the basis of quality and feasibility of proposals. PNPM Mandiri emphasizes local people's participation in the planning, implementation, and maintenance of the projects, and the amount of financial allocation for subsequent years is competitively allocated in accordance with village performances against a certain set of indicators. PNPM Mandiri's emphasis on participation and empowerment elements particularly appeals to donors who try to incorporate the same items in development projects through their community-driven development approach. The effectiveness, measured by the costs of the project, also attracted donors' attentions. The PNPM Support Facility, a government institution to support PNPM projects, discloses that building infrastructure through PNPM Mandiri mechanism costs 30–56% less than those executed by contractors. In some instances, the projects contribute to job creation by employing local people. Women's participation in the village and intervillage meetings is worth mentioning. All these results are attractive enough to donors, thereby not only leading donor aid to the PNPM Mandiri projects to drastically increase, but also contributing to expanding the coverage of the PNPM Mandiri (Wisnu 2013).

Donors' increased involvement has also had an adverse effect on the responsiveness of cash transfer programs to the needs of the poor. In the initial phase, contributions from the central government accounted for a significant share of the budget for PNPM Mandiri. Over time, however, aid from foreign donors has become the primary source of financing for PNPM Mandiri. Technical assistance is also dominated by international agencies, which often establishes community development programs in ways that do not reflect the priority needs of the poorest. Also, the government tends to select simple projects with visible outputs rather than focus on what people might need to earn income or to handle complex problems such as pollution, the results of which are not easily quantified within a short time frame. Also, PNPM Mandiri tends to be awarded to those poor who can present project ideas and defend them in the selection process, which tends to exclude those in chronic poverty who usually lack the capacity and time to make a well-crafted project plan.

In this process of selection based on the quality of the proposal, PNPM Mandiri becomes dominated by a few number of skills-making project proposals initiated by consultants from outside and constraining the participation of the poorest and most vulnerable in the village. It cements the power or stratification structures to generate inequality and exclusion in the villages, which was detrimental to the efforts to create social capital and make solidarity-based community self-help groups. The impact on the living standards and empowerment of the marginalized and vulnerable groups is not positive either. For instance, the living standards of women-headed households with low education attainment have not improved significantly enough to lift them out of poverty, and positive impact on employment opportunities is only temporary (Triwibowo 2017). A variety of factors ranging from donors' over-intervention in the program design and intervention in the method of selecting projects for granting has a negative impact on the ecosystem of SSE which could have been a sound basis for SSE growth in Indonesia.

INTERFACES IN PRACTICE: PARTNERSHIP

Since the 1970s, scholars and practitioners have been arguing that "development is not possible without partnership approaches" (Brinkerhoff 2002, 1; Pearson 1969). Partnership in development discourses and practices has been a buzz word for a long time. The imperative of partnership was once again clearly manifested in the SDGs, which emphasize the interlinkages and integrated nature of the 17 goals and 169 targets. Both goals and targets are closely interlinked like a web network in which goals are often associated with cross-cutting issues in policy-making. They cannot be addressed in isolation, given the fact that they often transcend the boundaries of administratively defined or established policy sectors and do not correspond to the purview of individual ministries or departments (Meijers and Stead 2004). The fact that it is impossible to achieve these goals and targets with siloed approach implies that a partnership between multistakeholders is imperative. The partnership between multiple and diverse actors—including NGOs, community-based organizations, governments, intergovernmental organizations, donors, and the private sector—becomes the norm in order to enhance development outcomes through treating causes of underdevelopment and addressing systemic forces that preserve the status quo (Brown and Ashman 1996).

Partnership contains processes to produce relational elements. In addition to enhancing outcomes, it creates synergistic rewards which are defined as the increase in performance of the combined elements over what those elements are already expected or required to accomplish independently (Boyer 2008; Brinkerhoff 2002; Sirower 2000). Development stakeholders, particularly international donors and national governments, envision partnerships which can produce enhanced and synergistic outcomes. Voluntary sector or third sector parties are also particularly encouraged and promoted to partner with the government in delivering social service by the international donor agencies and national governments. Resource constraints that the voluntary sector faces are also a push factor for its entrance into partnerships with the government in the areas of social service delivery such as housing, welfare, and employment services.

The impacts of partnership on social service delivery are mixed. Some report that partnership between the third sector and the government has been cost effective while others point out significant deficiencies in either the structure or operations. Partners involved in development projects might elevate the possibility of perverse incentives and pass the buck to others when projects fail; therefore, partnership needs organizational inputs for democratizing the relationship of development partners and driving them to work for common goals in the face of the enduring enticement of perverse incentives (Mulgan 2003; Gilson et al. 2005; Kim 2017). Many summaries of the research on public-private-partnerships (PPP) report that convincing evidence for or against the cost-effectiveness of PPP is rare, and available evidence, if there is any, is contradictory (Rees et al. 2011). Measuring outputs of partnerships with a focus on cost-effectiveness is methodologically problematic since the measurement is unable to take into account or control various intervening variables affecting the final outputs. One way to avoid this methodological problem is to identify and measure the set of resources partners mobilize through partnerships since the value added of partnership does not include only the increase in performance of the combined elements but also the improvement of capacities of the partners.

Community-based mutual health insurance schemes, which have rapidly increased since the 2000s, offer an excellent opportunity to examine whether and how social policy and SSE could mobilize additional resources through partnerships. Partnerships for community-based mutual health insurance policy involving various levels of government and community organizations have been established to enable members of the community to get easy access to health care and reduce social costs arising from the unequal distribution of services and misallocation of scarce resources (Prasad 2008; Yi et al. 2015). These small-scale community-centered insurance schemes are characterized with voluntary membership, nonprofit objectives, risk pooling, and mutual aid/solidarity. Multiple and diverse institutions and organizations such as health facilities in both public and private sectors, member-based organizations, local communities or cooperatives firmly rooted in the community play a significant role in initiating these schemes and become main actors to own and run them. These institutions and organizations usually negotiate with public or private service providers over terms and conditions (Bastagli 2013).

One important feature of these schemes is effective interactions between representative organizations implementing them and beneficiaries who those organizations target. The interactions through various forms such as seminars, training and education courses, and participatory workshops enhance the negotiating capital of the partners such as local community organizations and cooperatives representing communities with both public and private partners, particularly private health care providers. It consequently contributes to making this insurance scheme closer to public rather than private goods. For instance, in Rwanda, from 1999, the government promoted community-based health insurance (CBHI) schemes whose long tradition dates back to the preindependent years of faith-based NGO-run community mutual schemes (Soors et al. 2010). The government mobilized the voluntarism of people and nongovernmental actors to organize CBHI schemes. Participation in CBHI schemes is voluntary and based on a membership contract between the CBHI and members. With organizational structures including general assemblies, the board of directors, surveillance committees, and executive bureaus to regulate contractual relations between members and service providers, CBHI schemes establish contractual relations with health care providers such as health centers and hospitals for the purchasing of health care services. Laws provide measures to minimize risks associated with health insurance such as adverse selection, moral hazard, cost escalation, and insurance fraud (Diop and Butera 2005).

Technical and financial assistance from foreign donors and the international financial instruments for health such as the Global Fund are mostly channeled through to CBHI schemes. After its pilot phase of 2008, the government established a specific legal framework, making affiliation with health insurance in principle mandatory for nationals and residents alike. CBHI members can access health care in any public and faith-based organization across the country. Population coverage increased from 7% in 2003 to 85% in 2008, and up to over 90% in 2010. Access to health care also increased from 31% in 2003 to almost 100% in 2012 (Nyandekwe et al. 2014; Soors et al. 2010). The increase of CBHI contributed to lifting the overall health insurance coverage of Rwanda up to 96.15% as of 2012 including other health insurance schemes.

Greater access for the poor to CBHI scheme benefits is in part a result of mobilizing network resources of partners for CBHI schemes. The partnership between CBHI schemes, grassroots associations, and micro-finance schemes (Banques Populaires) plays a significant role in facilitating access for the poor to health care services through the CBHI and increasing memberships through the inclusion of grassroots associations into CBHI schemes as a group. Local micro-finance schemes provide loans to help the poor members of associations to pay for their yearly contributions to CBHI schemes. Governments in collaboration with NGOs finance the enrollment of the poorest and most vulnerable groups based on the information provided by the community organizations.[5] Consequently, the Rwanda case shows both SSE and the government in the health care sector utilize various resources such as finance, networks, and information to generate meaningful outcomes such as health coverage and strengthen their institutional capacities.

The recent phenomena of the increasing role of not-for-profit, nongovernmental organizations in social service delivery in transition economies including China's signify different development trajectories of SSE in social service provision, specifically government-induced development of SSEs. In an attempt to create a better concerted social security system that covers the entire population regardless of their employment status, place of origin, or current residence, the Chinese government established a new law that relaxes control over CSOs. With this law, the government has promoted the involvement of CSOs in delivering social services such as care for the elderly and a broad range of social services for migrant workers. As a result of the relaxed regulations, by the end of 2014, the total number of CSOs reached 547,000, 9.6% more than that of the previous year. More than 3,000 charitable foundations were set up to support the operation of CSOs, and 6.37 million people were employed in them. One of the most interesting dynamics is that the current government agencies have started to enhance their administrative and managerial capacity by adopting knowledge and skills from CSOs. Although it is still arguable whether these CSOs can be defined as SSE given their limitations in the members' democratic control over the organizations, the development of CSOs in social service delivery in China may be the birth of another variant of SSE and its interaction with social policy (Li et al. 2015).

CONCLUSION

Although partnership between the government and nongovernmental actors (particularly private actors) in social service delivery is not a new phenomenon, the emergence of SSE which prioritize social goals over profits creates a new landscape of collaboration. The double expansion of social protection schemes and SSE creates an interesting policy interface across many developing countries with positive outcomes regarding jobs creation and overall improvement of living standards in some cases. Whether the interactions between the government and SSE in this interface strengthens each other's capacity—for example, the government's capacity to implement social policy and SSE's values and principles—remains, however, a crucial question for both social policy and SSE communities. The question is of particular importance since it is directly associated with the sustainability of social policies and SSE.

Selecting three kinds of interfaces in discourse and practice, with a focus on participation and partnership, we have examined how the interactions between social policy and SSE contribute to or hinder strengthening the capacities of the government and SSE organizations and actors. The support of international organizations for the social service project which bypassed the government in developing countries for much of the 1980s and 1990s deprived the government of the opportunities to enhance its governance capacities. It is questionable whether it nurtured the capacity of the third sector or SSE organizations, particularly the capacity to plan and act in the longer term and broader perspective.

The social turn and the emergence of SSE as a response to a series of multiple crises, however, created a new space of interactions between social policy and SSE. At this time, the state assumes itself as a development partner with nongovernment actors while SSE organizations and enterprises play a role of autonomous partner prioritizing public interests over profits.

The configuration of political, economic, and social institutions affects diverse nature of partnerships and varying degrees of participation which have ultimately impacted on the capacity building of the government and civil society. In the case of Kudumbashree in India, well-matched three-tier governance structure and synergistic relations with MGNREGS facilitated the participation of the poorest and marginalized—particularly, women—into policy-making process and generated a significant improvement of standard of living for the poor class. It is clearly evident that the set of institutions contributing to rebalancing the existing power relations and creating synergies with other sectoral programs is the key solution to establishing a successful ecosystem of SSE.

In contrast, the case of the Indonesian PNPM Mandiri demonstrates how the design of social policy, selection of projects based on merit without empowerment or training of the poor and marginalized can constrain participation and make the whole process dominated and captured by a few policy or project elites. The ecosystem of SSE which could otherwise have been a sound basis for SSE growth in Indonesia has been negatively affected by the institutions and processes that the PNPM Mandiri created.

Rwanda's CBHI schemes show how partnerships between and within government institutions and community-based SSE organizations can contribute to health outcomes regarding health coverage. Both the government and SSE could mobilize and utilize additional resources which they could not have mobilized independently. It shows that the interface became mutually beneficial to both partners. Given the strong influence of the government in creating this health partnership, however, to what extent community-level insurance organizations can be resilient and sustainable still remains a question.

The Chinese case of social organizations' entry into social service delivery also shows mutual benefits from additional resources. Government agencies adopt new skills and knowledge from social organizations while social organizations get financial support from the government. The nature of social organizations and the long-term impacts on the capacity of both parties, however, need further research.

To sum up, interfaces between social policy and SSE have expanded but not without challenges. The challenges are diverse since the distinctive forms and nature of social policy and SSE organizations and enterprises shape the nature of the challenges differently. Although the challenges in making synergistic relations between social policy and SSE are diverse, there are some common solutions crucial to maximizing the potential to scale up both social policy and SSE, such as addressing power asymmetry between and within the government and SSE organizations, and creating complementary institutions and policies. These findings and lessons particularly highlight the importance of issues such as internal governance of SSE, and relationships of SSE with a broad range of policies and institutions at various levels in making a better institutional environment for social development.

NOTES

1. This work was supported by the Ministry of Education of the Republic of Korea and the National Research Foundation of Korea (NRF-2015S1A3A2046224). Authors would like to express their appreciation to the staffs of UNRISD for their suggestions during the planning and development of this work.

2. This chapter is reprinted from Ilcheong Yi, Hyuk-Sang Sohn, and Taekyoon Kim. (2018). "Synergistic Interactions between Social Policy and SSE in Developing Countries: Interfaces in Discourse and Practice." *Development and Society* 47(2): 313–340.

3. Origins and evolutionary trajectories of SSE are inevitably diverse because the concept of SSE refers to various "forms of economic activity that prioritise social and often environmental objectives, and involve producers, workers, consumers and citizens acting collectively and in solidarity" (Utting 2015, 1). One of the oldest forms of surviving SSE is producer cooperatives which have existed since the beginning of the factory system in the West (Bonin et al. 1993).

4. Kudumbashree means the prosperity of family in India: http://www.kudumbashree.org/pages/178.

5. This observation does not deny there are problems in Rwandan CBHI schemes. First, undersupply or uneven distribution of health care providers, which is common in rural areas of developing countries, prevents people's willingness to participate in the schemes and negatively affect the scheme's sustainability. Second, there is substantial evidence supporting the schemes' exclusion of the poorest of the poor in Rwanda's *Mutuelles.*

REFERENCES

Agg, Catherine. 2006. "Trends in Government Support for Non-Governmental Organizations: Is the "Golden Age" of the NGOs Behind Us?" In *Civil Society and Social Movements Programme Paper No. 23.* Geneva: UNRISD.

Arnstein, Sherry R. 1969. "A Ladder of Citizen Partnership." *Journal of the American Institute of Planners* 35(4): 216–224.

Barrientos, Armando, and David Hulme. 2009. "Social Protection for the Poor and the Poorest in Developing Countries: Reflections on a Quiet Revolution." *Oxford Development Studies* 37(4): 439–456.

Bastagli, Francesca. 2013. "Feasibility of Social Protection Schemes in Developing Countries." In *Directorate-General for External Policies.* Brussels: European Union.

Bateman, Milford. 2015. "Rebuilding Solidarity-Driven Economies After Neoliberalism: The Role of Cooperatives and Local Developmental State in Latin America." In *Social and Solidarity Economy: Beyond the Fringe*, edited by Peter Utting. London: Zed Books.

Bonin, John P., Derek C. Jones, and Louis Putterman. 1993. "Theoretical and Empirical Studies of Producer Cooperatives: Will Ever the Twain Meet." *Journal of Economic Literature* 31(3): 1290–1320.

Boyer, Robert. 2008. "Growth Strategies and Poverty Reduction: The Institutional Complementarity Hypothesis." *Working Paper No. 2007-43.* Paris: Paris School of Economics.

Brinkerhoff, Jennifer M. 2002. "Government-Nonprofit Partnership: A Defining Framework." *Public Administration and Development* 22: 19–30.

———. 2007. "Partnership as a Means to Good Governance: Towards an Evaluation Framework." In *Partnerships, Governance and Sustainable Development: Reflections on Theory and Practice*, edited by Pieter Glasbergen, Frank Biermann, and Arthur P. J. Mol. UK: Edward Elgar.

Brown, L. David, and Darcy Ashman. 1996. "Participation, Social Capital, and Intersectoral Problem-Solving: African and Asian Cases." *World Development* 24(9): 1467–1479.

Cernea, Michael. 1985. *Putting People First: Sociological Variables in Rural Development.* Oxford: Oxford University Press.

Corragio, José Luis. 2015. "Institutionalising the Social and Solidarity Economy in Latin America." In *Social and Solidarity Economy in Fringe*, edited by Peter Utting. London: Zed Books.

Corry, Olaf. 2010. "Defining and Theorizing the Third Sector." In *Third Sector Research*, edited by Rupert Taylor. New York: Springer.

Deacon, Bob. 2007. *Global Social Policy & Governance*. London: Sage.

Deakin, Nicholas. 2001. *In Search of Civil Society*. London: Routledge.

de Sousa Santos, Boaventura, and César A. Rodriguez-Garavito. 2007. "Introduction: Expanding the Economic Canon and Searching for Alternatives to Neoliberal Globalization." In *Another Production Is Possible*, edited by Boaventura de Sousa Santos. London: Verso.

Diop, François Pathé, and Jean Damascene Butera. 2005. "Community-Based Health Insurance in Rwanda." In *Findings 256*. Washington, D.C.: World Bank.

Ehmke, Ellen, and Khayaat Fakier. 2016. "Making Public Employment Schemes Work: Insights from Civil Society Engagement in India and South Africa." In *Research Note*. Geneva: UNRISD.

Evans, Peter. 1995. *Embedded Autonomy: States and Industrial Transformation*. Princeton: Princeton University Press.

———. 2014. "The Korean Experience and the Twenty-First-Century Transition to a Capability-Enhancing Developmental State." In *Learning from the South Korean Developmental Successes: Effective Developmental Cooperation and Synergistic Institutions and Policies*, edited by Ilcheong Yi and Thandika Mkandawire. Basingstoke: Palgrave Macmillan.

Evers, Adalbert. 1995. "Part of the Welfare Mix: The Third Sector as an Intermediate Area." *Voluntas* 6(2): 159–182.

Fine, Ben. 2017. "The Continuing Enigmas of Social Policy." In *Towards Universal Health Care in Emerging Economies: Opportunities and Challenges*, edited by Ilcheong Yi. Basingstoke: Palgrave Macmillan.

Ghimire, Kléber B. 2005. "The Contemporary Global Social Movements: Emergent Proposals, Connectivity and Development Implications." In *Civil Society and Social Movements Programme Paper No. 19*. Geneva: UNRISD.

Gibson, Clark C., Krister Andersson, Elinor Ostrom, and Sujai Shivakumar. 2005. *The Samaritan's Dilemma: The Political Economy of Development Aid*. Oxford: Oxford University Press.

Girad, Jean-Pierre. 2014. *Better Health & Social Care: How Are Co-Ops & Mutuals Boosting Innovation & Access Worldwide?* Montreal: LPS Productions.

Grindheim, Jan Erik, and Per Selle. 1990. "The Role of Voluntary Social Welfare Organisations in Norway: A Democratic Alternative to a Bureaucratic Welfare State?" *Voluntas* 1(1): 42–61.

Hecht, Robert M., and Vito L. Tanzi. 1994. *The Role of Non-Governmental Organizations in the Delivery of Health Services in Developing Countries*. Washington, D.C.: World Bank.

Isaac, T. M. Thomas, and Patrick Heller. 2003. "Democracy and Development: Decentralized Planning in Kerala." In *Deepening Democracy: Institutional Innovations in Empowering Participatory Governance*, edited by Archon Fung and Erik Olin Wright. London: Verso.

Josselin, Daphné, and William Wallace (eds). 2001. *Non-State Actors in World Politics*. Basingstoke: Palgrave.

Kadiyala, Suneetha. 2004. "Scaling Up Kudumbashree: Collective Action for Poverty Alleviation and Women's Empowerment." *Food Consumption and Nutrition Division (FCDN) Discussion Paper Brief.* Washington, D.C.: International Food Policy Research Institute.

Kendall, Jeremy. 2003. *The Voluntary Sector: Comparative Perspectives in the UK.* London: Routledge.

Kim, Taekyoon. 2008. "The Social Construction of Welfare Control: A Sociological Review on State-Voluntary Sector Links in Korea." *International Sociology* 23(6): 819–844.

———. 2017. "On Global Accountability: A Theoretical Revisit to Accountability for Development Partnerships." *Development and Society* 46(2): 317–339.

Lakshmanan, P. 2006. "Participatory Planning Process in Kerala." In *Decentralized Governance and Poverty Reduction: Lessons from Kerala,* edited by P. P. Balan and M. Retna Raj. Thrissur: Kerala Institute of Local Administration.

Li, Bingqin, Lijie Fang, and Jing Wang. 2015. "Community-Based Social Service Delivery in China: Reshaped by Social Organisations?" Prepared for the UNRISD Methodology Workshop New Directions in Social Policy, Geneva, Switzerland.

Meijers, Evert, and Dominic Stead. 2004. "Policy Integration: What Does It Mean and How Can It Be Achieved? A Multi-disciplinary Review." Prepared for Berlin Conference on the Human Dimensions of Global Environmental Change: Greening of Policies—Interlinkaged and Policy Integration, Berlin, Germany.

Migdal, Joel S. 1998. *Strong Societies and Weak States: State-Society Relations and State Capabilities in the Third World.* Princeton, NJ: Princeton University Press.

Mkandawire, Thandika. 2004. "Social Policy in a Development Context: Introduction." In *Social Policy in a Development Context.* Basingstoke: Palgrave.

Mukherjee, Ananya. 2012. "From Food Security to Food Justice." *The Hindu.*

Mukherjee-Reed, Ananya. 2015. "Taking Solidarity Seriously: Analysing Kerala's Kudumbashree as a Women's SSE Experiment." In *Social and Solidarity Economy: Beyond the Fringe,* edited by Peter Utting. London: Zed Books.

Mulgan, Richard. 2003. *Holding Power to Account: Accountability in Modern Democracies.* Basingstoke: Palgrave.

Nyandekwe, Médard, Manassé Nzayirambaho, and Jean Baptiste Kakoma. 2014. "Universal Health Coverage in Rwanda: Dream or Reality." *Pan African Medical Journal* 17(2–8): 232.

O'Brien, Robert, Anne Marie Goetz, Jan Aart Sholte, and Marc Williams. 2000. *Contesting Global Governance: Multilateral Economic Institutions and Global Social Movements.* Cambridge: Cambridge University Press.

Paul, Samuel. 1987. "Community Participation in Development Projects: The World Bank Experience." *World Bank Discussion Paper No. 6.* Washington, D.C.: World Bank.

Pearse, Andrew, and Matthias Stiefel. 1980. *Inquiry into Participation: A Research Approach.* Geneva: UNRISD.

Pearson, Lester B. 1969. *Partners in Development: Report of the Commission on International Development.* New York: Praeger.

Pisani, Elizabeth. 2014. "Indonesia in Pieces: The Downside of Decentralization." *Foreign Affairs* (July/August).

Prasad, Naren. 2008. "Overview: Social Policies and Private Sector Participation in Water Supply." In *Social Policies and Private Sector Participation in Water Supply: Beyond Regulation*, edited by Naren Prasad. Basingstoke: Palgrave Macmillan.

Rajan, J. B. 2006. "Kudumbashree: A Forum for Gender Mainstreaming." In *Decentralised Governance and Poverty Reduction: Lessons from Kerala*, edited by P. P. Balan and M. Retna Raj. Thrissur: Kerala Institute of Local Administration.

Rees, James, David Mullins, and Tony Bovaird. 2011. "Third Sector Partnerships for Service Delivery: An Evidence Review and Research Project." *Third Sector Research Centre Working Paper 60*. TSRC Informing Civil Society.

Ringen, Stein, Huck-Ju Kwon, Ilcheong Yi, Taekyoon Kim, and Jooha Lee. 2011. *The Korean State and Social Policy: How South Korea Lifted Itself from Poverty and Dictatorship to Affluence and Democracy*. New York: Oxford University Press.

Robison, Richard, and Vedi R. Hadiz. 2004. *Reorganising Power in Indonesia: The Politics of Oligarchy in an Age of Markets*. London: RoutledgeCurzon.

Roginsky, Sandrine, and Sally Shortall. 2009. "Civil Society as a Contested Field of Meanings." *International Journal of Sociology and Social Policy* 29(9/10): 473–487.

Rossel, Cecilia. 2015. "State and SSE Partnerships in Social Policy and Welfare Regimes: The Case of Uruguay." In *Social and Solidarity Economy: Beyond the Fringe*, edited by Peter Utting. London: Zed Books.

Salamon, Lester M. 1995. *Partners in Public Service: Government-Nonprofit Relations in the Modern Welfare State*. Baltimore: Johns Hopkins University Press.

Scholte, Jan Aart. 2011. "Global Governance, Accountability and Civil Society." In *Building Global Democracy? Civil Society and Accountable Global Governance*, edited by Jan Aart Scholte. Cambridge: Cambridge University Press.

Sellers, Jefferey M. 2011. "State-Society Relations." In *Sage Handbook of Governance*, edited by Mark Bevir. London: Sage Publication.

Sirower, Mark L. 2000. *The Synergy Trap: How Companies Lose the Acquisition Game*. New York: The Free Press.

Smith, Jackie, Marina Karides, Marc Becker, Dorval Brunelle, Christopher Chase-Dunn, Donatella della Porta, Rosalba Icaza Garza, Jeffrey S. Juris, Lorenzo Mosca, Ellen Reese, Peter Smith, and Rolando Vázquez. 2016. *Global Democracy and the World Social Forum*. Abingdon: Routledge.

Soors, Werner, Narayanan Devadasan, Varatharajan Durairaj, and Bart Criel. 2010. "Community Health Insurance and Universal Coverage: Multiple Paths, Many Rivers to Cross." *World Health Report (2010) Background Paper 48*. Geneva: WHO.

Stiglitz, Joseph E. 2009. "Is There a Post-Washington Consensus Consensus?" In *The Washington Consensus Reconsidered: Toward a New Global Governance*, edited by Narcis Serra and Joseph E. Stiglitz. Oxford: Oxford University Press.

Triwibowo, Darmawan. 2017. *PNPM Mandiri: Promotes Participation Without Empowerment?* Jakarta: Tifa Foundation.

UN DPADM. 2017. *Online Glossary on Governance and Public Administration.* New York: Division of Public Administration and Development Management, UNDESA.

UNRISD. 2003. *Research for Social Change.* Geneva: UNRISD.

———. 2016. "Policy Innovations for Transformative Change." *UNRISD Flagship Report.* Geneva: UNRISD.

———. 2017. *Potential and Limits of Social and Solidarity Economy.* Geneva: UNRISD.

UNTFSSE. 2014. *Social and Solidarity Economy and the Challenge of Sustainable Development.* Geneva: UN Inter-Agency Task Force on Social and Solidarity Economy.

Uphoff, Norman Thomas. 1979. *Feasibility and Application of Rural Development Participation: A State-of-the-Art Paper.* Ithaca: Cornell University Press.

Utting, Peter. 2015. "Introduction: The Challenges of Scaling Up Social and Solidarity Economy." In *Social and Solidarity Economy: Beyond the Fringe*, edited by Peter Utting. London: Zed Books.

Uzzaman, Wahed. 2010. "Value of People's Participation for Good Governance in Developing Countries." *Transforming Government: People, Process and Policy* 4(4): 386–402.

Varier, Megha. 2016. "The Kudumbashree Story: How Kerala Women's Grassroots Scheme Grew into a Multi-Crore Project What Makes Kudumbashree Relevant in 2016?" In *Women Power*, edited by The News Minute. India: The News Minute.

Ware, Alan. 1989. *Between Profit and State: Intermediate Organizations in Britain and the United States.* Cambridge: Polity Press.

Wolch, Jennifer. 1990. *The Shadow State: Government and Voluntary Sector in Transition.* New York: Foundation Center.

World Bank. 2015. *The State of Social Safety Nets 2015.* Washington, D.C.: World Bank.

Yi, Ilcheong, Hyuk-Sang Sohn, and Taekyoon Kim. 2015. "Linking State Intervention and Health Equity Differently: The Universalization of Health Care in South Korea and Taiwan." *Korea Observer* 46(3): 517–549.

Yi, Ilcheong, and Taekyoon Kim. 2015. "Post 2015 Development Goals (SDGs) and Transformative Social Policy." *Oughtopia* 30(1).

Chapter 3

Mapping Social Economy Organizations in Northeast Asia

Euiyoung Kim and Hiroki Miura

INSTITUTIONAL MAPS OF SOCIAL ECONOMY

The concept and model of social economy has attracted the attention of both scholars and practitioners in recent years. Innovative cases have continuously emerged and spread worldwide, extending from an alternative business model of social enterprises and private companies to a model of collaborative governance between the government and social economy organizations (SEO) for more effective social service provision and inclusive community development. In academia, a number of comparative studies examined the empirical realities of social economy in different countries, identified various enabling conditions, and disseminated successful models and effective policy tools (Defourny and Develtere 1999; Shragge and Fontan 2000; Gunn 2004; Noya and Clarence 2007; Osborne 2008; Amin 2009; ILO 2011; EU 2012; Bridge et al. 2014; Defourny et al. 2014; Utting 2015; Pun et al. 2016).

This chapter focuses on the organizational dimension of social economy by analyzing the terrain of SEOs in Northeast Asia. The organizational terrain is not only one of substantial aspects of social economy, but it is also a useful tool to analyze interstate and interregional differences and similarities. Previously, an in-depth understanding of the organizational dimension of Northeast Asia remains insufficient in the ongoing global comparative studies with some exceptional pioneering works.[1] In order to complement this research vacuum, we try to provide a more precise and comparative analysis on the organizational terrains based on a rigorous methodology.

A brief note on the conceptual background is in order. The definition, range, and classification of a SEO are considerably diverse and controversial. In the early 1990s, the major institutional forms were simply defined as cooperatives, mutual societies, associations, and foundations (CMAF).[2] The organizational terrain has become ambiguous and complex since the emergence and spread of various types of social enterprises in the 2000s. At the same time, the rapid development of alternative models of social economy such as micro-credit, fair trade, public-private partnership, and collaborative governance has further diversified the range and nature of social economy. Recently, a leading group of researchers suggested "SE mountain range" and "SE field," denoting a close relationship among similar concepts such as social enterprises, solidarity economy, social entrepreneurship, third sector, and nonprofit sector (Defourny and Pestoff 2013; EMES 2016). Others prefer to use the concept of "social and solidarity economy," with an emphasis on the value of democratic solidarity inherent in the concept (ILO 2011; Laville 2013; Utting 2015).[3] Scholars developed a variety of institutional maps to portray the diverse and complex nature of the social economy in a schematic fashion (Pestoff 1998; Ninacs 2002; Pearce 2003; Borzaga and Ermanno 2007; Bridge et al. 2014). Figure 3.1 is an example of such attempts.

In South Korea, the concepts of the nonprofit sector and civil society, and the social economy became fashionable in the late 1990s and mid-2000s, respectively. Self-support enterprises (*jahwal gieob*) and nonprofit, nongovernmental organizations (*biyeongri mingan danche*) were institutionalized in the early 2000s, followed by the enactment of the Promotion Law of Social Enterprises in 2006 and the Framework Act on Cooperatives (FAC) in 2012. According to Joo (2010), the main forms and activities of the social economy are located around the juncture of the traditional state-market-society triangle (figure 3.2). In contrast, Lee and Kim (2015) classified the old and new generations of SEOs in a domestic and historical context. The old organizations

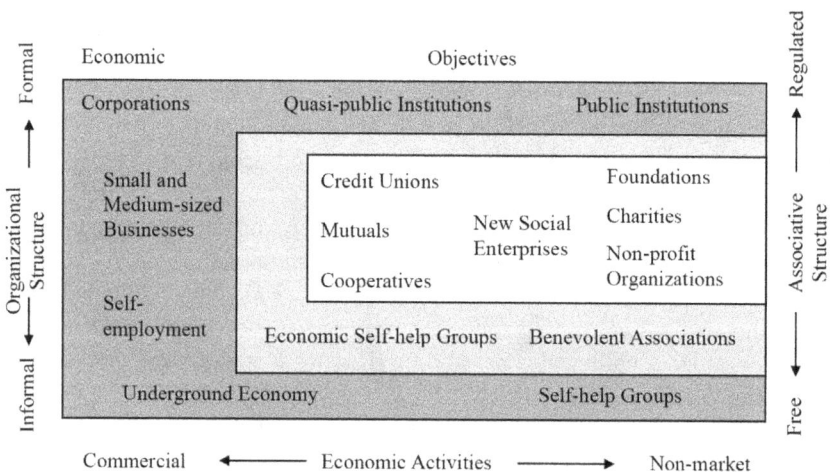

Figure 3.1 **The Social Economy Quadrilateral.** *Source*: Adapted from Ninacs (2002, 7).

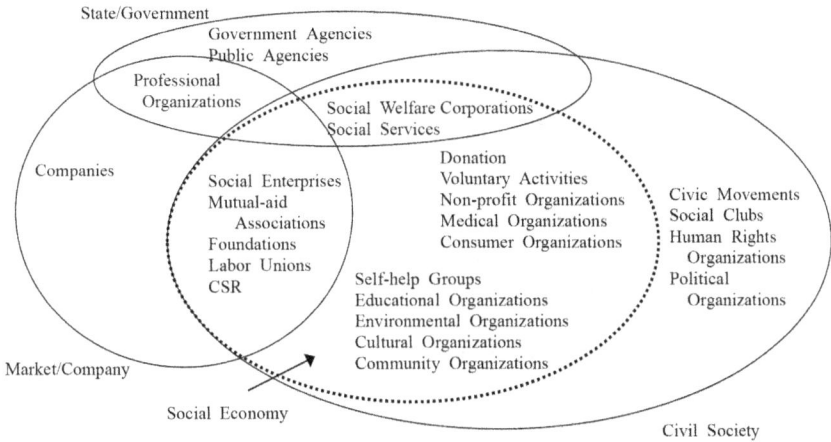

Figure 3.2 Realm of the Social Economy in South Korea. *Source*: Adapted from Joo (2010, 23).

include the government-led, traditional producer cooperatives, which have spread nationwide in the 1950s and 1960s, constituting a hierarchical and umbrella structure.[4] The new organizations include various legal entities such as certified social enterprises (*injung sahoijeok gieob*), self-support enterprises, community enterprises (*maul gieob*), and general and social cooperatives (*ilban hyeobdong johab, sahoijeok hyeobdong johab*). In contrast with the old ones, they are commonly characterized as voluntary and autonomous. Park et al. (2016) alternatively discuss that these old and new generations, together with the nonprofit sector organizations, constitute the broader "third sector" in South Korea. Social economy bills recently submitted to the National Assembly define the organizational terrain from an even broader perspective, including all of the abovementioned forms.[5]

In Japan, the concepts and practice of social enterprise, social entrepreneurship, and social innovation began to acquire popular recognition in the early 2000s. Afterward, the government and practitioners started to mention "social business" and "community business" in their official documents and projects.[6] This conceptual development or transformation has been intertwined with multiple epoch-making social trends. First, "community building" (*machi zukuri*) has emerged and spread since the 1970s. Some types or tools of community building activities such as car-sharing, local currency, and neighborhood care system came to be regarded or classified as a community business in the 1990s and 2000s. Second, the nonprofit sector was developed and institutionalized in the 1990s. Grassroot civic organizations have rapidly increased since the enactment of a Law to Promote Specified Non-profit Activities in 1998. The law provided conditions to establish specified nonprofit activity corporations (*NPO hojin*) and deliberately permit them to engage in profit-making activities to a limited degree and in the case of necessity for continuing nonprofit activities. Consequently, some non-profit organizations (NPOs) developed hybrid service programs integrating both nonprofit and profit-making activities, which was regarded as a typical form of social business in Japan in the 2000s. The total number of established NPOs reached about 51,000 in 2020. There is also a unique tradition in Japan since the 1980s that local governments and private companies jointly set up an enterprise called "third sector organization" (*daisan sekuta kikan*) to effec-tively cope with various public and social issues.[7] The development of Japan's social economy has been generally described as a result of the multiple flows of these similar concepts, institutions, and practices (Pekkanen 2006; Laratta et al. 2011; Kurimoto 2011; Ushiro 2011; Tsujinalka et al. 2013).

According to Tanimoto (2006), a leading researcher in this field, various types of social enterprises in Japan can be explained on a two-dimensional map (figure 3.3).[8] A survey conducted under this conceptual framework shows that 46.7% of "social business organizations" acquire a form of NPO, followed by stock companies (20.5%), individual enterprises (6.8%), differ-ent types of cooperatives (6.8%), workers cooperatives (1.7%), and limited liability companies (0.4%) (METI 2008).

The concept of social enterprise and social entrepreneurship began to gain popular attention in the mid-2000s in China (Yu 2011; Zhao 2012; Lee 2012; FYSE 2012; Zhao 2013). The rise of China's social economy is deeply entangled with multiple institutional reforms and social changes that appeared simultaneously in the 2000s. First, farmer specialized coopera-tives (*nongmin zhuanye hezuoshe*) were institutionalized in 2007 to restore

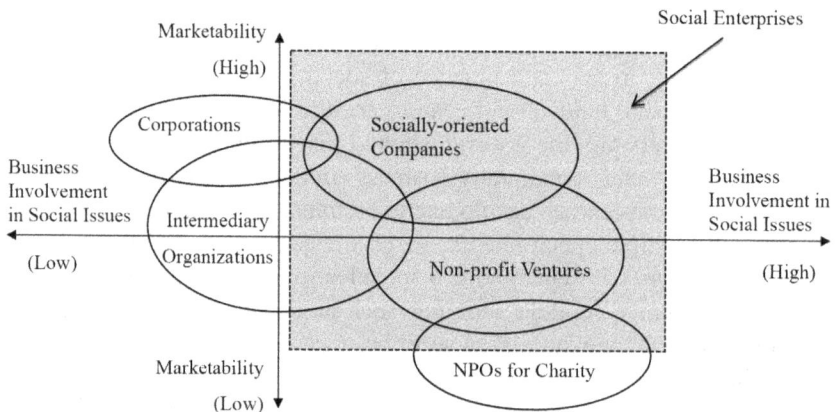

Figure 3.3   Position of Various Types of Social Enterprises in Japan. *Source*: Adapted from Tanimoto (2006, 15).

the diverse forms of agricultural cooperatives, farmers' groups, and related commercial entities in the rural area. More than one million cooperatives have been established under this legal framework. Second, increasing social needs for more effective welfare services resulted in the development of social service organizations (*shequ fuwu jiguo*) founded at the district or street level in the 2000s. The residential committee (*jumin weiyuanhui*), villagers' committee (*cunmin weiyuanhui*), and various types of voluntary grassroot groups were also expanded. Third, the legal system of corporation was largely reformed, and various private organizations emerged under the political vision of "small state, big society." The private nonenterprise units (*minban feiqiye danwei*) were institutionalized in 1999 and the autonomy of private foundations (*jijinhui*) was strengthened in 2004. The privatization of educational institutions (*minban jiaoyu jiguo*) was also promoted in the early 2000s. Fourth, the concept, practice, and business contest of social innovation (*shehui chuangxin*) have spread especially in the urban area. The Communist Party of China has hosted the biannual "China Social Innovation Award" through which innovative and creative business and community models were continuously introduced and disseminated. As a result of these multiple developments, researchers have started to examine the concept and model of social economy and its possibility in China (Wang and Zhu 2010; Zang et al. 2012; Zhao 2013; Yan and Pan 2014). For example, Yu (2011) suggested an institutional classification of Chinese social enterprises, based on the characteristics of five legal dimensions and five-point scale evaluation (table 3.1). The point 2 emphasized in the table means an ideal institutional condition of social enterprise.

ANALYTICAL FRAMEWORK

Ideal Type of Social Economy Organization

The institutional maps and classifications above are meaningful attempts to capture and portray the diverse and complex nature of the social economy in general and their manifestations in China, Japan, and South Korea. However, a more comprehensive and integrated methodology for mapping and classification is needed to compare their distinctive features and the regional characteristics of the social economy in Northeast Asia.

We use the following ideal type and operational definition of a social economy organization for our analysis. First, all SEOs basically share the organizational platform, which consists of democratic, economic, and social domains.[9] The hybridity among the three domains is their core institutional characteristics. In addition, the most ideal form of SEOs is one that realizes the

Table 3.1 Five Legal Dimensions of Social Enterprise and Their Ideal Condition

	Nature	Ownership	Tax-Exempt Status	Profit Distribution	Autonomy
3	—	Quasi-state owned	—	—	—
2	**Entirely nonprofit**	**Purely socially owned**	**Strongly favorable**	**Fully prohibited**	**Strongly autonomous**
1	Moderately nonprofit	Moderately socially owned	Moderately favorable	Rather restricted	Moderately autonomous
0	Neither for-profit or nonprofit	Neither private or socially owned	Neither unfavorable or favorable	Neither allowed or prohibited (no regulation)	Neither supervised nor autonomous (unregistered)
−1	Moderately for-profit	Moderately privately owned	Moderately unfavorable	Moderately allowed	Moderately supervised
−2	Entirely for-profit	Purely privately owned	Strongly unfavorable	Fully allowed	Closely supervised

In the five-point scale, point 2 means an ideal condition of social enterprise.
Source: Adapted from Yu (2011, 25).

high level of hybridity among the three domains. Second, the three domains are subdivided into six substantial subelements: ownership, establishment, main activity, profit distribution, institutional mission, and target problems (table 3.2).[10] This subdivision premises that ownership and establishment are relevant to the democratic domain. The main activity and profit distribution are related to the economic domain and the institutional mission and target problems are concerned with the social domain. Third, it is widely recognized that, being a hybrid organization, SEOs cannot be defined by a single feature or criterion. The patterns of hybridity among their multiple domains or features have remained as a central debate (Evers 2008; Bills 2010; Pestoff 2014; Donnelly-Cox 2015). We try to draw an alternative institutional map of social economy for China, Japan, and South Korea based on a detailed analysis of their degree and patterns of organizational hybridity. Our approach consists of the following three steps: evaluation, categorization, and mapping.

Evaluating the Six Subelements of Various Legal Entities

Our methodology is legal-institutional in nature. We analyze the three countries' governing laws and regulations of various legal entities and evaluate

Table 3.2   Forms and Conditions of the Six Subelements of Social Economy Organizations

Democratic Domain	
Ownership	*Establishment*
A • Organizations are owned by the members themselves and their decision-making is based on the one-person, one-vote rule.	• Organizations are established voluntarily and they can obtain their legal status through a simple procedure such as a declaration or a registration based on the freedom of association.
B • Organizations are owned by the members and regulated by the one-person, one-vote rule. However, they are under the substantial control of central agencies or hierarchical structure. • Organizations are owned collectively and decision-making is based on other democratic principles such as members' general conference and representatives' conference.	• Organizations are established voluntarily and they can obtain their legal status by a screening procedure such as administrative approval, permission, or other discretional judgment. • Organizations are established voluntarily and they can obtain their legal status through a simple procedure. However, the high level technical or structural conditions are required for their establishment.
— • Organizations are owned by the investors or stockholders and the voting rights are based on stock or the amount invested. • Organizations are owned by the state or the central or local governmental agencies. • Clear regulations are not provided concerning organizational ownership or decision-making principle.	• Organizations are established by government investments or with a specific policy purpose. • Organizations are established compulsory or semi-mandatory based on special administrative laws. • Clear regulations are not provided concerning organizational establishment.

Economic Domain	
Main Activity	*Profit Distribution*
A • A main activity is specified as an economic activity such as the production of goods or service provision.	• Social reinvestment of surplus is articulated as a requirement. • Clear standards or regulations are provided to limit the for-profit business.
B • Organizations mainly play supportive roles for the economic activities of other organizations. • A main activity is limited to the promotion of a specific policy or institutional purposes or broadly provided extending from economic to supportive or charity activities.	• Profit distribution is partially restricted. • For-profit business is partially restricted.

(Continued)

Table 3.2　Forms and Conditions of the Six Subelements of Social Economy Organizations (*Continued*)

Economic Domain	
Main Activity	Profit Distribution
— • A main activity is specified as the practice or dissemination of a political or religious belief or social ideologies. • Clear regulations are not provided concerning the main activity of organizations.	• Surplus is distributed to investors and other stakeholders. • Surplus is returned to government agencies. The budget of organizations mainly comes from governmental subsidies. • Clear regulations on surplus or limitation on for-profit are not provided.

Social Domain	
Institutional Mission	Target Problem
A • Social mission of organizations is clearly defined, providing that they must serve for the public interest or interests of the mass.	• Organizations are institutionalized to solve specific social problems that have a significant impact on society.
B • Missions and the range of activities are basically defined as a nonprofit business. • Organizations pursue social needs or interests of their members.	• Organizations are institutionalized to solve specific social problems, the impacts of which are limited to certain groups, regions, or policy fields. • Organizations are institutionalized to deal with multiple social problems, and their roles and functions are broadly defined.
— • Clear regulations are not provided concerning the social mission of organizations. • The mission of organizations is basically profit making.	• Organizations are institutionalized to solve specific social problems. However, the problems have been already solved to some extent or alternative policies have been already introduced. • Organizations do not have clear relevance to important social problems.

their relevance to the three domains and their six subelements. The range of the target legal entities in each country is defined from a holistic perspective and selected as important service providing organizations in each domestic context. At the same time, our research excludes the legal entities, which are institutionalized at the local government level or for the sake of very specific policy goals. As a result, we obtained twenty to thirty legal entities in each country for evaluation and the list is shown in Appendix I. We conducted a legal-institutional analysis on all relevant laws and regulations in China,

Japan, and South Korea in order to code their modes of organizational hybridity in terms of the democratic, economic, and social domains and their six subelements.

Categorizing the Legal Entities according to the Degree of Hybridity

A, B, and — in table 3.2 indicate the ranked evaluation of the subelements in each domain. A means that the regulations or the operational conditions of an organization stipulated in the relevant law satisfy the ideal state of a domain. B is the intermediate level, meaning that the regulations or the operational conditions of an organization neither satisfy the ideal state, nor deny the minimum conditions of a domain. — means that the regulations or the operational conditions of an organization do not satisfy even the minimum conditions of a domain. The degree of the hybridity can be estimated by aggregating the ranked evaluation in each of the six subelements. We sort out the different levels of hybridity into the following four categories.

* Major SEOs:
    The organizations ranked A in at least one subelement in the three domains, respectively, belong to this category. They have a high level of organizational hybridity and are thus regarded as leading SEOs in each country. Their relevance to the social economy is both high and direct.
* Quasi-SEOs:
    The organizations ranked A across any two domains belong to this category. They have an intermediate level of hybridity and their relevance to the social economy depends on case by case.
* Social Organization I:
    The organizations that do not satisfy the above two conditions but have four A or B ranks in total among the six elements belong to this category. Though they may have a certain degree of organizational hybridity, their governing laws cannot be viewed as relevant to the social economy. They may create and spread meaningful business models at a practical level. However, they are generally regarded as ordinary social organizations, not as SEOs, at a legal-institutional level.
* Social Organization II:
    The organizations that do not satisfy all of the above conditions belong to this category. The level of organizational hybridity is minimal, and they have specific social functions other than those of the social economy.

Mapping Major and Quasi-SEOs Based on Organizational Resource and Target Beneficiary

We also apply two other axes on our map: the principal organizational resource (human resource or solidarity/monetary resource or subsidy) and the principal target beneficiary (specific groups or individuals/local community). These two organizational features are also essential for understanding the basic characteristics of SEOs. Every legal entity has its own institutional characteristics or basic regulations between each pole of the two axes, and therefore, different coupling patterns will appear. The most complex entities will be located at the center of the map. We will locate the major and quasi-SEOs in the Northeast Asian countries on the map and discuss their common and different characteristics.

MAPPING AND COMPARING THE SEOS IN NORTHEAST ASIA

Categorization and Location of Relevant Legal Entities

The detailed evaluation of the six subelements for about eighty legal entities of China, Japan, and South Korea is presented in Appendix II. They could be categorized into four groups based on the analytical framework (table 3.3). The 2, 5, and 7 entities in China, Japan, and South Korea, respectively, are categorized into major SEOs. Various NPOs, private companies, and producer cooperatives are categorized into quasi-SEOs.

The results show the following notable characteristics and patterns. First, there is no legal entity ranked as A on all six subelements. That is, there is no organization that has a perfect hybrid platform. Specified nonprofit corporations or NPOs of Japan have the highest level of hybridity among all legal entities. However, their governing law does not stipulate economic functions or service provisions as their "main activities." Instead, twenty fields of nonprofit activities are specified. They can engage in for-profit businesses to some degree while profit distribution is clearly prohibited. Thus, they can be viewed as a typical form of so-called "earned income" organizations or "trading NPOs." South Korea's general cooperatives and social cooperatives have the second highest level of hybridity. General cooperatives have low-level regulation with respect to profit distribution and institutional mission. Social cooperatives are officially authorized by the government and thus, weak in terms of the freedom of association. Farmer specialized cooperatives of China are also low in terms of profit distribution and institutional mission. All major SEOs have certain democratic, economic, and social features, but lack some important subelements. This reality implies that the multifaceted aspects

Table 3.3   Categorization of the Major Legal Entities in the Northeast Asian Countries

	China	Japan	South Korea
Major SEOs	• Farmer specialized cooperatives • Social welfare enterprises	• Specified nonprofit corporations • Approved specified nonprofit corporations • Public interest incorporated associations • Public interest incorporated foundations • Consumer cooperatives	• Certified social enterprises • Precertification social enterprises • Consumer cooperatives • General cooperatives/social cooperatives • Self-support enterprises • Community business organizations
Quasi-SEOs	• Private nonenterprise units • Public fundraising foundations • Nonpublic fundraising foundations • Joint stock limited companies • Limited liability companies • Shareholding cooperative enterprises • Community service organizations • Rural credit cooperatives • Rural mutual cooperatives	• Social welfare corporations • Social medical care corporations • Producer cooperatives (agricultural, fisheries, forestry, and small-medium enterprises) • Shinkin (community) banks • Stock companies/ limited liability companies • Third sector organizations • Town management organizations (TMO) • Councils for the revitalization of central urban districts	• Nonprofit, nongovernmental organizations • Social welfare corporations • Producer cooperatives (agricultural, fisheries, forestry, and small-medium enterprises) • Credit unions/ community credit cooperatives • Stock companies/ limited companies • Partnership companies/ limited partnership companies • Limited liability companies • Rural community enterprises • Local credit guarantee foundations

(Continued)

Table 3.3   Categorization of the Major Legal Entities in the Northeast Asian Countries (*Continued*)

	China	Japan	South Korea
Social Organizations I	• Social organizations • Producer cooperatives (supply and marketing, industrial, and handicraft) • Rural township enterprises • Urban township enterprises • Social service organizations • Villagers' committees • Urban Residents' committees	• Incorporated education institutions • Medical corporations' juridical persons for offender's rehabilitation • Mutual aid associations • Labor unions • Authorized neighborhood associations	• Incorporated associations • Incorporated foundations • Public service corporations • Medical corporations/school juridical persons • Mutual aid associations/labor unions • Residential autonomous committees
Social Organizations II	• Labor unions • State-owned enterprises • Public institutions	• General incorporated associations/ foundations • Religious corporations • Neighborhood associations • Independent administrative agencies • Special corporations/ special civil corporations	• Confucian school foundations • Public agencies/ public enterprises • Local public enterprises

and specific patterns of hybridity are essential characteristics of the SEOs in Northeast Asia.

Second, concerning the mixture of subelements in the major and quasi-SEOs, four elements among six are particularly interconnected. However, there are some exceptions. Most of the hybrid platform consists of the ideal level of establishment, main activity, institutional mission, and target problem. These are common characteristics in the Northeast Asian countries in that they have weak or negative regulations concerning ownership and profit distribution. Specifically, the regulations on profit distribution are quite ambiguous in the case of most legal entities in China.

Third, the quasi-SEOs share two prominent patterns in their hybrid platform components. The first pattern is a mixture of freedom of association and economic activity, which appears in the private companies in particular. The second pattern is a mixture of economic activity and targets social problems. This pattern appears in the case of producer cooperatives and various community development organizations.

Table 3.4 shows the location of major and quasi-SEOs on a two-dimensional map. If we consider the two organizational features based on organizational resource and target beneficiary, Northeast Asian SEOs can be roughly recategorized into five types: (1) Work Integration Social Enterprises (WISE), (2) cooperatives, (3) private companies, (4) multipurpose complex organizations, and (5) community complex organizations. This result shows a similar but slightly broader image of the organizational terrain than that of Defourny and Kim (2011).[11] The result also provides a more inclusive and detailed list of organizations than "the Asian third sector organizations" discussed by Bhat and Hassan (2010).[12]

According to our legal-institutional analysis, the NPO-FPO (for-profit organization) partnership is not sufficiently institutionalized as the social economy, but various forms of private companies show a certain level of hybrid nature. Particularly, it should be noted that small-scale companies such as limited liability companies have been commonly institutionalized and have been increasing in China, Japan, and South Korea. They flexibly provide specific social or economic goods or services and are governed in a fair and cooperative manner by their core constitutive members.

South Korea's self-support enterprises and China's social welfare enterprises can be identified as WISE in Northeast Asia. These organizations are generally recognized as the most important in the discourse and policy discussion of the social economy. However, it should be also noticed that the NPOs and cooperatives are playing an important role in the employment of the handicapped, aged, or socially vulnerable in Japan. Therefore, organizational forms of WISE should be understood flexibly and broadly in Northeast Asia.

Community development enterprises can be viewed as one of the community complex organizations. There are also various legal forms in this category. The common characteristics of organizations in this category are that most are not corporations or juridical persons, but legal entities introduced and governed by the certification or approved system of local or central government. Thus, the relationship with or the intervention by the governments are the essential factor for the social economy at the community level.

Table 3.4　A Map of Major and Quasi-SEOs in China, Japan, and South Korea

		Main Organizational Resource		
		Human Resource/ Solidarity	*Complex*	*Monetary Resource/ Subsidies*
Main Target Beneficiary	Specific Groups/ Individuals	[WISE, Venture enterprises] **(C) Social welfare enterprises** **(K) Self-support enterprises** (C) Limited liability companies (J) Limited liability companies (K) Partnership companies (K) Limited partnership companies (K) Limited liability companies (K) Partnership Companies		[Companies] (C) Joint stock limited companies (J) Stock companies (K) Stock companies (K) Limited companies (Public agencies, Public-private Partnership organizations)
	Complex	[Cooperatives] **(C) Farmer specialized cooperatives** **(J) Consumer cooperatives** **(K) Consumer cooperatives** **(K) Social cooperatives** **(K) General cooperatives** (J) Producer cooperatives (Agricultural, Fisheries, Forest, etc.) (K) Producer cooperatives (Agricultural, Fisheries, and Forestry) (K) Credit unions (K) Community credit cooperatives	[Multipurposes complex organizations] **(J) Approved specified/ specified nonprofit corporations** **(J) Public interest incorporated associations/ foundations** **(K) Certified/ precertification social enterprises** (C) Private nonenterprise units (C) Foundations (C) Shareholding cooperative enterprises (J) Social welfare corporations (J) Social medical care corporations (K) Nonprofit, nongovernmental organizations (K) Social Welfare Corporations	
	Community	[Residential organizations]	[Community complex organizations] **(J) Approved specified/specified nonprofit corporations** **(J) Public interest incorporated associations/ foundations** **(K) Certified/precertification social enterprises** (C) Private nonenterprise units (C) Foundations (C) Shareholding cooperative enterprises (J) Social welfare corporations (J) Social medical care corporations (K) Nonprofit, nongovernmental organizations (K) Social welfare corporations	

(C): China, (J): Japan, (K): South Korea.
Major SEOs are indicated in bold text. Quasi-SEOs are indicated in plain text.

The multipurpose complex organizations may be the most remarkable in Northeast Asia because this category has the largest numbers of legal entities including all of the important NPOs in China, Japan, and South Korea. In terms of organizational resource and target beneficiary, the organizations in this category utilize both human and monetary capital and provide social services to both specific individuals and the whole community simultaneously. Such complex and multipurpose organizations are actively institutionalized and are increasing in Northeast Asia.

A Comparison between Northeast Asia and European Countries

Table 3.5 compares major SEOs of China, Japan, and South Korea with the corresponding organizational forms that are considered by the public to belong to the field of the social economy in the European countries (i.e., CMAF: cooperatives, mutuals, associations, and foundations). Other country-specific forms are also presented in the table. The first impression of the comparison would be that Northeast Asia still lacks organizational diversity. Mutuals, associations, and foundations have not been sufficiently institutionalized in China and South Korea as SEOs. Although Japan's major SEOs include associations and foundations, no other country-specific institutional forms are identifiable. The degree of organizational diversity looks low in comparison to France, Germany, and Spain, and the organizational terrain of China, Japan, and South Korea looks similar to that of Eastern European countries such as the Czech Republic, Poland, and Croatia.

However, if we consider the quasi-SEOs, the comparative view would radically change. Associations and foundations would be included for China and South Korea, and a variety of different forms would also be added as SEOs for Japan. In other words, the organizational diversity and dynamic development of the social economy may look more prominent in Northeast Asia than Europe if we include quasi-SEOs. Thus, in order to understand the unique regional characteristics of the social economy, it is necessary to pay attention to the broad aspects of its organizational terrain.

Another feature of the Northeast Asian region is that the mutual organizations have not sufficiently institutionalized in terms of the three domains and six subelements. It is a fact that the mutual organizations have been providing important social goods in China, Japan, and South Korea and their organizational scale and membership have been particularly increasing in Japan and South Korea. However, their legal regulations on ownership, establishment, and institutional mission are either ambiguous or insufficient to be included as an ideal SEO. As a consequence, the commercialization of the mutual

Table 3.5   Comparison of Major SEOs in Northeast Asia and Europe

	Cooperatives	Mutuals	Associations	Foundations	Other Forms of SEO
China	*	—	—	—	Social welfare enterprises
Japan	*	—	*	*	
S. Korea	*	—	—	—	Social enterprises, self-support enterprises community business organizations
Denmark	*	*	*	*	Social enterprises
Sweden	*	*	*	*	
France	*	*	*	*	Comités d'entreprise, voluntary social protection
Germany	*	—	*	*	Volunteer services and agencies, social firms for disadvantaged people, alternative enterprises of the women's and environmental movements, self-help organizations, sociocultural centers, work integration companies, local exchange and trading systems, neighborhood and community enterprises
Ireland	*	*	—	—	Credit unions
Italy	*	*	*	*	Volunteering organizations, associations of social promotion, family associations, community foundations, nongovernmental organizations, Istituzionidi Pubblica Assistenza e Beneficenza (IPAB)
Spain	*	*	*	*	Sociedades Laborales, Empresas de Inserción, Centros Especiales de Empleo, ONCE, Sociedades Agrarias de Transformación
UK	*	*	*	*	Community interest company (CIC)
Czech Republic	*	—	—	—	Association of common benefits
Hungary	*	*	*	*	Nonprofit enterprises
Poland	*	—	*	—	Centers of Socio-Economic Integration
Rumania	*	*	*	*	Authorized protected units
Croatia	*	—	*	*	
Slovakia	*	*	*	*	Sheltered workshops, social services

* means the major SEOs in each country.
For the source of the European countries, see EU (2012). The survey question for Europe is "which of the following institutional forms do you consider to belong to the field of the 'social economy' in your country or, if applicable, to a related concept that you consider more widely accepted?".

organizations has been commonly progressing in China, Japan, and South Korea.

CHALLENGES FOR THE DEVELOPMENT OF SOCIAL ECONOMY IN NORTHEAST ASIA

Taking Quasi-SEOs Seriously

The abovementioned regional characteristics imply some challenges for the development of social economy in Northeast Asia. We briefly discuss two notable implications of our analysis. It is true that the major SEOs are generally recognized by the public as belonging to the field of social economy and thus take a symbolically important position for the development of social economy in China, Japan, and South Korea. They are, in fact, playing innovative and leading roles in the field. However, the role of the quasi-SEOs should not be underestimated. The number of organizations and employees of the quasi-SEOs is much larger than that of the major SEOs in the three countries. Case-by-case activities of the quasi-SEOs can help spread the model of social economy throughout society. In order to realize a more effective social service provision and the creation of social values, the major SEOs alone are not enough. The role of the quasi-SEOs is also important, and it is necessary to seek for ways to enhance mutual complementarities between the major and quasi-SEOs.[13] These include, for example, corporate social responsibility practices of private companies, various participatory programs provided by community complex organizations, and community-level social relations of producer cooperatives. The horizon of social economy can be expanded by effectively combining the resources and models of the quasi-SEOs with those of the major SEOs.

Inclusive Institutional Reform

Northeast Asia may need institutional reforms for a more balanced and inclusive development of SEOs. The cases in point are the mutual organizations and the residential organizations, which were excluded from a wave of institutional reforms for promoting social economy in the 2000s in China, Japan, and South Korea. Thus, they remain as "Social Organizations I" on our map. With some institutional complements, they would easily be able to serve as quasi-SEOs. It would be necessary to strengthen the democratic ownership or freedom of association aspects of mutual organizations, while residential organizations need more detailed regulations on their economic activities or profit control. The institutional reforms of its nature would help enrich the organizational diversity of Northeast Asia.

In this respect, the South Korea government has partially and provisionally institutionalized the residential self-governing associations (*jumin jachihoi*) in 2013 to promote more diverse and autonomous activities at the community level. According to the policy guidelines, they are democratically owned among the residents and can engage themselves in community businesses while profit distribution is regulated to a certain degree.[14] The platform for residential and community organizations is also evolving in China and Japan. They are considered to be emerging in the region as a potential driving force for promoting social economy and social change (Read and Pekkanen 2009).

NOTES

1. Some pioneering comparative studies analyzed specific organizational forms or subjects such as social enterprises in East Asia (Defourny and Kim 2011), social economy programs in Asia (Yoo et al. 2015), Asian solidarity economy (Jayasooria 2013), Asian third sector (Hasan and Onyx 2010), Asian civil institutions (Weller 2005), Asian local organizations (Read and Pekkanen 2009), and corporate social responsibility in Asia (Low et al. 2014).

2. The Social Economy Unit was established under the European Commission in 1989, focusing on the "four families of social economy." The Unit was developed into the CEP-CMAF (European Standing Conference of Cooperatives, Mutual Societies, Associations and Foundations) in 2000.

3. A number of new concepts, models, and theories are emerging in this context. These include democratic innovation (American Political Science Association 2012), social ecosystem (Chen and Mohamed 2010), creative economy (Gates 2008), and inclusive business (UNDP 2008).

4. Some representative organizations of the old generation SEOs include agricultural cooperatives (*Nonghyup*), fisheries cooperatives (*suhyeob*), forestry cooperatives (*sanrim hyeob*), and small-medium enterprise cooperatives (*jungso gieob hyobdong johab*).

5. Three bills were consecutively submitted to the National Assembly through April–November 2014. The bill submitted by the ruling party, the Framework Act of Social Economy, provides seventeen legal entities with the legal capacity to participate in the subsidiary programs and development plans of the national social economy.

6. The Japanese government set up the "Social Business Research Group" as a policy consultative meeting affiliated to the Ministry of Economy, Trade, and Industry in 2007. As a result, the Ministry founded "Social Business and Community Business Promotion Council" at the local level by a public-private partnership method in 2008 and "Social Business Network" in 2010 as a private network of leading social enterprises and social entrepreneurs in Japan.

7. Japan implemented a comprehensive reform of corporation system in the 2000s by amending the civil act and newly introducing the companies act. New forms

of corporation include public interest corporation (*koeki hojin*), general corporation (*ippan hojin*), limited liability company (*godo gaisha*), and independent administrative agencies (*dokuritsu gyosei hojin*).

8. In his understanding, they share three key features: marketability of goods or service that an organization produces or provides, involvement in social issues, and innovative characteristics in its activity or structure. The map reflects two of these features.

9. In prior comparative studies, Defourny (2001, 16–18) focused on two features (social and economic) of social enterprises, Coraggio et al. (2015, 239–44) suggested three indicators (economic, social, and political) for evaluating an ideal type of solidarity-based social enterprise, and Bills (2010) directly argued for five subelements of hybrid organizations without categorizing or integrating them into broader domains.

10. The abovementioned comparative studies (note 9) also discussed the main domain and subelements as follows. Defourny (2001, 16–18) suggested eight subconditions of social enterprises: a high degree of autonomy; a significant level of economic risk; a minimum amount of paid work; an explicit aim to benefit the community; an initiative launched by a group of citizens; a decision-making power not based on capital ownership; a participatory nature, which involves the persons affected by the activity; and limited profit distribution. Coraggio et al. (2015, 239–44) argued for detailed nine criteria: hybridization of economic principles and logic of solidarity; consistency of economic, social, and environmental commitment; valorization of work; objective of transformation and repair; democratic solidarity; autonomy; public dimension; intermediate public sphere; and institutional entrepreneurship and political embeddedness. Bills (2010) discussed five core elements of hybrid organizations: ownership, governance, operational priority, distinctive human resources, and distinctive other resources. Our analytical framework rearranges these elements in terms of an aspect of legal regulations.

11. Defourny and Kim (2011) pointed out five major models of social enterprise in East Asia: (a) trading NPO-NPOs looking for other sources of income or seeking to achieve financial sustainability through the delivery of social services (other than work integration); (b) WISE provision of (stable or temporary) job opportunities with training and/or employment services; (c) nonprofit cooperative-collective self-employment and innovative responses to unmet needs based on cooperative tradition; (d) NPO-FPO partnership involvement of private companies (or company foundations) to support NPOs or joint initiatives with a social mission; and (E) community development enterprise multistakeholder partnerships (NPO, FPO, and public) promoting local participation.

12. Bhat and Hassan (2010) categorized the third sector organizations in Asian countries into three types: associations, foundations, and cooperatives. They also add nonprofit or charitable companies, religious trusts, and trade unions as minor categories.

13. The significance of interorganizational complementarity and effective synergy has been discussed under various theoretical labels including "co-production," "shared value," and "collaboration economy" (Porter and Kramer 2011; Lowitt 2013; Pestoff 2014).

14. Residential self-rule associations were excluded from the major legal entity in our analysis because their governing law was introduced provisionally and effective in only some designated local municipalities.

REFERENCES

American Political Science Association. 2102. *Democratic Imperatives: Innovations in Rights, Participation, and Economic Citizenship (Task Force Report).* Accessed June 30, 2020. http://www.apsanet.org/democraticimperatives.

Amin, Ash (ed.). 2009. *The Social Economy: International Perspectives in Economic Solidarity.* London: Zed Books.

Bhat, Iswara, and Samiul Hasan. 2010. "Legal Environment for TSO Governance: A Comparative Overview of Six Asian Countries." In *Comparative Third Sector Governance in Asia: Structure, Process, and Political Economy*, edited by Samiul Hasan and Jeney Onyx, 36–69. New York: Springer.

Bills, David. 2010. "Toward Understanding Governance in Hybrid Organizations." In *Hybrid Organizations and the Third Sector: Challenges for Practice, Theory and Policy*, edited by David Bills, 46–69. New York: Palgrave Macmillan.

Borzaga, Carlo, and Ermanno Tortia. 2007. "Social Economy Organisations in the Theory of the Firm." In *The Social Economy: Building Inclusive Economies*, edited by Antonella Noya and Emma Clarence, 23–60. Paris: OECD.

Bridge, Simon, Brendan Murtagh, and Ken O'Neill. 2014. *Understanding Social Economy and the Third Sector* (2nd Edition). London: Palgrave.

Cheng, Willie. 2010. "The Social Ecosystem: Transition within the Ecosystem of Change." In *The World that Changes the World: How Philanthropy, Innovation, and Entrepreneurship Are Transforming the Social Ecosystem*, edited by Willie Cheng and Sharifah Mohamed, 7–36. San Francisco: Jossey-Bass.

Defourny, Jacques. 2001. "Introduction: From Third Sector to Social Enterprise." In *The Emergence of Social Enterprise*, edited by Carlo Borzaga and Jacques Defourny, 1–28. London: Routledge.

Defourny, Jacques, Lars Hulgård, and Victor Pestoff. 2014. "Introduction to the 'SE Field.'" In *Social Enterprise and the Third Sector: Changing European Landscapes in a Comparative Perspective*, edited by Jacques Defourny, Lars Hulgård, and Victor Pestoff, 1–14. New York: Routledge.

Defourny, Jacques, and Marthe Nyssens. 2010. "Conceptions of Social Enterprise and Social Entrepreneurship in Europe and the United States: Convergences and Divergences." *Journal of Social Entrepreneurship* 1(1): 32–53.

———. 2012. "The EMES Approach of Social Enterprise in a Comparative Perspective." *EMES Working Paper* 12/3.

Defourny, Jacques, and Patrick Develtere. 1999. "Social Economy: The Worldwide Making of a Third Sector." In *Social Economy North and South*, edited by Jacques Defourny, Patrick Develtere, and Bénédicte Fonteneau, 17–47. HIVA: KU Leuven.

Defourny, Jacques, and Shin-yang Kim. 2011. "Emerging Models of Social Enterprise in Eastern Asia: A Cross-Country Analysis." *Social Enterprise Journal* 7(1): 86–111.

Donnelly-Cox, Gemma. 2015. "Civil Society and Governance: Hybridization within Third-Sector and Social Enterprise Domains." In *Civil Society, the Third Sector and Social Enterprise: Governance and Democracy*, edited by Jean-Louis Laville, Dennis R. Young, and Philippe Eynaud, 30–44. London: Routledge.

EMES. 2016. "Focus Area." Accessed June 30, 2020. http://emes.net/focus-areas.

EU. 2012. *The Social Economy in the European Union*. Brussels: EU.

Evers, Adalbert. 2008. "Hybrid Organization: Background, Concept, Challenges." In *The Third Sector in Europe: Prospects and Challenges*, edited by Stephen Osborne, 279–292. London: Routledge.

FYSE. 2012. *China Social Enterprise Report*. Accessed July 31, 2018. http://www .fyse.org.

Gates, Bill. 2008. "A New Approach to Capitalism in the 21st Century." Presentation at World Economic Forum, January 24, Davos, Switzerland.

Gunn, Christopher. 2004. *Third Sector Development: Making Up for the Market*. Ithaca: Cornell University Press.

Hasan, Samiul, and Jeney Onyx. 2010. *Comparative Third Sector Governance in Asia: Structure, Process, and Political Economy*. New York: Springer.

ILO. 2011. *Social and Solidarity Economy: Our Common Road towards Decent Work*. Turin: ILO.

Jayasooria, Denison. 2013. *Developments in Solidarity Economy in Asia*. Malaysia: JJ Resources.

Joo, Sung Su. 2010. *Social Economy: Theories, Institutions, Policies* [*Sahoijeok Gyoenje: Iron, Jedo, JeongJaeg*]. Seoul: Hanyang University Press.

Jose Coraggio, et al. 2015. "The Theory of Social Enterprise and Pluralism: Solidarity-Type Social Enterprise." In *Civil Society, the Third Sector and Social Enterprise: Governance and Democracy*, edited by Jean-Louis Laville, Dennis R. Young, and Philippe Eynaud, 234–259. London: Routledge.

Kurimoto, Akira. 2011. "Statistics of Japan's Social Economy." [Nihonno Shakaiteki Keizaino Tokeiteki Haakuni Mukete]. In *Future of Social Economy* [*Shakaiteki Keizaiga Hiraku Mirai*], edited by Osama Mari. Kyoto: Minerva.

Laratta, Rosario, Sachiko Nakagawa, and Masanari Sakurai. 2011. "Japanese Social Enterprises: Major Contemporary Issues and Key Challenges." *Social Enterprise Journal* 7(1): 50–68.

Laville, Jean-Louis. 2013. *The Social and Solidarity Economy: A Theoretical and Plural Framework*. Geneva: UNRISD.

Lee, Eun Ae, and Young-Sik Kim. 2013. *Social Economy and Public Policy Development: A South Korean Case*. Montreal: Chantier de L'économie Sociale.

Lee, Rebecca. 2012. "The Emergence of Social Enterprises in China: The Quest for Space and Legitimacy." *Tsinghua China Law Review* 2: 79–99.

Low, Kim Cheng Patrick, Samuel O. Idowu, and Sik Liong Ang (eds). 2014. *Corporate Social Responsibility in Asia: Practice and Experience*. New York: Springer.

METI. 2008. *Report of Social Business Research Group.* Tokyo: METI.

Ninacs, William. 2002. "A Review of the Theory and Practice of Social Economy." *SRDC Working Paper Series* 2-2.

Noya, Antonella, and Emma Clarence (eds). 2007. *The Social Economy: Building Inclusive Economies.* Paris: OECD.

Osborne, Stephen. 2008. *The Third Sector in Europe: Prospects and Challenges.* London: Routledge.

Park, Tae-gyu, Gu-hyeon Joeng, In-chun Kim, and Chang-sun Hwang. 2016. *The Third Sector in South Korea [Hangugui Jesamsegteo].* Seoul: Samsung Economic Research Institute.

Peace, John. 2003. *Social Enterprise in Anytown.* London: Calouste Gulbenkian Foundation.

Pekkanen, Robert. 2006. *Japan's Dual Civil Society Members without Advocacy.* Redwood: Stanford University Press.

Pestoff, Victor A. 1998. *Beyond the Market and State: Social Enterprises and Civil Democracy in a Welfare Society.* Aldershot: Ashgate.

————. 2014. "Hybridity, Innovation and the Third Sector: The Co-Production of Public Services." In *Social Enterprise and the Third Sector: Changing European Landscapes in a Comparative Perspective*, edited by Jacques Defourny, Lars Hulgård, and Victor Pestoff, 250–270. New York: Routledge.

Porter, Michael E., and Mark R. Kramer. 2011. "The Big Idea: Creating Shared Value." *Harvard Business Review* 89(January/February): 62–77.

Pun, Ngai, Ben Hok-bun Ku, Hairong Yan, and Anita Koo. 2016. *Social Economy in China and the World.* London: Routledge.

Read, Benjamin L., and Robert Pekkanen. 2009. *Local Organizations and Urban Governance in East and Southeast Asia: Straddling State and Society.* London: Routledge.

Shragge, Eric, and Jean-Marc Fontan (eds). 2000. *Social Economy: International Debates and Perspectives.* Montreal: Black Rose Books.

Tanimoto, Kanji. 2006. *The Rise of Social Enterprise [Sosharu Entapuraizu: Shakaiteki Kigyouno Taito].* Tokyo: Chuo Keizai.

The Youido Institute. 2014. "Management of Cooperatives and Their Implications." *Policy Paper Series* 11.

Tsujinaka, Yutaka, et al. 2013. "The Formation and Existence of Groups in Japan." [Nihonni Okeru Dantaino Keiseito Sonzai]. In *Political Functions of Contemporary Social Groups [Gendai Shaiasyudannno Seijiteki Kinou]*, edited by Yutaka Tsujinaka, et al. Tokyo: Bokutakusya.

UNDP. 2008. *Creating Value for All: Strategies for Doing Business with the Poor.* Paris: UNDP.

Ushiro, Fusao. 2011. *The Category and Management of the Japanese Third Sector [Nihonni Okeru Sadosekutano Hannito KeieiJittai].* Tokyo: Research Institute of Economy, Trade and Industry.

Utting, Peter (ed.). 2015. *Social and Solidarity Economy: Beyond the Fringe.* London: Zed Books.

Wang, Ming, and Xiaohong Zhu. 2010. "An Outline of Social Enterprises." [Shehui Qiye Lungang]. *Chinese Journal of Non-Profit Organization* 6(2).

Weller, Robert P. 2005. "Introduction: Civil Institutions and the State." In *Civil Life, Globalization, and Political Change in Asia: Organizing Between Family and the State*, edited by Robert P. Weller. London: Routledge.

Yan, Hairong, and Yi Pan. 2014. *Social Economy in China: Beyond the Imagination of Capitalist* [*Shehui Jingji Zai Zhongguo*]. Beijing: Social Science Academic Press.

Yoo, Chung Sik, Ki Jian, and Kyu Jae Kee. 2015. *Case Studies on Poverty Alleviation and Social Economy*. Seoul: CM Press.

Yu, Xiaomin. 2011. "Social Enterprise in China: Driving Forces, Development Patterns and Legal Framework." *Social Enterprise Journal* 7(1): 9–32.

Zang, Shuguan, et al. 2012. "Social Economy in China." [*Shehui* Jingji Zai Zhongguo]. *Open Times* 9(1).

Zhang, Xiaomin. 2013. "Challenges Facing the Development of Farmers' Specialized Cooperatives in China." In *Cooperative Growth for the 21st Century*, edited by Bruno Rolelants, 19–22. International Cooperative Alliance. Accessed June 30, 2020. https://www.ica.coop/en/co-operative-growth-21st-century.

Zhao, Li. 2013. "Conceptualizing the Social Economy in China." *Modern Asian Studies* 47(3): 1088–1123.

Zhao, Meng. 2012. "The Social Enterprise Emerges in China." *Stanford Social Innovation Review* (Spring): 30–35.

Chapter 4

Grassroots Economies, Empowering Local Communities

Case Studies from Three ASEAN Countries

Denison Jayasooria

INTRODUCTION

The dominant economic model in Asia and in majority of South East Asian countries is big business and multinational companies dominating in a free market economic environment. National economic policies seem to favor big business and capital investments. This movement of capital to low-wage countries in manufacturing is popular and this is impacting micro and small business communities in a negative way. While there are increased employment opportunities in many Asian countries, nonetheless, it is creating inequalities, disempowering, and alienating the bottom sections of our societies.

It is in this unequal and unfriendly business environment we see all over Asia, the rise of local grassroots economies which are operating at the bottom catering the needs of the ordinary people, providing goods and services to this section of the communities. We could see these developments as counter socioeconomic grassroots initiatives in the South East Asian countries in response to the "dominant business models which marginalise and alienates the vast majority of the people. Solidarity economy is an alternative economy that is people empowering, and promotes equitable share of economic growth as well as sustainable use of the natural resources" (Jayasooria et al. 2015, 2).

There is a close correlation between grassroots economies and the informal sector as these are not part of mainstream or formal economies. In this context, it is significant to note that the International Labour Organisation (ILO) has recognized the potential of the informal sector and grassroots economies, noting that the informal sector is still central to the ILO mandate for social justice (Bangasser 2000). In a recent press release, ILO notes that more than 68% of the employed population in Asia pacific are in the informal economy. This reiterates its importance; however, national public policy and State intervention tend to favor private big business (ILO 2018). Another, international development organization, Asia Foundation (2011) also recognizes that "throughout Asia, small businesses area a critical component of local economies." While recognizing this potential, Asia Foundation (2011) also notes the policy environmental challenges such as regulations and procedures which are not favorable to creating a favorable policy environment for business development.

Within Asia, South East Asian countries are seeing economic prosperity and also the flourishing of grassroots economics including the informal sector. It is significant to that five of these countries, namely Malaysia, Indonesia, Thailand, Philippines, and Singapore, jointly established in 1967, ASEAN—the Association of South East Asian Nations. From five countries, ASEAN is now a socioeconomic regional grouping of ten countries. These now represent a collective population of 620 million people and is strategically located in South East Asia between India and China. One can say that ASEAN is "one of the most successful regional organisations in the world" (Anthony 2017, 275). In ASEAN, there is a clear policy toward a people- and community-centered ASEAN by 2025 which has some parallel complementarities with Sustainable Development Goals (SDGs) 2030 Agenda (ESCAP 2017).

The SDGs with its five foundational principles of people, planet, prosperity, peace, and partnership correspond closely with the five guiding frameworks of SSE. This theme is well articulated by Benjamin Quinones and cited by Denison Jayasooria (2016). Quinones highlights five major attributes of SSE (responsible governance, edifying values, and triple bottom line—people, profits, and planet) which could also serve as the common framework for measuring and evaluating solidarity economy performance. We can therefore utilize these five dimensional frameworks as a way of evaluating the various community and social enterprises. In addition, the SDGs' framework can also be utilized for enhancing income of the bottom 40 (B40) in addressing inequality and eliminating discrimination (SDG10:3), ensuring access to justice (SDG 16:3), and creating space in decision-making (SDG 16:7).

These are illustrated by the case studies from ASEAN countries. It is within these ASEAN countries that we will illustrate the dynamic movement at the grassroots. These businesses are micro and small organizations with less than five workers. In the community and cooperative setting, the numbers will be larger. However, it is right to say that these are grassroots micro community organizations which are working with disadvantaged and marginalized communities within their societies. They could be also operating in a value chain supporting each other and therefore much bigger than just one unit but rather a chain or business which has community support. The first case study is a Thai example of the informal sector in Bangkok. The second is an Indonesian example of alternative financing for business development and poverty eradication, and finally the third, indigenous people in an organic farm project.

From Thailand, the case of HomeNet in Bangkok, an organization working with the informal sector, who are undertaking economic activities by the streets to create wealth at the bottom and the conflicts with enforcement for their rights for the space to make a living. From Indonesia, the case of Dompet Dhuafa, an Islamic philanthropic and investments institution which seeks to empower rural communities through micro create and community development. From Malaysia, the case of OA Organics (YKPM) in Pekan, Pahang. An initiative of indigenous forest-based communities, who are making the transition from nomadic life to organic farms. Their struggles in farming as well as the conflicts faced on land ownership alongside their rights to shift from charity approach toward empowerment and dignity. These alternative stories are innovative initiatives of people empowerment who are seeking local solutions in addressing their challenges through mutual cooperation and self-determination. SSE is enhancing their collective expressions for transformation emerging from the grassroots.

INFORMAL—HOME-BASED WORKERS, THAILAND EXPERIENCE

Context and Location

Bangkok[1] is the capital of Thailand with 8.28 million people and it is regarded "as one of the largest metropolises in the world" (Sarosa and Arifin 2012, 322). Bangkok is a cosmopolitan city, home to people from around the world. There are 2.7 million small enterprises which has contributed USD 8.6 billion or 25% of Thailand's total GDP +5 (Mandhachitara and Allapach 2017, 1). Therefore, the city of Bangkok has a striving informal and formal business sector creating wealth and providing a decent living for all.

Target Group

The target group can be categorized by class, gender, and type of business or trade-based group largely among informal and home-based workers at the bottom of the socioeconomic pile. They are at the B40 and among the urban poor. Gender is a key component as a large percentage of informal and home-based workers are women. They are home-based workers, informal workers, and street vendors who are seeking to survive in the city, at its fingers. They are also among the poor who migrated from the rural areas to urban centers in search for jobs, better income, and quality of life.

It could be said that they are people with low economic capital and low educational qualifications. They are a group, that policy makes and rich often underestimate as powerless. However, we see great resilience among them to survive in the city and they are innovating to create wealth at the bottom of the socioeconomic pile. They are providing services that city dwellers need such as good, tasty but at the same time cheap food. It is also important to recognize that these informal workers "produce a wide range of low and high-end good and services for both domestic and global markets" (Chen and Singha 2016, 1).

Issues Encountered

While the urbanization rate of Thailand is low compared to other ASEAN countries, nonetheless the movement of rural people into the city of Bangkok, into high density neighborhoods is creating issues of employment for the poor and low-income families. They are there for resorting to informal economy for their livelihood support.

A large section of Bangkok city business fall in the informal sector and they were not organized. They are individuals operating micro business and therefore do not have a collective bargaining position in a free market economy. As there is the need for collective action and networking, for in numbers they could be strong in collective action against Bangkok city officials as well as formal business which were better connected with political forces on the top.

One group among the informal sector namely, street vendors faced the eviction notice on hawking by the streets which took place in 2014. Aljazeera journalist Bemma (2018) documented the clash between Bangkok city official and street vendors. While Bangkok is known as the "number one city in the world for street food" (Bemmna 2018), the Bangkok Metropolitan Administration since 2014 introduced a policy for citywide clearance campaign entitled "return the pavement to pedestrians." The city officials' intention was to get rid of food carts and stalls by the Bangkok streets. It is estimated that about 300,000 street vendors in Bangkok generate around 450 million Baht (USD 14 million) per day in income. Public policy is not favorable to the informal sector and city officials seem pro formal business and not facilitating and ensuring the informal sector strives in the city.

Chen and Sinha (2016, 2) describe the critical challenges faced by the informal and home-based workers. They state these "workers do not enjoy adequate economic opportunities, legal rights, social protection or representative voice . . . [in the case of home based workers they are] largely invisible and undervalued. . . [they are also] . . .overlooked by policy makers" (Chen and Sinha 2016, 2).

Innovation

There are three innovations that HomeNet Thailand (HNT) was involved in. Their success has been seen as collective action of the people in community solidarity. These are as follows:

First, organizing the informal sector into associations and collective movements on the ground.

HNT organized various informal worker groups into a federation which is very significant for public advocacy and mutual support. The effort here was to build and strengthen organizations of informal workers and to promote the legal and social protection of informal workers. To support its organizing and advocacy activities, HNT forms alliances with other civil society organizations (CSOs) and with academics and lawyers, undertakes research studies, and has worked with the national statistical office to generate improved statistics on informal workers.

The Federation of Informal Workers was established in 2016 comprising two registered associations and two nonregistered networks, each of which have constitutions and elected leaders, as follows:

The Association of Home-Based Workers was founded in 1992. This association has 5,000 members across Thailand. The association is engaged in efforts to implement ILO Convention 177 and the national Act on Homeworkers. With the ILO Regional Office in Bangkok, the association is currently involved in a study of fair piece rates for homeworkers and in drafting a model employment contract for homeworkers.

The Association of Motorcycle Taxi Drivers was founded in 2010. This association has 3,000 members across Bangkok. The association advocates for more supportive city policies toward motorcycle taxi drivers. The 2014 Footpath Policy in Bangkok not only banned street vendors from footpaths but also motorcycle taxi queues. Out of 1,000 motorcycle taxi queues across the city, only 300 are currently allowed to park their motorcycles on footpaths. The association estimates that there are 130,000 motorcycle taxi drivers in Bangkok who jointly generate about 200 million Baht (USD 6.2 million) income per day.

The Network of Domestic Workers founded in 2010 has 600 members, of which 400 are Thais and 200 Burmese domestic workers. This network is engaged in efforts to implement ILO Convention 189 and the national resolution on domestic workers, including drafting of a model employment contract for domestic workers and their inclusion under Article 33 of the Social Security Act of Thailand.

The Network of Thai Street Vendors for Sustainable Development was founded in 2018. This network has 7,500 members. All members of 7,500 preexisting local associations of street vendors.

Second, innovation is the policy advocacy initiative undertaken to improve the quality of working condition of the informal and home-based workers.

Over the years, HNT has helped achieve several successes for informal workers on the national policy front together in alliance with other CSOs. Two public policies were introduced through the campaign efforts of HNT.

The first such success was the universal health coverage scheme for informal workers and other groups not covered by formal health insurance. According to Tulaphan, "Thailand stands out for its decade-long inclusion of civil society organizations in an alliance for health reform, with HNT and one of the partners, who contributed to the campaign for what became known, initially, as the 30 Baht Scheme. When the 30 Baht Scheme was replaced by the free Universal Coverage Scheme, the alliance of civil society networks including HNT, were again involved in the design of the scheme, in the legislation, and thereafter in facilitating, monitoring and evaluating implementation" (Tulaphan 2019a).

The second success achieved was the Homeworkers Protection Act, which entitles Thai homeworkers (subcontracted home-based workers) to minimum wage, occupational health and safety protection, and other fundamental labor rights. "HNT made a concerted effort to inform homeworker leaders and homeworkers about their rights under the Act through workshops with lawyers and government officials, posters, newsletters and other documents. In 2014, as a direct outcome of these struggles, three home-based workers supported by HNT were included in the tripartite committee" (Tulaphan 2019a).

The third is the organizing of street protest to exercise the rights of the informal sector as citizens and rights to livelihood by the streets.

Faced with eviction notice, a citywide counter campaign and protest was organized by the network of street vendors and informal workers in 2017, to fight street hawking evictions. About 10,000 were mobilized for street protest. This protest was supported by HNT and WIEGO Focal City. On September 4, 2018, over 1,200 members rallied to the Government House to negotiate with the government to stop banning street hawking policy. They called for a committee to solve these problems which will include street vendor representatives.

The Thai government responded with the formation of a committee to deal with the street vendor issues, chaired by the Ministry of the Interior. The network seeks representation on and action by the committee. Another positive outcome is also the creation of the Network of Thai Street Vendors for

Sustainable Development—NEST in 2018. According to Tulaphan, "the network's objective is to provide support and solidarity to vendors and to protect their rights" (Tulaphan 2019b). The dialogue between the street vendors and the government is ongoing but "up to now nothing has moved" or changed (Tulaphan 2019b). The street vendors are still operating but the lesson is that they made their stand and exerted their rights as citizens.

Organization

HNT was established in 1996. It has its roots in the ILO support project on social protection for home workers which began in 1992. HNT members and partners formed the Foundation for Labour and Employment Promotion (Foundation), which now has become the support institution to the membership-based societies of home and informal workers. Internationally HNT is associated with WIEGO, a global network focused on securing livelihoods for the working poor, especially women, in the informal economy.

Lessons Learned

Building the collective partnership of all the informal and home-based workers is most critical for their empowerment, as a collective voice for self-help and self-advocacy. Governance in this federation of formal and informal associations and networks is most essential, as each association and network elects a representative to serve on the executive committee of the Federation of Informal Workers and pays an annual membership fee to the Federation. The street vendors in the Federation also sell T-shirts to help raise funds for the Federation. Through the Federation, with support from HNT, these associations and networks seek to raise awareness of the contributions and concerns of informal workers and to demand benefits and protection for informal workers in Bangkok and across Thailand.

According to Tulaphan (2019a), "being a member of the federation, according to the leaders of the associations and networks, enhances their awareness of how the policy and regulatory environment impacts other informal worker groups; enhances their bargaining power through strength in numbers; and reduces their sense of isolation. Together, they are fighting for recognition that domestic workers, home-based producers, motor cycle taxi drivers and street vendors provide essential services and goods and that street vendors especially are part of the charm and attraction of Bangkok, to tourists and to citizens alike."

We note in the Bangkok case study that the approach enhances a very strong rights-based framework. Within the limited democratic space of Thailand, the informal micro business people acted to demonstrate they have a voice and say in the city. Their collective self-organizing eventually facilitated their collective action in street protest forcing the Thai government to invite them for a dialogue and a committee established to resolve the issues. The HNT groups were able to demonstrate that they were exercising their rights for their right to earn an income through their street hawking businesses.

FAITH-BASED FINANCES—INDONESIAN EXPERIENCE

Context and Location

Indonesia is the largest Muslim populated country in the world with 191 million Muslims. They form 87% of 220 million people in Indonesia. One of the religious pillars of Islam is the financial giving to the poor which is known as Zakat, which is a religious obligation. It is estimated that 40% of Indonesian Muslims or 76.5 million make contributions which is collected by Zakat institutions, who then redistribute the collected funds to the poor.

Very little of this faith-based initiative has been discussed in social solidarity literature. This is one form of collective, community-based financing pool to assist and support the poor in local communities. This Indonesian case study explores the potential of Islamic financing for economic empowerment and common good in the community of believers.

Target Group

The main target groups are the poor, disadvantaged person, and their families. Based on the 2010 Indonesia Census, there are about 33.9 million poor people living below the poverty line throughout Indonesia. Said and Purwakananta (2010) state that the current figures estimate that about 26 million or 9.82% of the Indonesian population can be considered poor. Of these, a majority (estimated twenty million) live in Java. It is also estimated that 50.1% of these are poor women. The contemporary public debate is on the poverty line income which is regarded as too low and unrealistic.

"In Indonesia, people live below the poverty line when their average spending is Rp 401,220 (USD 27.72) a month, or around Rp 11,000 (USD 0.76) a day. In the capital of Jakarta, the numbers are slightly higher: people are poor when they spend Rp 578,000 per month (USD 39.93) or Rp 19,000 (USD 1.31) a day" (Said and Purwakananta 2010). The critics say "the government's ridiculously low standards of poverty is baffling in this economy where no one can fulfil their basic needs with Rp 20,000" (Said and Purwakananta 2010).

Dompet Dhuafa, the organization working among the poor, targets the poor living below the poverty line and who are also entitled as zakat beneficiaries. Since its founding in 1993 it has helped more than sixteen million people through one of its many programs for socioeconomic development (Jakarta Post 2018).

Issues Encountered

Access to credit is one major issue faced by the Indonesian poor. It is pointed out by Aligori (2017) that banks are unable to touch poor people. This is because they are commercial, profit-oriented entities. These banks "only choose the potential clients who are able to return the money and were able to generate revenue for the bank. "Bank tends to be reluctant to serve low-income households, because they are considered not 'bank able'. Consequently, many people who are trapped by trapping money lenders who give high-interest loans" (Aligori 2017). The net result of this lack of access forces the poor to seek alternative funding largely through moneylenders with their high interest. Based on Islamic teaching there is a need to break-through usury (interest) and in Arabic it is called *riba*, which is religiously prohibited.

Innovation

Fund mobilization is one of the major innovations through funds raised as a result of Islamic religious obligation. These contributions are institutionally collected and are now utilized in an empowering way. This is a unique feature of this faith-based initiative, where the collective action by the majority is directly providing alternative financing for wealth creation among the poorer sections of that faith community.

Since its founding, Dompet Dhuafa has undertaken many programs of empowerment through the efficient and productive use of zakat funding. According to Said, social programs are established "to provide social security making the poor get a proper access to obtain the services of health, education and settlement be able to fulfil the needs in an emergency and urgent conditions" (Said 2010, 3). In this context, Dompet Dhuafa has established different programs to cater health, education, disaster management, and address unemployment issues. These therefore could be reviewed from the multidimensional approach of SDG goals and viewing poverty beyond income the agenda.

However, their most significant initiative in this context is their economic programs in assisting the poor to get them out of poverty. They provide capital through microcredit and assisting the small-scale business in the villages. There are special initiatives for the promotion of organic agriculture among farmers, as well as building the network of animal breeders. In addition to loans, capacity building in improving productivity and marketing the produce has been introduced. A business division was established to promote and market the products produced so as to ensure higher economic returns.

Dompet Dhuafa seeks to be a solution for poor people to develop themselves and their economy. From the beginning, Dompet Dhuafa resolved not to give the funds as cash to the poor community. However, they decided to channel it through entrepreneurship programs which provide grants, loan capital, training skills, and mentoring. "This empowerment program is expected to develop well and be a provision for a business community. Finally, beneficiaries are required to establish a cooperative based Sharia system and they are able to make this cooperative as members' enterprise development" (Aligori 2017).

It is significant to note that there are priority thrust areas. The first is the Farm Livestock economic program where the focus is in increasing income through livestock breeding. The second is in Healthy Agricultural program which is helping small farmers through community farming enterprises and the introduction of postharvest technology.

Aligori (2017) notes that one positive outcome is the emergence of local institutions such as community cooperatives which will ensure self-sufficiency communities. A significant creation is the development of nonbanking sharia finance emerging from the community economic empowerment programs. Five economic pillars are recognized in the community empowerment program conducted by Dompet Dhuafa, namely, "the value of the humanities, law and justice, economy and wellbeing and Institutional Governance. It means that the concept of empowerment should refer to Sharia" (Aligori 2017).

Organization

As noted in the website, Dompet Dhuafa was established in 1993 and it is an Islamic philanthropy institute or board, where the funds are sourced from Zakat contributions and other halal funding rechanneled to the needy person and family. Dompet Dhuafa is the largest Amil Zakat (LAZ) organization in Indonesia. The objective is to empower the poor and create an empowered society. Its approach is a religious and cultural one based on philanthropic and humanitarian activities. There is a recognition for prophetic social entrepreneurship or prophetic sociotechnopreneurship. They rely on local resources and seek to foster a fair system (Dhuafa 2019). In addition to economy, Dompet Dhuafa undertakes programs pertaining to health, education, and social development.

According to Haryono (2019), Dompet Dhuafa operates in 22 provinces and in more than 140 villages in Indonesia. Its economic empowerment program currently reaches out to 30,775 households such as farmers, fishermen, breeders, and small ventures. While there is a thrust toward economic empowerment, they adopt a multidimensional approach including economic, educational, health, and community empowerment.

Lessons Learned

This Indonesian Islamic model of collective financing for the poor is from the country with the largest Muslim population in the world. This is very encouraging and highlights the potential of faith-based communities and their collective financial pooling and action in addressing poverty and inequality in modern societies. The pooling of funds raised from the Muslim community and its management can signify alternative community-based financing for socioeconomic development including community solidarity and empowerment. This faith-based initiative is also values based, such as our common humanity and motivated from religious obligations. Here, is an institutional approach for fund collection and utilization which can be empowering for the common community good during the collective management of these resources. Zakat funds are only used for addressing poor communities within the Muslim community as they are a very needy group in many Muslim societies. The Indonesian example and experience is not a charity handout model but an empowering model for economic wealth creation and redistribution.

Chandra and Rahman (2010) in writing about the Dompet Dhuafa note that they have changed the goal of the fund distribution, from a consumption purpose to that of production. This according to them means that their economic assets are now generating returns, which will benefit the beneficiaries. The newly generated income can be invested for other socioeconomic objectives too for the common good such as providing free education and health needs, alleviation of poverty, and creation of jobs.

INDIGENOUS PEOPLE—MALAYSIAN EXPERIENCE

Context and Location

Ulu Gumum[2] village is located in Malaysia, in the state of Pahang and in the district of Pekan, about four kilometers from Tasik Chini which is the second largest freshwater lake in Malaysia and a UNESCO Biosphere Reserve. This is also a popular tourist spot. It is about 225 kilometers from Kuala Lumpur.

Target Group

The target group are among the aboriginal community of Peninsula Malaysia whom are known as the Orang Asli or original people. According to Nicholas et al. (2010, 9), "they are the descendants of the early inhabitants of the peninsula before the establishment of the Malay kingdoms." The Orang Aslis form 0.05% of the Malaysian population and are about 150,000, but other sources now estimate it at 180,000 (Kon 2019).

Within the Orang Asli community, are the Jakuns who are one of the eighteen subethnic groups comprising about 27,448 (Nicholas et al. 2010, 9–11). They are the second largest subethnic group. They fall within the proto Malay tribe and they were largely hunters and gathers living within the forest till 2008. According to Kon (2019), "the shift had begun earlier but there was a gradual change to settled small holders. A minority still practice shifting cultivation and they stay in a place for a couple of years and then move on."

The target group of Jakuns living in Ulu Gumum comprise 33 families and about 120 people. Ulu Gumum is a hamlet from the larger village of Tasik Cini, which consists of about eighty families. They share the same headman who is based in Tasik Cini. There is a local representative head resident in Ulu Gumum.

Issues Encountered

There are some major issues which confront this community. One major issue is their income source. While many undertake traditional roles of hunting and gathering, they need to do some other jobs to supplement their incomes. Some participate in the oil palm scheme managed by a government agency through which they receive a monthly dividend of RM 600 or more (USD 143.48) depending on the crop, rubber or oil palm. The Orang Aslis do not do any work but this is an equity payment for the use of six acres of their land. This is a disempowering project as they are not being equipped to become small holders. In the case of others who are collecting forest produce or working as contract workers, they seem to be exploited by the middle men as they lack the capacity to access the markets directly.

There are many other socioeconomic issues, such as lack of internet connectivity and rubbish disposal system, although basic facilities such as low-cost housing, water, and electric supply are available. Educational achievements are very low, with children dropping out after primary school education at twelve years of age.

Land is precious and the Jakuns have a very close relationship with their land and natural resources. According to Kon Onn Sein, "their lands and resources are significant not only as a means of livelihood but also as part of their spiritual and cultural life and form part of their identity as peoples. The ancestors are buried in the vicinity and it is believed that these spirits act as guardians of the land and form an important part of their lives" (Kon 2019).

All the lands in the Orang Asli villages belong to the individuals in the community, which they inherited over the years and their memory of occupation of these lands go back to 1942. "Customary land rights continue to plague the Orang Asli. Many of their customary land is not given adequate legal protection and about 80% of such lands are not gazetted as Orang Asli reserve. This puts them in a vulnerable position as tenants at will" (Kon 2019). A fuller description of the land rights issues can be found in the Human Rights Commission's land inquiry report (SUHAKAM 2013).

Innovation

Since 1992 Kon Onn Sein had been working with the Orang Asli communities and by 2000 when he gave up his legal career, YKPM had an outreach to fifteen villages undertaking literacy programs and building houses. However, in December 2015 it was soon realized that one of the villages was ready to undertake income generation projects, namely, to develop an organic farm.

A small start was made and the village folks received some seeds and discovered that one of them had green thumbs. Their product was sold in the market to get the best price. After a few months, the price for their mustard greens went up from RM 2 to RM 4 (USD 0.48–0.96 cents) per kilogram. This rise in revenue attracted others. From individuals the village began a collective approach in organizing an organic farm as a social enterprise called OA Organics. A local village committee was established after collective discussion and decision-making. They identified a plot of land and begun cultivation on one area. The foundation provided some support, including recruiting a team of volunteers to provide agricultural and markets support.

According to Kon, "OA Organics is the trading name and partnership between the Orang Asli farmers and the marketing cooperative" (Star 2017). Initially they produced and sold about 300 kilograms of vegetables per month which eventually reached 900 kilograms. In October 2017, a major supermarket chain, Jaya Grocer, adopted OA Organics as part of its corporate social responsibility (CSR) and sells the produce at its outlet in Kuantan town which is about 60 kilometers further east from Ulu Gumum. OA Organics now has a guaranteed fair trade market.

The project has already made an impact on the farmers' lives. With OA Organics they are receiving about RM 800 (USD 191.25) per person per month. However, Kon recognizes that their "current challenge is to expand the farm to five acres to reach economy of scale and help them earn RM 1,200 (USD 286.88) per month. One way is to invest in mechanization so that they can achieve this goal."

OA Organics also received the support from a private sector construction company called Gamuda which undertook a CSR contribution of thirty engineers and staff to help the community build greenhouses to boost production, and CIMB has provided a grant to set up a chicken farm.

Organization

The organization working with the Jakun community is the Foundation for Community Studies and Development (YKPM), which was founded on September 22, 1993, with the aims of empowering poor communities, both rural and urban, by working alongside them. YKPM's current major project is the partnership with the Jakun community in Ulu Gumum, Pekan, Pahang in undertaking economy projects (eco farm and eco-tourism). This partnership is with twelve families in this community who have established a 2.5-acre organic farm. Kon Onn Sein, general manager of YKPM, was chosen as one of the ten winners of this year's Star Golden Hearts Award for the work in setting up an organic farm to increase the income of the local community.

Lessons Learned

While the beginning is slow, it is important to note that these are first-generation organic farmers. Prior to this they were hunters and gatherers. There is a major transition toward settled and organized farming for cash.

According to Kon (2019):

> OA Organics is the brand for the chemical- and pesticide-free vegetables grown by the Orang Asli farmers. OA Organics also embodies a Fair Trade Plus partnership between the OA farmers and a non-profit marketing cooperative. In short, the farmers are given a fair trade price for their farm produce, and additionally, profits from the marketing network is ploughed back into the OA community fund for the benefit of the wider community.

It is also told that the village farmers had to go through an amazing journey of learning multidisciplinary skills. "From organic farming skills, to human organisation, business management and marketing skills. For the OA, with low literacy backgrounds, they had to learn all of this within 12 months."

The project saw the resilience of the local community, who took ownership of the project. Kon (2019) noted that "the first 6 months was extremely challenging for the farmers. They had no salary from the farm and had to hold other jobs whilst preparing the farm. After 6 months of back breaking work, they finally reaped their first harvest and pay."

It is also noted that the local people have a role of conserving the forest. Kon (2019) recognizes this "the OA are natural guardians of the forest. Their lives are intertwined with the forest. They have a sacred respect for the forest and take only what is necessary for their needs. Their simple lifestyle lends naturally to them protecting the forest. But they are being denied this role and deprived of their traditional livelihoods due to a highly consumptive society. The OA become impoverished as a result of the unrelenting demands of development that continue to destroy their forest."

CONCLUSION

From the three ASEAN country case studies, we can draw five major lessons:

Grassroots Communities

First, grassroots communities are innovating ways to survive the markets. In all the three case studies, the local communities begun key innovations. The dimension of collective action of individual business actors is key for their collective success. We see this in the informal sector in Bangkok through the formation of associations and networks. We note this in the Indonesian example of collective pooling of voluntary religious contributions toward the poor, and in the case of the Malaysian example their economic activities are collectively owned at the village level. Here we recognize that micro business needs the support of other partners to survive in the open market system.

Business Development from a Rights-Based Approach

Second, we can note that businesses development cannot isolate itself from a rights-based approach as revealed in the Bangkok case study where the informal sector which undertook micro business was prepared to exercise their fundamental rights to organize a protest to affirm their rights in a very politically restrictive democratic environment. The SDGs, especially SDG 10 on addressing inequality and discrimination, call for the protection of rights to wealth creation and collective rights of the people. In all the three case studies, we see the wider application of development and rights to other socioeconomic development such as gender equality, health care, education, and overall quality of living in modern societies.

Alternative Financing—Community-Based Faith Initiatives

Third, the approach undertaken is sourcing for alternative financing, for example, the Indonesia Islamic funding is one good alternative source for people in that faith. This is a local community source which can be effectively collected and utilized for the socioeconomic empowerment of the poor rather than making the poor passive recipients.

Through the Dompet Dhuafa example that they collect the *zakat* (Muslim obligatory giving) and also manage the *waqf* (an endowment made by a Muslim for a religious, educational, or charitable cause). It is significant to note that this philanthropic institution, which is an autonomous nonprofit organization receiving the financial support from various public community groups, has effectively redistributed to those in need. In addition, from the funds raised they undertake sociocommunity activities promoting education, health, poverty eradication, and research. Based on the write-ups, the Dompet Dhuafa is managed honestly and with dedication, so as to win the respect of the Muslim community in Indonesia (Chandra and Rahman 2010).

It is necessary for the social solidarity community to capture other models of community-based financing and in this case by faith-based organizations. In the SSE world both European examples and the Latin American ones are most popularly referred to. We need to look to other models emerging from faith- and cultural-based communities where mutual aid and support is also addressing the inequalities created by the markets. Islamic finance has emerged as a major alternative financial system based on *shariah* (Islamic) principles and ethnical, financial, and investment agenda.

In this context, the work of Mohd Daud Bakar is useful. He devoted a chapter on socially responsible investing (SRI), Corporate Social Responsibility (CSR), and Environment, Social, and Governance (ESG) (Bakar 2016, 117–20). He notes that this aspect is not well articulated and is a relatively new concept. However, he recognizes the need to address the contemporary challenges especially "society's response towards excessive capitalistic practices in the Western financial system" (Bakar 2016, 117). The challenges of values rest in ESG which "underpins the importance of the private sector to subscribe to some non-commercial values, which are healthy to the whole ecosystem of modern society" (Bakar 2016, 117). There is therefore a need to emphasize accountability, transparency, and incorporation of social responsibility which are also at the heart of Islamic considerations. He further notes the other pillars of human rights as equitable and respectable treatment for all, labor practices, safe and healthy working conditions, anticorruption, fairness in business, consumer issues, promoting sustainable consumption, and community involvement (Mohd Daud Bakar 2016, 118). Impact assessment is another aspect of Shariah-based ESG index.

Changing Lifestyles and Income Generation

Fourth, in all the case studies we note that they can organize themselves, learn business principles, and generate income. The most unique example is the Malaysian first generational organic farmers. We note that there must be attitudinal changes among the target group as well as among policy-makers.

On policy-makers, the Bangkok street protest shows that the policy-makers were not sensitive to the urban poor and micro business by the streets which is not just a tourist attraction but also source for cheap but good food in the city. It is noted that all the Bangkok street hawker's link with HNT do undergo medical checks and take cleanliness seriously. A major breakthrough is in the way religiously motivated funds are not just given as charity but now being utilized for wealth creation is another aspect of mind-set change from handouts to finding a way out in the tradition of teaching how to fish rather than giving the fish.

Impacting National Policies by Creating an Enabling Policy Environment

Fifth, we can recognize that governments must develop national-enabling policies which encourages and sustain their micro grassroots businesses rather than suppress them in the interest of big–mega business. We see the strong co-relations in the case of the informal sector as supported by ILO policies as well as Thai policies. This is also noted in the case of Indonesia. However, in the case of the Malaysian example, seeking the native communities in organic farming is still in the early stages but public policy will in due course adopt empowering strategies for all communities.

While these three case studies from three ASEAN countries are encouraging and setting a new trend of community business, however these social solidarity-oriented projects face an uphill task as public policies and contemporary business biases are toward big investment-oriented projects in contemporary societies. The dominant business models are toward foreign investment and neoliberal market policies. In this context, too, while ASEAN has made a strong commitment to ASEAN Economic Community 2025 and drawn parallels with SDGs' 2030 Agenda, and a focus on "people oriented," however, the thrust is still toward "trade liberalisation agenda" including liberalizing and facilitating investments. The regional and national policies are not really recognizing SSE approaches as viable alternatives to the dominant economic models. Therefore, in this context, access to credit, a conducive policy environment, as well as movements of community-based products will be a challenge within the ASEAN region. Another aspect we need to recognize is that business schools and Master in Business Administration are still dominated by the old business philosophy toward big business. We therefore face challenges in this context but do recognize the rise of people's movements from the ground which are setting alternative models. Over the next ten years, we will see these developments from the grassroots emerge with success as alternatives providing holistic results enhancing quality of life, reducing inequality, empowering the poor, and safeguarding the environment in a more sustainable way.

NOTES

1. Information gathered from Ms Poonsap Tulaphan (HNT) based on her notes shared and other materials as indicated.
2. Information gathered from Mr. Kon Onn Sein (YKPM) on this project based on his notes shared and other materials as indicated.

REFERENCES

Aligori, Ahsin. 2017. "The Effectiveness of Zakat Fund Through Empowerment Program For Enhancement of Social Welfare 1." *Research Gate.* November. Accessed May 2019. https://www.researchgate.net/publication/320826540_the_effectiveness_of_zakat_funding_through_empowerment_program_for_enhancement_of_social_welfare_1.

Asian Foundation. 2011. "Unleashing Small Business Growth - The Asian Foundation Experience in Indonesia." *Asian Foundation.* Accessed May 2019. https://asiafoundation.org/resources/pdfs/indoSME.pdf.

Bakar, Mohd Daud. 2016. *Shariah Minds in Islamic Finance* . Kuala Lumpur: Amanie Media.

Bangasser, Paul E. 2000. *The ILO and the Informal Sector: An Institutional History.* Employment Paper 2000/9, Geneva: International Labour Organization. https://www.ilo.org/wcmsp5/groups/public/---ed_emp/documents/publication/wcms_142295.pdf.

Bemma, Adam. 2018. "Thai Street Food Sellers Battle Bangkok's Clearance Campaign." *Aljazeera.* October 21. Accessed May 2019. https://www.aljazeera.com/indepth/features/thai-street-food-sellers-battle-bangkok-clearance-campaign-181021072146310.html.

Caballero, Anthony Mely. 2017. "A People-Centred Agenda: ASEAN at 50." In *ASEAN Future Forward Antipating The Next 50 Years*, edited by Mari Elka Pangestu and Mohd Isa Rastam, 275–294. Kuala Lumpur: ISIS.

Candra, Hari, Ab Asmak, and Asmak Ab Rahman. 2010. *WAQF Investment: A Case Study of Dompet Dhuafa Republika, Indonesia.* Accessed May 2019. https://www.researchgate.net/publication/265409999_WAQF_INVESTMENT_A_CASE_STUDY_OF_DOMPET_DHUAFA_REPUBLIKA_INDONESIA.

Chen, Martha, and Shalini Sinha. 2016. "Home-Based Workers and Cities." *Environment & Urbanisation* 28(2): 343–358.

ESCAP. 2017. *Complementarities Between the ASEAN Community Vision 2025 and the United Nations 2030 Agenda for Sustainable Development.* Bangkok: ESCAP.

Haryono, Arif Rahmadi. n.d. "Towards Sustainability Development through Empowerment Program." *Socioeco.* Accessed May 2019. http://base.socioeco.org/docs/indonesian_case_study1.pdf.

ILO. 2018. "Informal Economy: More than 68 Per Cent of the Employed Population in Asia Pacific are in the Informal Economy." *International Labour Organization.* May 2. Accessed May 2019. https://www.ilo.org/asia/media-centre/news/WCMS _627585/lang--en/index.htm.

Jayasooria, Denison. 2016. "Developing Solidarity Economy in Asia. Innovations in Policy and Practice." In *Social Economy in China and the World*, edited by Ngai Pun, Ben Hok-bun Ku, Hairong Yan, and Anita Koo, 156–174. New York: Routledge.

———. 2019. "Grassroots Empowering Themselves To Ensure No One Is Left Behind." *Socioeco.org.* March. Accessed May 2019. http://www.socioeco.org/b df_fiche-document-6537_en.html.

Jayasooria, Denison, Benjamin Jr Quinones, and Saifuddin Abdulla. 2015. *Fostering An ASEAN Community Through Solidarity Based Community Enterprises.* Bangi: KITA-UKM.

Kon, Onn Sein. 2019. *Background Information and Organic Farm Report.* Ulu Gumum.

Mandhachitara, Rujirutana. 2017. "Small Business Performance in Thailand: Key Success Factors." *Emerald Publishing Limited.* October 23. Accessed May 2019. https://www.emeraldinsight.com/doi/pdfplus/10.1108/JRME-06-2016-0018.

Nicholas, Colin, Jenita Engi, and Yen Ping Teh. 2010. *The Orang Asli and the UNDRIP: from Rhetoric to Recognition.* Subang Jaya: Center for Orang Asli Concerns (COAC).

Oorjitham, Santha. 2017. "A Heart of Gold and a Green Thumb." *The Star Online.* November. Accessed May 2019. https://www.thestar.com.my/news/nation/2017 /11/18/a-heart-of-gold-and-a-green-thumb-former-lawyer-dedicated-to-improving -orang-asli-lives-with-organic/#oEX2gxxRzsv6VlQY.99.

Renaldi, Aldi. 2018. "Poverty Isn't Decreasing, Indonesia's Official Poverty Line Is Just Too Low." *Vice.* July 23. Accessed May 2019. https://www.vice.com/en_a sia/article/ev8z7w/poverty-isnt-decreasing-indonesias-official-poverty-line-is-just -too-low.

Said, Ismail A., and Moch Arifin Purwakananta. 2010. "Indonesia Islamic Integrated Community Development: Indonesian Concept on Poverty Eradication of Zakat Dimensioned Community." First Forum of World Conference on Zakat, Yogyakarta.

Saidurrahman, Saidurrahman. 2013. "The Politics of Zakat Management in Indonesia: The Tension Between BAZ and LAZ." *Journal of Indonesia Islam* 7(2): 366–382.

Sarosa, Wicaksono, and F. P. Anggriani Arifin. 2012. "Contexts and Challenges in Engaging Local Governments for Sustainable Urban Development in Southeast Asia." In *Urbanization in Southeast Asia*, edited by Yap Kioe Sheng and Moe Thuzar, 320–340. Singapore: ISEAS Publishing.

SUHAKAM. 2013. *Report of the National Inquiry into the Land Rights of Indigenous Peoples.* KL: SUHAKAM.

The Jakarta Post. 2018. "Dhuafa: 25 Years of Spreading Kindness." *The Jakarta Post.* July 3. Accessed May 2019. https://www.thejakartapost.com/adv/2018/07/03/dompet-dhuafa-25-years-of-spreading-kindness.html.

Tulaphan, Poonsap. 2019a. "HomeNet Thailand Profile and Notes."

———. 2019b. "Advocacy for Inclusive Street Vendor's Policy." *Asia Pacific People Forum for Sustainable Development (APPFSD).*

YKPM. 1993. *Foundation for Community Studies and Development*. Accessed May 2019. https://ykpmblog.wordpress.com.

Part II

CASE STUDIES OF
ASIAN COUNTRIES

Chapter 5

Dance with the State

The Case of a Chinese Social Service Organization

Xiaoshuo Hou and Siqi Chen

The term "social economy" can be traced back to the nineteenth century. However, it was rekindled in the late 1970s when neoliberalization began. The reemergence of the social economy was to respond to the crisis in the welfare state in which social needs were not satisfactorily supplied and to the increasing atomization of workers in the capitalist economy (Avila and Campos 2007; Moulaert and Ailenei 2005; Shin 2016).

The social economy initiatives include primarily cooperatives, associations, and mutual societies with the objective to prioritize social rather than economic goals (Defourny 2014; Defourny and Develtere 2009; Shin 2016). By the 1990s, with the development of the social economy, terms such as "third sector," "solidarity economy," "alternative economy," "nongovernmental organizations," "nonlucrative sector," "nonprofit sector," "not-for-profit sector," and "voluntary sector" appeared often as a synonym for the social economy (Moulaert and Ailenei 2005). Social economy organizations (SEOs) in various parts of the world often adopt different logics and forms to connect the public and private sectors (Avila and Campos 2007; Defourny 2014; Moulaert and Ailenei 2005).

Scholars have different views on the relationship between the social economy, the state, and the capitalist market. The emancipatory perspective regards social economy as a new economic system that can potentially transcend the capitalist and statist hegemony (Borowiak 2015; Jessop et al. 2013) and "serve social and environmental needs, empower producers and consumers and reinforce human solidarity and moral care" (Shin 2016, 159). The complementary perspective, on the other hand, characterizes the social economy as reformist. Although it can be an alternative to the market and the state, it does not challenge the overall social configuration (Shin 2016, 160). Social economy is proposed as "a new model for the utilization and distribution of resources" (Shin 2016, 160) and sites of "both social reintegration and provision for social need" (Defourny et al. 2014). Both perspectives affirm the contribution of the social economy in delivering social needs excluded or marginalized by the government and the market while differing in their views on how much social economy challenges existing power dynamics. A third, more critical view of the social economy perceives it as an integral part in the neoliberalization of the state and suggests that the social economy has become increasingly coopted by the state or the market (Corbett and Walker 2012; Curtis 2008; Hulgård 2014, 80–81; Shin 2016, 160–61).

Compared to Western countries, the social economy in China is still emerging and its boundary is not clear-cut. In addition, China has a history of three-decade state socialism under which the state was the sole provider of welfare benefits and acted as the central planner in the economy. As a result, discussion of social economy in China, like elsewhere, has to take into account its historical and social context rather than to simply transplant Western definitions and perspectives. The Seventeenth National Congress of the Communist Party of China in 2007 formally replaced all previously used terms such as "NGO," "NPO," "third sector," "nonprofit sector," "civil society," and "people's organization" with the term "social organization" (*shehui zuzhi*) (Sun 2009 in Smith 2016, 7). In this chapter, we thus use the term "social organization," even though scholars we cite may use other terms in their writings. Not all social organizations match the ideal-type SEOs, and one of the goals of our chapter is to shed some light on the boundary of SEOs within the Chinese context.

When the Communist Party gained power in China in 1949 it "eliminated anything that stood between the state and the individual, including churches, trade unions, and independent associations" (*The Economist* 2014, 2), and as a result, no autonomous social organizations existed. Since the reforms started in 1978, the Chinese state has focused more on the growth of the economy through the decollectivization of agriculture and the privatization of state-owned industries. With the introduction of market mechanisms, the state could no longer provide all social needs to its citizens through central planning, and employment and welfare benefits such as housing, education, and health care have become increasingly privatized. This has led to a surge in social inequality and the creation of new vulnerable groups. As a result, the state has started to encourage the development of social organizations to fill the vacuum left by the retreat of the state from welfare provisions (Ma 2002; Urio 2016). Although there had been some progress in the development of social organizations since 1978, it was not until 1988 when the state officially began to legalize such organizations. It was not until 2004 that three categories of social organizations—social groups (*shehui tuanti*), private nonenterprise units (*minban feiqiye danwei* or *minfei*), and foundations (*jijinhui*)—were officially recognized. In the newly launched 2016 Charity Law, "private non-enterprise unit" was renamed as "social service organization" (*shehui fuwu jigou*) (see table 5.1 for a more detailed history of the regulatory development regarding social organizations in China since 1978).

Social organizations in China have to operate under their specific political context and navigate the legal space granted by the state. At the beginning, the only groups allowed to operate were "state entities parading as non-state ones" (*Economist* 2014). The collapse of the Soviet Union and the Tiananmen Square protests alerted the Chinese state of the political risks of having private organizations (*Economist* 2014). Therefore, social organizations in China were put under a dual control system where they were required to be affiliated with (*guakao*) and supervised by a government agency in their functional area and subject to complicated and time-consuming registration procedures (Guo et al. 2012; Ma 2002; Urio 2016). They are also only allowed to operate in the local jurisdiction where it is registered according to central state regulations; establishing branch organizations in other locations is prohibited in order to prevent social organizations from scaling up (Guo et al. 2012). The strict registration and administration rules ensure that such organizations are localized and fragmented (Spires 2011). Under the close supervision of the state, only a small portion of social organizations are able to formally register, while the rest may stay as unregistered or look for alternative paths such as registering as a for-profit company or accept patronage or sponsorship from government-registered organizations to serve as their second-tier organizations (Guo et al. 2012; Lu 2009; Spires 2011). Since 2013 four types of social organizations have been able to directly register with the Ministry of Civil Affairs and its local branches in a number of provinces without the need to seek approval from their professional supervisory units (*yewu zhuguan danwei*), that is, trade associations, organizations dedicated to promoting science and technology, charities and foundations serving the public good, and community service organizations (*Economist* 2014; Smith and Zhao 2016).

Changes in the legal status of social organizations indicate that while the government welcomes the fact that social organizations are assuming more responsibility for providing social services, state support is often limited to the types of organizations that are deemed as politically safe and not potentially challenging to regime stability. Howell (2015) calls this selective openness to civic organizations "welfarist incorporation" that relaxes registration rules for social organizations that assist with welfare provision yet keeps the corporatist regulatory framework intact to maintain social control. For

Table 5.1   Regulatory Changes on Social Organizations in China

Year	Regulation	Categorization of Social Organizations
1988–1989	Measures for the Management of Foundations; Measures for the Registration and Management of Social Groups; Provisional Regulations on the Administration of Foreign Chambers of Commerce	Institutional restructuring took place in the State Council, and a division specialized in the management of social organizations was set up within the Ministry of Civil Affairs; only one type of social organizations was officially recognized—social groups.
1996	Circular of the General Offices of the Communist Party Central Committee and State Council On Strengthening the Management of Social Groups and Private Non-Enterprise Units	Started to separate social groups and private nonenterprise units and specify ways of managing those organizations through the joint forces of the organizations' affiliated units (guakao danwei), professional supervisory units (yewu zhuguan danwei), and civil affairs departments.
1998	Provisional Measures for the Registration and Management of Private Non-Enterprise Units	Started to register private nonenterprise units as the second category of social organizations.
2004	Regulation on Foundation Administration	Foundations became an independent category, and private firms were allowed to use assets donated by individuals or organizations to set up private foundations.
2013	Plan for the Institutional Restructuring of the State Council and Transformation of Functions	Four types of social organizations were allowed to register directly with the Ministry of Civil Affairs and its local departments without approval from their professional supervisory units: trade associations, organizations dedicated to promoting science and technology, charities and foundations serving the public good, and community service organizations.
2016	The Charity Law of the People's Republic of China	Regulations on charitable activities, fundraising, and donation in charitable organizations (cishan zuzhi) including foundations, social groups, and social service organizations.

example, advocacy organizations are under more suppressive institutional environment with heavier state regulations, closer monitoring, and less financial support than are service-oriented organizations (Zhang et al. 2011), even though the boundary between the two is not always clear-cut as service-oriented organizations may eventually start advocating for the people that they serve (*Economist* 2014). Moreover, the fragmented nature of China's authoritarian state means that it is often up to the local governments and officials to interpret and implement central policies, which leads to variations in the local environment facing those organizations (Spires 2011). As a result, social organization leaders often have to cultivate close relationships with local officials in search for allies and resources (see, e.g., Hildebrandt 2013).

Under the political and legal context in China, SEOs in China are more likely to focus on their nonstate ownership and non-capital-driven nature than the principles of democratic decision-making and community or multi-stakeholder participation, when comparing to their Western counterparts (Hildebrandt 2013; Yu 2013; Zhao 2013). Rather than being politically independent, social organizations in China often have a co-dependent relationship with the state, and their leaders are more likely to be motivated and impacted by both political and economic factors (Hildebrandt 2013; Spires et al. 2014). Therefore, some scholars argue that the expansion of social organizations in China under the control of the state has a more likely effect of helping the authoritarian regime persist rather than challenging it (Hildebrandt 2013). Other scholars, however, discuss the difference between autonomy and independence under the Chinese context, pointing out that social organizations in China may have more autonomy than how they are perceived and a closer relationship with the state may add to rather than reduce the organization's autonomy in its operation and its bargaining power vis-à-vis the state (Lu 2009).

While previous literature on Chinese social organizations often focuses on how autonomous they really are or whether they can be change agents to help democratize the Chinese state and empower its people, in this study we do not make any assumptions about the normative stand or social visions of such organizations. Instead, we are more interested in the questions of how social organizations sustain themselves, how they balance their economic and social goals, and more importantly, the strategies that they come up with in order to navigate the political and legal space to achieve their goals. Like Hildebrandt (2013), we do not see Chinese social organizations as either mere puppets maneuvered by the state or the market or fighters that defy the state and the market. However, unlike him, we do not take a rationalist approach to assume that actors in social organizations are rational, at least not in the narrow sense of instrumental rationality. We would like to grant agency to people working in these social organizations and understand the political and legal context through their eyes and voices. We specifically focus on the type of social organizations that are faced with looser state supervision and relatively favorable policy environment to see how they perceive their autonomy and their relationship with the state. Finally, previous discussions of China's social economy often focus on its rural cooperatives (see, e.g., Pun et al. 2014, 2016). We hope that our study could offer some insight into the potentiality of SEOs in urban China, and how they are similar to and different from their Western counterparts.

METHODOLOGY

Data in this study are mainly based on interviews and participant observation at a registered private nonenterprise unit or social service organization, Happy Living, located in Hangzhou City in Zhejiang province, which is among the wealthiest cities in China, boasting the internet giant Alibaba. Happy Living has been registered for six years since 2012. It primarily focuses on providing social services to two demographics: (1) the elders to enhance their community participation and improve their lives; and (2) the teenagers, especially marginalized teenagers such as children of migrant workers and juvenile delinquents, to facilitate their social and cognitive development. Because of regulatory restrictions, private nonenterprise units cannot establish branch organizations, and Happy Living thus registers under two different names in two separate districts in Hangzhou, one focusing on youth services and one on aging services. The two registered entities, however, share resources and have overlapping personnel.

One of the authors worked as an intern at Happy Living for five weeks in the summer of 2017, participating in organizing summer camps for migrant children, and wrote down her observations and reflections at the end of her internship. In June 2018, semi-structured interviews were conducted with three of the eight members, including two founders of the organization and one employee who has worked for the organization for over a year. In addition, in June 2018 and January 2019, two previous members were interviewed—both worked for Happy Living for over a year and have started to work for a spin-off of the organization in another district since early 2018, which we call Happy Living B in this chapter. The spin-off organization has its independent financial and administrative structure that is separate from Happy Living, and one of the two members we interviewed in this new organization serves as its founder. The initial round of interviews lasted between two and three hours. Three rounds of follow-up interviews were conducted between June 2018 and February 2019, clarifying certain points and/or getting more detailed views on some questions.

Our initial questions focused on exploring the interviewees' understanding of the concepts of social enterprise and social organization, how the organization balances its economic and social goals, and the achievements and challenges they experienced working in a social organization. After the initial round of interviews, we narrowed down the questions to get more information on how the organization deals with formal institutions and what they do to secure funding and sustain its operation. All the interviews were conducted in Mandarin and transcribed by one of the authors. The authors then independently coded the data and compared and combined coding to minimize biases. Important themes and patterns emerged from those interviews, specifically concerning funding, professionalization, and social organizations' strengths and limitations in relation to the state.

DATA ANALYSIS

As an eight-member organization, Happy Living has a flat and flexible organizational structure. Members are divided into two teams, one focusing on aging services and the other youth services. The two founders each leads one team and is in charge of research and planning; the members are responsible for execution and implementation. Depending on the workload, members from one team can be drawn to help the other team. In addition, the organization also recruits volunteers and interns to assist with event organization.

Aging services mainly include organizing activities and providing a platform for the elders to socialize and develop interest groups to enrich their lives and strengthen their communities. In terms of service models, over the years Happy Living has moved from home visits to encouraging the elders to leave their homes and engage in their communities. This change was spurred by three things: (1) home visits require having a large number of volunteers that make operations costly and quality control difficult; (2) demands of the elders are changing and offering companionship is no longer enough; (3) while the elders were seen as the weak that need assistance in the previous model, the current model focuses on discovering, developing, and utilizing the elders' strengths and talents.

Youth services, on the other hand, include bringing art classes such as dance, singing, drawing, and musical instruments to migrant children to equalize educational opportunities and increase their feeling of belongingness in the city, and offering after-school programs, especially to low-income families. In addition, Happy Living also organizes summer camps for low-income families and rural left-behind children whose parents have left their home villages to work in urban cities, and provide legal and emotional support to juvenile offenders.

Happy Living B currently has four full-time members, and it also offers aging and youth services in a wide range of programs such as after-school programs, day care for older adults, community self-governance initiatives, and programs that involve children in public and community services.

Funding—Interactions between Formal and Informal Institutions

Funding is the primary challenge for Happy Living. According to one of the founders, Happy Living needs to raise at least 1.2 million *yuan* (about USD 180,000) per year to ensure the survival and functioning of such an eight-person organization. As a community service organization, Happy Living's major source of funding comes from government contracts, accounting for between 60% and 80% of their total budget. State funds can be gained through two ways—venture philanthropy projects (*gongyi chuangtou*) and government purchase of services (*zhengfu goumai fuwu*), and can come from the municipal (*shi*), district (*qu*), or subdistrict (*jiedao*) level of government. The rest of their budget comes from either corporate sponsorship, foundations, or public donations.

The current legal framework in China limits the ways in which organizations like Happy Living can raise their funds. For example, as a private nonenterprise unit, Happy Living cannot charge membership fees and has to be nonprofit. In our interviews with the two founders of Happy Living, they admitted that the difference between their organization and a social enterprise is their inability to generate profits and be self-sustaining, but they also pointed out the lack of legal status for social enterprises in China. Registration for social enterprises is in its experimental stage in cities like Beijing and Chengdu and does not comprise a separate legal category, even though certified social enterprises may receive certain tax benefits or other forms of government support such as providing funding or office space. Nonetheless, they have made efforts to transform their organizations into de facto social enterprises, designing marketable service products, such as after-school care and after-school curricula, to generate revenue and subsidize free services provided to marginalized youths. Similarly, Happy Living B now offers paid services like classes on performance improvisation, study tours, and volunteer travel programs that can subsidize and be incorporated into its free programs.

Dependence on government funding means less flexibility in budget allocation and more state supervision. For example, limits are set on how much can be spent on transportation and promotional materials, and no money can be spent on purchasing equipment or building infrastructure. Such restrictions are designed to make sure that more money will be spent on the beneficiary groups. Our interviewees also indicated that it was initially stipulated in government contracts that no more than 10 % could be spent on stipends and some projects did not even allow including stipends in the budget. This rule is directly transposed from fiscal allocation in the public sector. While the low percentage of stipends allowed will not affect state-sector employees who have fixed salaries, it poses a huge challenge for workers in social service organizations whose incomes largely rely on those projects. It also makes it difficult for organizations like Happy Living to financially survive, because staff salaries comprise the biggest area of expenditure and human capital is the most important asset of such organizations. One of the founders suggested that stipends should account for at least 30–50 % of the budget for it to be viable for social service organizations.

In order to sustain income payments for its workers, Happy Living has come up with several strategies. The most direct and legitimate way is to try to raise more funds from corporations and foundations that do not have restrictions on budgetary spending or to bid for bigger or more projects from the government. Creating revenue-generating programs is another way of reducing dependency on government funds. In addition to diversifying the sources of revenue, creative accounting is used as coping strategies. For government projects that prohibit any budget for stipends, they usually allow volunteer expenses, which could then be converted into subsidies for full-time employees. Another way to subsidize staff income is to offer bonuses or meal allowances through Alipay or WeChat, which are electronic payment platforms that are similar to PayPal. For Happy Living B, when a project is won with a significantly lower budget than what they have requested for in the proposal, it means that the organization will not be able to offer all the services or events that it has promised without bearing a financial loss, and in that case creative accounting is used to make the government believe that it has delivered everything in the proposal. The latter three could be seen as informal institutions developed by the organization in response to restrictions in the formal institutions.

Both founders of Happy Living revealed that as a result of social organizations' call for increasing the percentage allowed for stipends, in some districts and for some government projects stipends can account for 50% or even 70% of the total budget, indicating policy changes that reflect social service organizations' interests and local variations in budgetary restrictions. They admitted that such changes make their accounting easier.

However, even with the increase in percentage, because funds are only partially paid to organizations at the start of the project and do not always arrive in a timely manner, sometimes when a project's upfront costs exceed the allocated amount, money will have to be moved from other projects, resulting in capital chain rupture that could affect Happy Living's financial stability and its ability to pay its employees.

In addition, all of the interviewees mentioned the shrinking funds and inconsistent availability of government projects that greatly affect their ability to maintain a steady stream of revenue. First of all, policy shifts or adjustment in government leadership could result in changing preferences over different categories of services and the availability of funds that specifically target aging and youth services.

Second, for projects that Happy Living have successfully bid for several consecutive years, not only is there no adjustment for inflation, but the amount of money available could be decreasing each year, making it difficult to offer quality programs or sustain their services. Moreover, because government contracts in Hangzhou are signed on a yearly basis, there is often a lack of continuity, as there is no guarantee that the same project will be available each year or the same organization will get the contract for the same project. This also means that government-funded projects do not necessarily achieve their intended social outcomes, especially because bringing meaningful changes or assistance to the beneficiary groups require a long-term commitment. The leader of Happy Living B mentioned that in Guangzhou, for example, a government-funded project could last two or three years, while in Hangzhou the default project cycle is only one year.

Third, in Hangzhou the maximum amount for municipal-government-funded projects is 200,000 *yuan*, much lower than other cities in the region like Shanghai and Suzhou that often have the upper limit set at 500,000 *yuan*. At the district level, project funds are even lower. This means that organizations in Hangzhou have to bid for more projects to survive; however, the number of projects available is not increasing.

Lastly, the bidding process is not always transparent. For example, some projects are designed with specific organizations in mind so that no other organizations are qualified, and details regarding expert scoring (*zhuanjia pingfen*) are not publicly disclosed. Besides, officials often favor organizations with which they are familiar or sometimes grant contracts to organizations that have not provided services in the particular area. Interviewees also pointed out that it is extremely difficult for organizations not registered in a specific subdistrict or district to win projects funded by that particular subdistrict or district, as local governments prioritize the survival of organizations within their jurisdiction. As a result, maintaining a good relationship with local officials and keeping a large social network is an important part of the founders' work.

Even though all of our interviewees expressed their hope that the government could expand the pool of money and the number of projects available for social organizations, they also talked about the problems that come with increasing the funds for each project. One of the founders said, "Social organizations do not have the ability to spend (too much money)."[1] This is because a 300,000 *yuan* project may require the engaged social organization to provide services to the whole city, whereas most social organizations only serve a district or a subdistrict. Projects with higher funds are also often more specialized and exclusive as they require having skilled professionals trained in the field, while community service organizations like Happy Living do not necessarily have such qualifications. Clearly, the institutional environment that prevents social organizations from scaling up and becoming more professionalized also affects their revenue generation and financial stability.

When asked about why moving the youth service part of the organization toward the direction of a social enterprise, one of the founders said that the decision has nothing to do with increasing the organization's autonomy but is merely a different way of managing and developing the organization to commercialize the service products, because government purchases are imperfect competitions, while social enterprises are more engaged in market competitions. The former involves satisfying the needs of the government and the beneficiaries, whereas the latter targets individual or groups of consumers, but the two are not mutually exclusive. For him, both social organizations and social enterprises have autonomy, albeit in different forms. The founder of Happy Living B, on the other hand, discussed the motivation behind creating more revenue-generating activities as to become less passive and to have more choices in the organization's operation so that it does not need to be constrained by the projects that the government perceives as important but could focus more on realizing its own vision of social services. However, he, too, admitted that no matter where the revenue comes from, maintaining a good relationship with different levels of the state is necessary and becoming a social enterprise does not mean that it will not participate in bidding for government-funded projects.

The Double Edges of Professionalization

Except for the founders who have been with Happy Living since its establishment, members working at Happy Living have only been with the organization for one or two years. One of the founders said that it seems that three years is the longest time that a member would stay, and he attributed the retention problem mainly to the relatively low salary. The employees, on the other hand, thought that their salaries were reasonable for entry-level jobs like theirs. One of the employees, nonetheless, complained about the lack of an increase and inconsistency in salary and bonuses, as their incomes heavily depend on the number of government contracts acquired each year. The high living cost in Hangzhou also makes it more difficult to economically survive. Employees, in particular, talked about the lack of professional development and training opportunities and did not see themselves working in the organization for a long period of time, even though they like what they do and feel proud of being able to help others. They intend to apply to graduate schools in the next couple of years. None of the two employees that we interviewed majored in social work or related area in college—one majored in mass communication and the other in TV editing and directing, and they had no clear idea of what a social service organization was prior to entering the field, although one of them said that she loved volunteering when she was in college.

All three founders pointed out the difficulty in attracting high-skilled professionals to the field of social organizations, as the field is still in its early stage of development and the limited revenue-generating sources and the low level of social recognition make it less appealing compared to the corporate or the state sector. Interviewees complained that people often confuse social service with volunteering and expect it to be free. Family members could also question the future of working in a social service organization and thus not support the decision to work for it. When one of the authors was interning at Happy Living, she heard an employee lamenting over not having a matching job category in the Chinese language other than social worker, which makes it difficult to describe and explain to outsiders what they really do.

However, all three founders also expressed that when recruiting they pay more attention to the employees' passion toward the job and their abilities to learn than their academic or professional background because the job is more experiential than theoretical and majoring in social work does not necessarily make an employee more suited for the job. It seems that while the interviewees hope that the field can be more professionalized to attract more talents and investment, their current work does not require a high level of skills or expert knowledge. Founder of Happy Living B discussed his plan to enhance the core competencies of the organization and his willingness to pay employees a higher salary if they have high professional qualifications, but he also said that the unwritten rule in the field is to offer a monthly salary between 3000 *yuan* (roughly USD 450) and 5000 *yuan* (roughly USD 750), even in cities like Guangzhou where the average income is high and social service organizations have had a longer history.

We have also observed from the interviews that founders are the ones that bring social networks and financial resources to the organization and they make key decisions, while members of the organization work on specific projects. Therefore, in our interviews founders were more likely to talk about policies and the macro environment facing social organizations and the grand social goals, while members were not familiar with policies regarding such things as taxation and budgetary restrictions and they were more likely to discuss goals in economic terms such as the number of government projects and the amount of income and in terms of their personal career goals. Similarly, members expressed their hope of collaborating more with and learning from other social service organizations and foundations, but founders said that they have already had plenty of collaborations with other social service organizations because they have formed their own circle and the capacity and power of any single social organization is limited. Perhaps one of the reasons why employees do not feel that they can commit to Happy

Living for a longer period of time is because they do not sufficiently participate in the decision-making process and there is not enough communication
over the organization's visions or sharing of organizational resources.

Nevertheless, the common passion toward helping those in need and the
camaraderie that has been built by working in such a small organization with
people of a similar age do bond the members together, so even though at
times salaries cannot be paid on time, employees choose to trust and stay.
One of the interviewees revealed that she did not even sign a formal labor
contract with Happy Living and only had an oral agreement, and for an organization of this size there is no standard labor contract issued by the state. One
of the founders described their work as "tiring but happy." Even though they
have to complete about fifteen to twenty projects each year and the workload for each person is thus often pretty high, there is not much bureaucratic
hierarchy within the organization and everyone collaborates to get the work
done. During her internship at Happy Living, one of the authors also found
the working environment collegial and full of energy.

In sum, although the founders expressed concerns over the field's lack of
appeal to high-skilled professionals and the longer time required for social
organizations to scale up compared to corporations as there is often not a large
sum of investment at the establishment of the organization and there is more
legal restrictions, the employees did not see much professional growth working
in the organization. Perhaps because of Happy Living's scope of services and
scale of resources it needs more of a generalist than a specialist. When projects
do require specialists, it will then collaborate with or outsource to other social
organizations. For example, at summer camps that offer drawing classes Happy
Living will invite trained professionals from other social organizations to be its
teachers or work with the social work programs at local universities to recruit
teachers. Increased professionalization may enable social service organizations like Happy Living to bid for larger government projects and attract more
state and corporate funding, but it also depends on whether they can compete
with the public and private sectors and offer comparable salaries to recruit
professionals in the first place. As previously mentioned, the legal and institutional environment also prevents social service organizations from scaling up,
restricting their scope of service to their registered district. In its current stage,
Happy Living attracts mostly fresh college graduates who are looking for their
first jobs, and their work is then supplemented by interns and volunteers.

Strengths and Limitations—Change Agent or Not?

When asked about whether they think that social organizations can lead to any
social change, all of the interviewees mentioned changes in the communities that
they serve. They perceive social service organizations to be more flexible and

efficient and to be able to better understand the beneficiary groups compared to government agencies that are more bureaucratic and removed from the communities. Because they directly serve the communities, their service is more targeted and down-to-earth (*jiediqi*). For example, Happy Living now provides a service menu for the elders to choose from. In one of the communities that they serve, they helped the elders build an accordion team, and the team members regularly meet to practice. When Happy Living organizes events, the elders on the team often offer to perform for free, and one of them even knitted a scarf to express her gratitude. Another example is when a sixteen-year-old minor was arrested for theft and was transferred to the Procuratorate, Happy Living stepped in to provide assistance. Because the minor caused minimum harm to society and expressed genuine repentance, he was not prosecuted by the Procuratorate. They also see changes in the migrant children that they serve, witnessing their growing confidence and elegance after taking the art classes. It is cases like those that make members of Happy Living see the value of their work. One of the employees said that even though working for a social service organization may not seem to be a glamorous job, she thought that in the future social service organizations would become an essential part of societal development.

In addition, the founders of Happy Living discussed their hope to be able to eventually participate in policy-making and influence policy. One of the founders gave the example of some environmental NGOs participating in drafting environmental standards in China, and said that through assisting juvenile offenders Happy Living was able to make local governments and judiciary institutions aware of the need for criminal justice social work and start to allocate funds in this area. The other founder said that the legalization of social service organizations in China marked the end of an era of focusing solely on economic development, and as the state started to recognize the importance of social, environmental, and other noneconomic issues, social organizations would shoulder more and more responsibilities. However, both founders pointed out the limited power of any single social organization and expressed the need for organizations to cooperate. They talked about the weak status of social service organizations compared to the state who controls policy and large sums of money and foundations who dominate social resources and private donations, which was echoed in the interview with the founder of Happy Living B. Interestingly, one of the founders mentioned the need for strengthening "party-building" (*dangjian*), meaning reinforcing the leadership of the Communist Party in social organizations, as social organizations can be a double-edged sword that can either assist the state to solve many social problems or be used against the state. He saw maintaining regime stability as important for China's development. Clearly, the founders see social organizations more as a bridge that connects and coordinates the state, the market, and society than an oppositional force.

Employees, on the other hand, discussed the challenges of balancing multiple stakeholders' interests in their work. For example, one of the after-school programs involves the subdistrict office that funds the project, the school that provides classroom space, and children and families that enroll in the program. The school, however, wanted to add more children to the program even when the program was already fully enrolled, which then required Happy Living to negotiate and coordinate. Employees also need to balance interests between corporate sponsors who want to market their products and display their logos and state agencies like neighborhood committees that are cautious of commercial activities negatively affecting the image of the communities. Because of the limited resources controlled by social service organizations, it seems that they lack the power and authority to be an equal partner in those projects, even though the state, foundations, or corporations may rely on social service organizations for their abilities to implement projects in specific local communities.

Employees also hoped that the state could issue more policies to regulate the sector and provide minimum wage and benefits to workers in social service organizations. They mentioned, for example, that in some other cities in the province the government would reimburse social service workers for taking social work licensing exams. In addition, there are huge variations in how social service organizations are managed in Hangzhou across different districts that some districts have more favorable policies and provide more resources including subsidized office space, while others do not value social service organizations as much. One of the employees suggested that more centralized management of social service organizations would help facilitate resource-sharing and coordination among organizations across different districts and better develop the sector. Our interviews reveal that currently collaborations among social service organizations are more task based. For example, if a corporate sponsor requires the organization to organize at least 200 events a year displaying the corporate logo, whereas Happy Living can only organize fifty events a year, it will then outsource the rest to other organizations.

The limited resources and fragmented and localized nature of social service organizations mean that their power to change is constrained, even though they may be able to offer more targeted services to beneficiaries and are less restricted by bureaucratic red tape compared to the state. When combined they may be strong, yet the policy environment does not offer much room for them to join forces in any substantial way.

FINDINGS

The case of Happy Living indicates a number of paradoxes between social service organizations, the state, and the market.

First, state support helps social organizations sustain, yet state control also constrains the sector's growth. Happy Living's major source of revenue comes from government contracts, even though efforts have been made to transform the youth service sector into a social enterprise. State support is the reason why social service organizations like Happy Living can emerge and survive. As previously mentioned, since 2013 the state has relaxed rules of registration for four types of social service organizations to allow them to directly register with local civil affairs departments without having to first get approved by their professional supervisory units. The central state has also issued policy to lower the financial threshold for registration. In response to the central policy, some districts in Hangzhou have, since 2014, removed any requirement of minimum registered capital for those social organizations. This indicates the need for such organizations from the state's perspective. However, the increasing number of social service organizations has led to more competition for government funds. When not many alternative ways of revenue exist, state control prevents social service organizations from scaling up or becoming financially more stable, especially when the bidding process is not transparent or purely market based but is more dependent upon relationships and *guanxi* networks and the availability of projects and funds is often a result of officials' preferences. Built upon the Western model of community foundations, some attempts have been made in the Shangcheng district in Hangzhou to pool government funds together and put into a foundation to offer venture philanthropy projects through that foundation. The ultimate goal is to use government funds to attract more private capital and donations so that the foundation can become a community foundation that can be used to strengthen ties among its residents and respond to communal needs. However, so far it has remained as a foundation solely funded by the state, so the bidding and approval process is still dominated by the state and is no different from any other government fund. As described by Hildebrandt (2013), the state and social service organizations have a co-dependent relationship, yet the state cares more about the entire field of social service organizations than any single social organization's survival, so for an organization of Happy Living's size, it has limited bargaining power vis-à-vis the state and keeping a good relationship with the state is essential.

Nonetheless, this does not mean that commercializing the organization will necessarily bring more autonomy to Happy Living. As the founders explained, it merely means satisfying different groups of stakeholders. For government-funded projects, the organization works to balance the budgetary requirements issued by the state, the needs of government officials for accumulating political capital, and the demands of the beneficiaries. For market-based projects, the organization has to design profitable service products that consumers are willing to pay, and navigating the state institution is still important. Ultimately the goal is the same—to generate enough revenue so that the organization can focus more on the projects that they would like to deliver rather than the projects that they have to do in order to survive.

Second, while Happy Living calls for increasing professionalization and specialization of the field of social service organizations to make it more competitive with the private and public sectors in order to attract high-skilled professionals and investment, its current work does not require a high level of training and staff salaries are only comparable to entry-level jobs for college graduates. The lack of career development opportunities makes it difficult to retain employees for a longer period of time, and people stay for the camaraderie and the satisfaction of serving those in need.

Lastly, collaborating with other organizations is essential for organizations of Happy Living's size and scope of service, but such collaborations currently remain task-based. Moreover, social and financial resources are kept at the hands of the founders and not shared with staff members, even though project implementation and execution is more decentralized.

The co-dependent relationship between Happy Living and the state means that social service organization's strengths lie more in its ability to provide more targeted services to its beneficiaries and to ultimately call the state's attention to issues that the organization cares about such as in the case of criminal justice social work. In that sense, Happy Living is somewhere between being coopted by the state and reforming the state, but it is far from challenging the state hegemony. Transforming into a social enterprise may help broaden its sources of revenue to make it less dependent upon government contracts, but it will not fundamentally change its relationship with the state, given the current legal and institutional framework in China.

For social service organizations like Happy Living to provide real alternatives to provisions by the state and the capitalist market, it will perhaps require more participation in the organization's operation and decision-making process by multiple stakeholders including staff members and the beneficiary groups, bringing back their agency. In addition, it will rely on more meaningful collaboration with other social service organizations beyond outsourcing certain tasks to integrate and coordinate the entire sector and develop solidarity. Nevertheless, the state deliberately keeps the sector fragmented and localized, and it seems that in the Chinese context only the state has the power and ability to coordinate the whole sector. It poses another dilemma for social service organizations.

NOTE

1. Interview on September 10, 2018.

REFERENCES

Borowiak, Craig. 2015. "Mapping Social and Solidarity Economy: The Local and Translocal Evolution of a Concept." In *Social Economy in China and the World*, edited by Ngai Pun, Ben Hok-bun Ku, Hairong Yan, and Anita Koo, 17–40. London and New York: Routledge.

Campos, José L. M., and Rafael C. Avila. 2012. "The Social Economy in the European Union." The European Economic and Social Committee. https://www.eesc.europa.eu/resources/docs/qe-30-12-790-en-c.pdf.

Corbett, Steve, and Alan Walker. 2012. "The Big Society: Back to the Future." *The Political Quarterly* 83(3): 487–493.

Curtis, Tim. 2008. "Finding that Grit Makes a Pearl: A Critical Re-Reading of Research into Social Enterprise." *International Journal of Entrepreneurial Behavior and Research* 14(5): 276–290.

Defourny, Jacques. 2014. *Social Enterprise and the Third Sector: Changing European Landscapes in a Comparative Perspective*. London and New York: Routledge.

Defourny, Jacques, and Patrick Develtere. 2009. "The Social Economy: The Worldwide Making of a Third Sector." In *The Worldwide Making of the Social Economy: Innovations and Changes*, edited by J. Defourny, P. Develtere, B. Fonteneau, and M. Nyssens, 15–40. Leuven and The Hague: Acco.

Ding, Kaijie. 2007. "From the Third Sector to Social Enterprises: Practices in China [从第三部门到社会企业: 中国的实践]." *Comparative Economic and Social Systems [经济社会体制比较]*. http://www.cctb.net/zjxz/expertarticle1/201604/t20160413_340064.htm.

Economist. 2014. "Beneath the Glacier: In Spite of a Political Clampdown, a Flourishing Civil Society is Taking Hold." April 12, 2014. https://www.economist.com/china/2014/04/12/beneath-the-glacier.

Guo, Chao, Jun Xu, David H. Smith, and Zhibin Zhang. 2012. "Civil Society, Chinese Style: The Rise of the Nonprofit Sector in Post-Mao China." *The Nonprofit Quarterly* 19(3): 20–27.

Hildebrandt, Timothy. 2013. *Social Organizations and the Authoritarian State in China*. Cambridge: Cambridge University Press.

Howell, Jude. 2015. "Shall We Dance? Welfarist Incorporation and the Politics of State-Labour NGO Relations." *The China Quarterly* 223(September): 702–723.

Hulgård, Lars. 2014. "Social Enterprise and the Third Sector—Innovative Service Delivery or a Non-Capitalist Economy?" In *Social Enterprise and the Third Sector: Changing European Landscapes in a Comparative Perspective*, edited by Jacques Defourny, Lars Hulgård, and Victor Pestoff, 66–84. London and New York: Routledge.

Jessop, Bob, Frank Moulaert, Lars Hulgård, and Abdelillah Hamdouch. 2013. "Social Innovation Research: A New Stage in Innovation Analysis?" In *International Handbook on Social Innovation: Collective Action, Social Learning and Transdisciplinary Research*, edited by F. Moulaert, D. MacCallum, A. Mehmood, and A. Hamdouch, 110–130. Cheltenham: Edward Elgar.

Lu, Yiyi. 2009. *Non-Governmental Organizations in China: The Rise of Dependent Autonomy*. London and New York: Routledge.

Ma, Qiusha. 2002. "The Governance of NGOs in China since 1978: How Much Autonomy?" *Nonprofit and Voluntary Sector Quarterly* 31(3): 305–328.

Moulaert, Frank, and Oana Ailenei. 2005. "Social Economy, Third Sector and Solidarity Relations: A Conceptual Synthesis from History to Present." *Urban Studies* 42(11): 2037–2053.

Pun, Ngai, Ben Hok-bun Ku, Hairong Yan, and Anita Koo, eds. 2016. *Social Economy in China and the World*. London and New York: Routledge.

Pun, Ngai, Hairong Yan, Ben Hok-bun Ku, and Anita Koo, eds. 2014. *Social Economy in China: Beyond the Imagination of Capitalism [社会经济在中国—超越资本主义的理论与实践]*. Beijing, China: Social Sciences Academic Press.

Shin, Changhwan. 2016. "A Conceptual Approach to the Relationships between the Social Economy, Social Welfare, and Social Innovation." *Journal of Science and Technology Policy Management* 7(2): 154–172.

Smith, David Horton, and Ting Zhao. 2016. *Review and Assessment of China's Nonprofit Sector After Mao: Emerging Civil Society?* Leiden: Brill.

Spires, Anthony J. 2011. "Contingent Symbiosis and Civil Society in an Authoritarian State: Understanding the Survival of China's Grassroots NGOs." *American Journal of Sociology* 117(1) (July): 1–45.

Spires, Anthony J., Lin Tao, and Kin-man Chan. 2014. "Societal Support for China's Grass-Roots NGOs: Evidence from Yunnan, Guangdong and Beijing." *The China Journal* 71(January): 65–90.

Urio, Paolo. 2016. "The Emergence of NGOs in China and the Changing Role of the Party-State." *The China Nonprofit Review* 8(2): 188–214.

Wright, Erik Olin. 2006. "Compass Points: Towards a Socialist Alternative." *New Left Review* 41: 93–124.

Yu, Xiaomin. 2013. "The Governance of Social Enterprise in China." *Social Enterprise Journal* 9(3): 225–246.

Zhao, Li. 2013. "Conceptualizing the Social Economy in China." *Modern Asian Studies* 47(3): 1083–1123.

Chapter 6

Emerging Nonprofit Corporations in Japan

Masanari Sakurai

THE JAPANESE CONTEXT OF THE TRANSITION OF NPOS AND EMERGING NEW NPO CORPORATIONS

This study examined Japanese nonprofit organizations (NPOs). NPOs, which have been widely researched around the world, were defined by Johns Hopkins University as organizations that were: (1) institutionalized to some extent, (2) institutionally separate from the government, (3) self-governing and equipped to control their own activities, (4) nonprofit, and (5) involving some meaningful degree of voluntary participation (Salamon and Anheier 1996).

Prior to 1995, the Japanese government had strictly limited the establishment of nonprofit corporations (Laratta et al. 2011) and had tightly regulated their activities. However, because of the excellent disaster relief work by volunteers in response to the disastrous 1995 Hanshin-Awaji earthquake, the Japanese government promulgated the "Law to Promote Specified Nonprofit Activities" (new NPO Law), which made it easier for citizens to establish Specified Nonprofit Corporations (SNCs). Within ten years of this NPO was enacted, over 35,000 NPOs primarily focused on social welfare or human care activities had been established, as shown in table 6.1, with each type operating under different laws and expected to focus on its proscribed purposes and activities. As can be seen, some public interest foundations, associations, and NPOs have a wide range of activities, while others have very specific activities.

There are three types of establishment and management government regulations for each nonprofit corporate status: permission, approval, or certification. As shown in table 6.1, permission corresponds to public interest corporations, and indicates that the establishment of the NPO is at the

Table 6.1   Main Legal Nonprofit Social Welfare Organizations in Japan (in early 2000s)

Name	Purpose, Activity	Government Regulation for Establishment and Management	Information Disclosure
Medical corporation	Narrow. Establishing a hospital, clinic, or an elderly health care facility.	Medium (Approval)	Narrow. Government and stakeholders only.
Social welfare corporation	Narrow. Providing social welfare services based on social welfare law.	Medium (Approval)	
Specified Nonprofit Corporation	Rather broad. Twenty fields of the new NPO Law.	Weak (Certification)	Wide. Many public. Documents.
Public interest corporations (associations and foundations)	Broad. No restrictions.	Strong (Permission)	Rather wide. General.

Source: Sakurai (2019). It should be noted that we also referred to this citation source largely in sentences that explains this table in this section.

discretion of the government administration. Approval is related to the establishment of medical and social welfare NPOs, the requirements for which are stated in the law, that is, if all requirements stipulated in the law are being complied with, the government administration will approve the NPO establishment. In practice, however, the government generally judges both compliance with the specified legal requirements and the financial and managerial operations with any changes in the articles of incorporation needing further government permission. The certification principle is applied to Specified Nonprofit Corporations (SNCs), the establishment requirements for which are also specified in law. In these cases, the government administration needs to only confirm that the NPO application satisfies the specified legal requirements. As certification is also needed if there are any changes in the articles of incorporation, administrative discretion is very narrow when establishing and managing nonprofits under this principle.

Moreover, there are institutional differences in the information disclosure requirements for each type of NPO. For example, Public Interest Corporations and SNCs are required to disclose their annual reports to the public, but only government administrations and stakeholders can request information from other nonprofit corporations. SNCs are required to accede to public inspection as part of their establishment application, with the new NPO law stating that the SNCs are required to disclose as much information as possible to obtain public trust. The new NPO law also stipulates that SNCs can only operate in twenty specific fields (Article 2 of the new NPO Law and Appended Table) and that the "specified nonprofit activities" must be included in the articles of incorporation (table 6.2).

An Authorized Specified Nonprofit Corporation (hereinafter referred to as "Authorized SNC") system was established in 2001 to further support donations from citizens and companies for SNC activities. An SNC that conforms with the criteria to contribute to promoting public good through appropriate organizational governance and activities can become an Authorized SNC. Individual or organizational donors to Authorized SNCs are given preferential taxation treatment and the Authorized SNC also is given preferential corporate tax treatment. Under the "authorization"

Table 6.2 Specified Nonprofit Activities and the Number of Corporations

Type of Activity	Number of Corporations
(i) Enhancing health care, medical care, and welfare	30,469
(ii) Promoting social education	25,183
(iii) Promoting community development	23,101
(iv) Promoting tourism	3,300
(v) Revitalizing rural areas or hilly and mountainous areas	2,697
(vi) Promoting science, culture, arts, or sports	18,227
(vii) Preserving the environment	13,819
(viii) Disaster relief activities	4,445
(ix) Regional security activities	6,350
(x) Protecting human rights or promoting peace	8,724
(xi) International cooperation activities	10,089
(xii) Promoting a gender-equal society	4,805
(xiii) Assisting with the sound development of children	23,672
(xiv) Developing an information-oriented society	5,879
(xv) Promoting science and technology	3,160
(xvi) Revitalizing the economy	9,162
(xvii) Supporting the development of vocational skills or the expanding employment opportunities	13,330
(xviii) Protecting consumers	3,110
(xix) Liaison work, or providing advice or assistance for the operations or activities of organizations engaged in any of the activities set forth in the preceding items	23,992
(xx) Activities specified by an Ordinance of a prefecture or designated city as being equivalent to the activities set forth in the preceding items	245

Source: Cabinet Office Homepage.

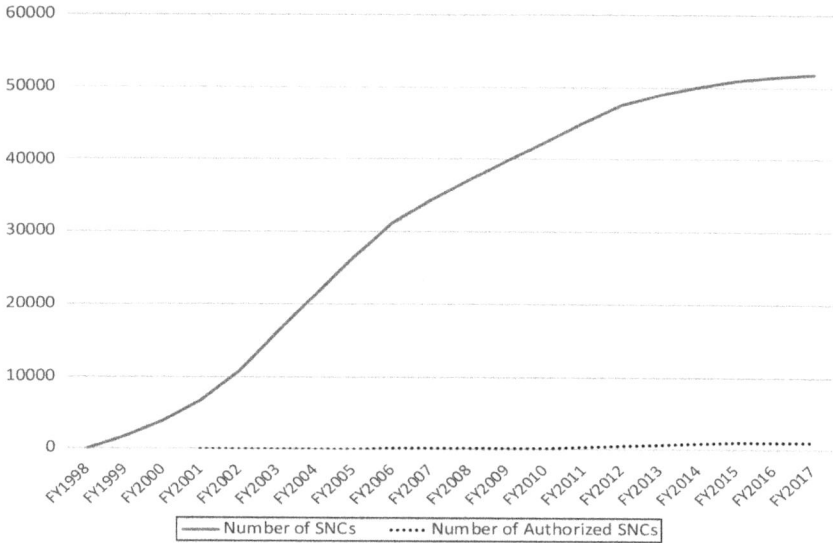

Figure 6.1   SNCs and Authorized SNCs in Japan. *Source*: Cabinet Office Homepage.

system, authorized SNCs must confirm that their organization and activities are appropriate and that they have a high public character by completing a "public support test."

Figure 6.1 shows the rising number of SNCs and Authorized SNCs in Japan. In the twenty years following the promulgation of the new NPO law, over 51,000 SNCs have been certificated. Although approval for the number of authorized SNCs was initially slow, over 1,000 organizations had been certified by 2017. This increase in Authorized SNCs appears to have been influenced by a relaxation in the accreditation requirements.

CURRENT SNC STATUS

In the following, the current NPO situation in Japan is discussed based on the results of the March 2018 Cabinet Office "State Survey on Activated Specified Nonprofit Corporations in 2017." The Cabinet Office (2018) survey was conducted with the aim of revising the Specified Nonprofit Activities Promotion Act.

From August 21, 2017, to October 18, 2017, a combination of mail surveys and online surveys was sent to 6,437 SNCs and Authorized SNCs nationwide, which were selected using a stratified two-stage random sampling of the districts and SNC and Authorized SNC corporate types, of which 53.8% were returned.

The SNCs and Authorized SNCs were asked to describe the most central specific nonprofit activities that were stated in their articles of incorporation, the results for which were as follows. The highest percentage of activities in both the SNCs (n = 2,551, 39.7%) and Authorized SNCs (n = 735, 35.5%) was related to health, medical care, or welfare, followed by activities to promote the sound development of children with 12.7% of the SNCs and 14.3% of the Authorized SNCs.

However, the third and fourth most frequent activities for the SNCs and Authorized SNCs were different. Around 11.0% of SNCs were involved in activities promoting academic, cultural, artistic, or sports activities and 9.2% were involved in promoting community development, whereas for 9.1% of the Authorized SNCs, the third and fourth most frequent activities were activities to conserve the environment and activities associated with international cooperation. The fifth most frequent activity (5.9%) in the SNCs was environmental conservation, but was the promotion of academia, culture, art, or sports in the Authorized SNCs (7.9%). The main activity field with the largest difference between the nonauthorized SNCs and the Authorized SNCs was international cooperation activities, being undertaken by 7.3% of the Authorized SNCs, which was possibly because the Authorized SNCs were receiving preferential tax treatment.

The survey also asked about the scale of activities in terms of the annual budget for the specified nonprofit activities. It was reported that 43.9% of SNCs (n = 1,198) and 67.9% of Authorized SNCs (n = 399) had annual budgets greater than 10 million yen, with 15% of SNCs and 30.8% Authorized SNCs having annual budgets greater than 50 million yen. Therefore, approximately 85% of the SNCs and about 70% of the Authorized SNCs have annual budgets of less than 50 million yen.

The revenue breakdown results showed that 83.8% of the revenue (service fee, consignment fee, etc.) for the nonauthorized SNCs (n = 1198) and 67.9% of the revenue for the Authorized SNCs (n = 750) were earned income. Around 15.9% of the revenue earned by the Authorized SNCs was from donations, which was significantly higher than for the SNCs' donations (2.1%). Overall, however, the ratio of earned income revenue was high at 77% on average across all surveyed corporations.

The staff number median for the SNCs (n = 2,534) was five, with the average being 10.3, and the median for the Authorized SNCs (n = 732) was seven, with the average being 18.3. In terms of gender, the SNCs had a median of three female staff and an average of 7.1, whereas the female staff average for the Authorized SNCs was five, with the average being 12.9. The median for paid staff was two for the SNCs (n = 2,318) with the average being 8.6, and median for paid staff was six for the Authorized SNCs (n = 715), with an average of 16.2. The median number of female paid staff members was two for the SNCs, with an average of 6.7 and the median number of female paid staff members was four for the Authorized SNCs, with an average of 12.4. Therefore, the percentage of female staff was higher and it appeared that both the SNCs and the Authorized SNCs tended to rely on females in their labor force.

Although the number of staff members was small overall, the staff sizes in the nonauthorized SNCs were smaller than in the Authorized SNCs and the proportion of paid staff in the SNCs was less than half the number in the Authorized SNCs, which indicated that the SNCs relied more on volunteers.

The survey then asked about the number of volunteers engaged in the organization's activities excluding those engaged in management and administrative work, which was calculated based on the number of volunteer participants in the activities multiplied by the number of engaged days of these participants. It was found that volunteers did not engage in 24.1% of SNC (n = 2,664) activities and also did not engage in 10.6% of Authorized SNC (n = 748) activities. More than half of the Authorized SNCs (54.8%) had 100 or more volunteers, while this was true for only 29.1% of the SNCs.

Based on the Act for the Promotion of Specified Nonprofit Activities, 49.6% of the SNCs (n = 2,666) claimed that they publicly disclosed information on their own organization's internet site, and 30.4% answered that they publicly disclosed information on the internet site managed by the Cabinet Office, the competent authorities, and private organizations. However, 87.2% of the Authorized SNCs claimed that they publicly disclosed information on their own internet sites; 52.8% claimed that they publicly disclosed information on the internet site managed by the Cabinet Office, the competent authorities, and private organizations; and 26.8% claimed that they had opened a public relations magazine. Only 1.3% of Authorized SNCs said that had not disclosed information other than the browsing documents compared to 15.8% of the nonauthorized SNCs, which indicated that the Authorized SNCs were more active in their information disclosure compliance than the SNCs.

The SNCs (n = 2,666) claimed that the main information disclosed on their own internet sites was activity reports (87.5%), board member lists (31.1%), their constitution (29.6%), and calls for donations (24.4%): whereas the Authorized SNCs (n = 750) claimed that the main information disclosed on their own internet sites was activity reports (93.0%), calls for donations (80.7%), and accounting documents (65.4%). Therefore, there was more information available on calls for donations and accounting documents by the Authorized SNCs than by the nonauthorized SNCs.

In summary, while the number of SNCs in Japan has been growing steadily, many have small budgets and few staff, most of whom are female, possibly because female salaries tend to be lower than male salaries in Japan. Furthermore, although many organizations appeared to be actively engaged in information disclosure, over 15% of the nonauthorized SPCs were found to be less compliant than required by the Specified Nonprofit Activity Promotion Law.

WHAT CAUSED THE INCREASE IN THE NUMBER OF SNCS? AN ANALYSIS OF THE MALDISTRIBUTION FACTORS

The SNCs have become a new type of social economy organization (SEO) in Japan. However, from the reviews of the establishment and the current situation, it is not clear why there has been such a rapid increase in the number of NPOs. The Comparative Nonprofit Sector Project from Johns Hopkins that was conducted in twenty-two countries during the 1990s (Salamon and Sokolowski 1999) outlined the historical contexts for the regulation and development of civil society organizations (CSOs). This approach treated the nonprofit sector "not as an isolated phenomenon floating freely in social space but as an integral part of a social system whose role and scale are a by-product of a complex set of historical forces" (Salamon and Anheier 1998, 245). Salamon and Anheier (1998) claimed that the contours for third-sector development went beyond the simple "large" versus "small" dimensions of standard empirical research and said that it was important to look at the prevailing social structures to identify the multiple routes leading to the development of nonprofit sectors of a certain size.

Based on this social origin hypothesis, Kerlin (2009) sought to classify the contexts of social enterprises in various regions using several comparative axes (Kerlin 2009). Based on considerations in Tsukamoto and Nishimura (2009), Kerlin (2009) stated in Chapter 8 of the same book that the government had a strategic development base for Japanese social enterprises. For example, rather than being a product of the government as in the United States, in Europe, the development of social enterprise was based on the EU as well as the governments in the various countries. In Japan, the market economy was incorporated into the social sector, with the results of the NPO activities expected to be both social and economic. Therefore, Kerlin (2009) suggested that the Japanese social enterprise models were different from other regions and countries as they were "civil society/market/nation" models.

Kerlin (2009) suggested that a social origin approach, in which the societal, political, historical, and cultural uniqueness of Japan is employed, could be used to analyze the development of NPOs in Japan. However, Kerlin (2009) was not clear which factors should be examined as only a hypothetical model was presented. Further, this type of model would not be able to sufficiently explain the domestic maldistribution of social enterprises in Japan or other countries. Therefore, to be able to fully explain this distribution, it is necessary to specify the factors that are driving the establishment of social enterprises in different areas. Under this reasoning, multiple independent variables were used to identify the differences in the number of SNCs in each Japanese prefecture.

In the following, the differences in the number of SNCs in Japan's prefectures were empirically analyzed, with the number of SNCs in each prefecture in the multiple regression analysis being the dependent variable, and with the independent variables being adopted from Kerlin (2009). It was assumed that the resources provided by the government, the market, and the civil society would explain the uneven distribution of the SNCs. As of December 31, 2018, there were 51,671 NPO Japanese corporations published on the Cabinet Office website, which included the NPOs certified by the prefectures and the NPOs certified by government-designated cities in each prefecture.

The explanatory variables were taken to be the main government, market, and civil society resources that influence the development of social enterprises (Kerlin 2009). The scale items for the government resources were the financial power index average in the municipalities in each prefecture (Fiscal 2017), and the number of facilities in each prefecture as of April 1, 2015, that had introduced a local government Designated Manager System. The financial power index shows the financial strength of the local public bodies; therefore, the higher the indicator, the more financially prosperous (the public service can be enhanced). The Designated Administrator System, the establishment of which is specified in Section 24 of Article 244 of the Local Autonomy Act, came into force in 2003 to provide an instrument to allow for the delegation of the management of public facilities to private business operators at the discretion of local governments. As SNCs can also accept outsourcing services, this was considered to be a suitable indicator for the impact by local governments.

To measure the influence of the market as a driving force in increasing the number of SNCs, the employer remuneration for each prefecture population (Fiscal 2015) and the average income per population in the prefecture (Fiscal 2015) were used. Employer remuneration refers to the amount of distribution to employers from the total value added from all production activities such as public and social services. Prefectural income is the sum of the income earned by citizens and companies in the prefecture, such as property income—interest, dividends, and corporate profit—as well as employer remuneration. Therefore, per capita income did not represent the level of personal incomes or salaries but the income level of the prefecture's overall economy. While neither indicator could be said to be an indicator that strictly measures the market effect as to whether NPO corporations have increasing market transactions, they indicate whether there are rich economic resources in the prefecture.

The number of volunteers in each prefecture (Fiscal 2016), the donations for the Community Cheas (Fiscal 2017), and the number of community voluntary firefighters (Fiscal 2015) were used as scale items to indicate the civil society resources, as volunteers and donations are important NPO resources. The number of volunteers used in this survey was based on the "Survey on Basic Social Life in 2016" (Statistics Bureau of the Ministry of Internal Affairs and Communications) that covered Japanese people over the age of ten, in which the volunteer activity referred to activities "to provide their labor force, skill, and time without any compensation aimed at promoting the welfare of local communities and individuals and groups" and if "payment of the actual expenses such as transportation expenses for activities is received, it is not regarded as compensation." While not all volunteers work in NPOs, because volunteer activities could be seen as being the driving force for the establishment of SNCs, this was taken as an indicator for the civil society. The Community Chest in Japan, also known as the Red Feather, is prescribed in the social welfare law[1] with donations to the Red Feather being 181 billion yen in FY 2016. Although it has not been clarified how much of this was allocated to SNCs, as fund-raising activities are being conducted in each prefecture, this was adopted as the donation performance index. The number of firefighter's indicator demonstrates the resident participation in the autonomous activities in the local communities in each prefecture.

However, if the social origin approach for treating NPOs "as an integral part of a social system whose role and scale are a by-product of a complex set of historical forces" were to be followed, only paying attention to the government, market, and civil society "resources" was deemed insufficient as it was also necessary to consider the possibility that differences in regional needs also affected the uneven SPC distribution in Japan. Therefore, the number of welfare recipients in each prefecture (Fiscal 2015) and the number of people receiving long-term care insurance (and support) were also selected as explanatory variables (Fiscal 2016) for the regional needs.

It was also speculated that there were specific variables that may have been affecting the growth in the number of SNCs in some regions. First, it was expected that a greater number of NPOs would be established in more highly populated areas; therefore, the population in each prefecture (as of October 1, 2017) was taken as a variable (control variable) to account for this possible influence. Second, since the NPO Act was enacted, Japan has experienced many major natural disasters. A previous study identified that the impact of large-scale disasters in East Asia led to the emergence of many social enterprises (Defourny and Kim 2011). Therefore, disaster restoration expenditure per capita (total of prefectural/municipal finance, the average of 2005, 2010, and 2015) per population was introduced into the model as an indicator for disaster influence, that is, the degree to which a prefecture had suffered from a major disaster in the previous year and whether this had led to an increase in the number of NPOs.

For the numerical values other than the financial power index, logarithmic transformations (natural logarithm) were performed before the analysis to reduce the influence of a biased distribution and outliers.

RESULTS AND DISCUSSION

Not all the explanatory variables for the multiple regression analysis model described above were used in the analysis as the variables were selected using the stepwise method and then put into the model. JMP 14.0 statistical software was employed and the variable reduction method (a method used to decrease the explanatory variables one by one from all explanatory variables the first time) is applied to select the explanatory variables that had a minimum Bayesian information criterion (BIC), the results for which are shown in table 6.3. The variance inflation factor (VIF) was calculated to assess the possible multicollinearity, from which it was found that the value was sufficiently low to reject any possible multicollinearity. The multiple regression analysis results are shown in table 6.3, from which it can be seen that the number of SNCs in each prefecture was significantly and positively affected by prefectural income per population, the number of volunteers (over ten years old), and the number of welfare recipients, but negatively affected by the municipal financial power index.

The survey results indicated that the driving force in Japan for the emergence of new SEOs was the civil society and the market as well as social needs. The influence of the government did not appear to coincide with the proportion of earned income in the SNC income structure. Also, in common with the previous survey results that found that the organizational staff relied on volunteers, the number of volunteers was also found to affect the number of SNCs in the analysis, which also indicated that a shortage of government support could be a bottleneck to any expansion in the activities of Japanese SEOs in the future. Therefore, it may be necessary to procure resources from the market and civil society to make up for the small government support, and SEOs may possibly need to campaign for greater government support to activate their advocacy and social activities.

The survey results revealed that the driving force in Japan for the emergence of new SEOs was the civil society, the market, and the recognition of social needs, which confirmed the views in Kerlin (2009). However, the negative results for the municipal financial power index average, the government factor, were not in line with Kerlin's (2009) model, which suggested that the government influenced the development of Japan's social enterprises.

Table 6.3 Multiple Regression Analysis (Dependent Value: The Number of SNCs in Each Prefecture)

		Standard β	p Value	VIF
Governmental factors	Municipal financial power index average	−0.132	0.025*	3.0
	Facilities introduced Designated Manager System	—	—	—
Market factors	Prefectural income per capita	0.118	0.014*	2.0
	Prefectural Employee Reward per capita	—	—	—
Civil society factors (community)	Volunteers (over ten years old)	0.837	<0.001*	4.2
	Donation for Community Chest	—	—	—
	Community voluntary firefighters	—	—	—
Social needs factors	Welfare recipients	0.206	<0.001*	2.5
	Long-term care recipients	—	—	—
Control variables	Disaster restoration budgets per capita	—	—	—
	Population	—	—	—
R^2	0.955			
F	222.6723			
AICc	−22.7998			
BIC	−13.7989			

* p<.05. *Source*: Made by the author.

Therefore, it could be concluded from this result that the weaknesses in the municipal budget have led to the increase in the number of NPOs in the area, that is, the NPOs in Japan are actively responding to the social needs the government has not been dealing with, which can be also explained using "government's failure" theory.[2]

CONCLUSION

This chapter examined the background to, the establishment of, and the growth in SNCs in Japan. Distinct from the nonprofit corporation system, the SNC system was established to make it easier for citizens to establish groups by minimizing regulatory authority management and emphasizing information disclosure, with Authorized SNCs, which receive preferential tax treatments, being allowed if they adhere to certain public interest standards and demonstrate strong citizenship.

Based on specific survey results, section 2 confirmed the activities and current status of SNCs and found that while the number of SNCs has been steadily growing in Japan, most have small budgets, and small, mainly female staff, possibly because female wages tend to be lower in Japan. While the Law for the Promotion of Specified Nonprofit Activities requires extensive information disclosure, particularly by the Authorized SNCs, around 15% of the non-authorized SNCs were not revealing full information. The income breakdown (revenue related to specific nonprofit activities) found that over 80% of earned income did not receive tax incentives and that earned income was becoming an important income source for the SNCs.

Using prefecture-specific data, section 3 analyzed the factors for the significant increase in SNCs across Japan in recent years. Employing the social origin approach, it was assumed that several "resource" factors were contributing to this increase. The analysis found that market factors (economic factors), civil society factors, and regional needs factors positively influenced the number of SNCs and that the municipal financial power index negatively influenced the number of SNCs, which tended to imply that the weaker the financial strength of the local governments in Japan, the greater the number of new SNCs. These survey results were consistent with the income structure of the SNCs being based largely on earned income, and the greater dependence of the Japanese SNCs on market and civil society resources rather than government resources to sustain and develop their activities.

As mentioned, even though the SNCs rely on civil society and market resources, around 15% were found to be deficient in their information disclosure; therefore, there may be issues with this low SNC transparency in the future.

The results indicated that the identified poor government support could restrict the expansion of the activities of Japanese SEOs as they need to seek resources from the market and civil society. Therefore, SEOs need better directed campaigns to encourage government support. Furthermore, this study revealed that the increase in SNCs across Japan has been in response to the lack of government support for social needs, which is of great significance for future nonprofit sector studies in Japan. The geographical imbalances in the number of SNCs were also found to be affected by several factors. Therefore, we feel that these findings have some significance for nonprofit organizational research in Japan and around the world.

NOTES

1. In the social welfare law, the Community Chest is "the entity that recruits of donations to be made only once a year within a period prescribed by the Minister

of Health, Labor and Welfare, with the prefecture's area as a unit, and allocates the donation to entities that operate project aiming for social welfare (excluding national and local public entities) for promoting community welfare within the area."

2. Government failure theory posits that nonprofits are most active in regions where the largest gap exists between the homogeneous supply of public service and heterogeneous citizen demands (Liu 2017). However, it should be noted that the population of prefectures did not influence the number of SNCs in this survey result. The needs of people will become more diverse as the population increases. As such, this finding that low local government budgets, regardless of population, is only partially supported by the government failure theory.

REFERENCES

Cabinet Office. 2018. *Actual State Survey Report on Specified Nonprofit Corporation in 2017*. Tokyo: Cabinet Office of Japan.

Defourny, Jacques, and Shin-Yang Kim. 2011. "Emerging Models of Social Enterprise in Eastern Asia: A Cross-Country Analysis." *Social Enterprise Journal* 7(1): 86–111.

Kerlin, Janelle A. 2009. *Social Enterprise: A Global Comparison*. Medford, MA: Tufts University Press.

Laratta, Rosario, Sachiko Nakagawa, and Masanari Sakurai. 2011. "Japanese Social Enterprises: Major Contemporary Issues and Key Challenges." *Social Enterprise Journal* 7(1): 50–68.

Liu, Gao. 2017. "Government Decentralization and the Size of the Nonprofit Sector: Revisiting the Government Failure Theory." *The American Review of Public Administration* 47(6): 619–633.

Salamon, Lester M., and Helmut K. Anheier. 1996. *Working Papers of the Johns Hopkins Comparative Nonprofit Sector Project: The International Classification of Nonprofit Organizations: ICBPO-Revision 1, 1996*. Baltimore, MD: Johns Hopkins Center for Civil Society Studies.

———. 1998. "Social Origins of Civil Society : Explaining the Nonprofit Sector Cross-Nationally." *Voluntas* 9(3): 213–248.

Salamon, Lester M., and S. Wojciech Sokolowski. 1999. *Global Civil Society: Dimensions of the Nonprofit Sector*. Baltimore, MD: Johns Hopkins Center for Civil Society Studies.

Tsukamoto, Ichiro, and Mariko Nishimura. 2009. "Japan." In *Social Enterprise: A Global Comparison*, edited by Janelle A. Kerlin, 163–183. Medford, MA: Tufts University Press.

Chapter 7

Development of Social Economy in South Korea

The Role of Civil Society

Eun Sun Lee

INTRODUCTION

As[1] the concept and the model of social enterprise continue to spread across the globe particularly in the twenty-first century, there has also been an unprecedented spike in interest in social economy. Theoretical discussions about social enterprise remain in progress, but at the very least, it is clear that social enterprises continue to proliferate and take roots in the United States and Europe as well as in Asian countries. Although scholars have tried to define the term "social enterprise," a general definition that exactly describes all global instances of the phenomenon does not yet exist. One of the closest definitions that reasonably explain the social enterprise would be that: a social enterprise is an organization that aims to improve public interest and make revenue (Campbell 1998; OECD 1999; Defourny 2001; Auteri 2003; Pearce and Kay 2003; Borzaga and Defourny 2004; Social Enterprise London 2004; Kerlin 2006). Existing accounts of social enterprises in Europe heavily rely on Social Economy theory (Pearce and Kay 2003; Borzaga and Defourny 2004; Kerlin 2006). One of the key elements of this theory is the existence of a well-developed third sector that provides and delivers various welfare services. In numerous European countries, central and local governments support and foster social enterprises by systematically collaborating with the third sector, which in turn provides welfare provision and job creation for their members, and tends to be established for labor integration (Dees 1998; Young 2003; Evers and Laville 2004; Aiken and Spear 2005; Aiken 2006; Defourny and Nyssens 2009). By contrast, the U.S. government does not deliberately nurture social enterprises. Rather, the market and the third sector cooperate with each other, resulting in a rapid proliferation of venture-style social enterprises promoted by a culture of philanthropy, donation, and the venture friendly market (Campbell 1998; Salamon and Sokolowski 2006; Bornstein 2007; Christopher et al. 2008; Defourny and Nyssens 2009). In South Korea, social enterprise emerged as a subject of academic discussion and debate around 2000. It was only after 2007 that the Korean government officially began recognizing and supporting social enterprises by benchmarking the UK and U.S. models. In 2007, fifty-five social enterprises were established in South Korea. In the past twelve years, the social economy sector has diversified into social enterprise, village enterprise, self-sufficiency enterprise, and (social) cooperatives in South Korea. The number of social enterprises has increased 52 times from 55 in 2007 to 2,865 in 2019. The number of all Social Economy Organizations (SEOs), including social enterprises, showed an explosive increase of 440 times from 55 in 2007 to 24,195 in 2019. These facts raise the question: what explains the rapid and successful development of SEOs in South Korea in the recent years? The dominant explanation points to the effective policies set by the central government, which sponsored and nurtured SEOs by creating relevant institutions and giving financial, organizational, and advisory support. In the early stage, social enterprise, which is the first official SEO, became rapidly known to the public through the government's active development policy together with intense promotion by the mass media as public service announcements. The speed of its development was comparable to a "boom" and many Korean scholars and members of the public began to accept the phenomenon as a type of popular trend and predicted that it would not be sustainable. Yet various SEOs including social enterprises in South Korea today are advancing both quantitatively and qualitatively. Despite the fact that the size of the third sector in South Korea has been small compared to that of the other OECD member countries and that the third sector previously did not appear as a substantive subject of government policy (Lee 2009), the third sector in South Korea played a dominant role in establishing and managing SEOs. Traditionally, the role of civil society in South Korea has been focused on the participation of "politics of protest," but recently as SEOs have been developed, the civil society organization (CSO) in South Korea has been transformed into a key actor of coproduction and cocreation.

This chapter utilizes the concept of "policy entrepreneurship" to assess how diverse governmental and nongovernmental actors have formed and forged dynamic strategic interactions with one another to contribute to the successful development of SEOs in South Korea. This chapter is organized as follows: it first discusses agenda setting to argue that existing public policy was transformed to incorporate social enterprise in South Korea. That follows an analysis of the role of the third sector as a policy entrepreneur in the field of social enterprise. It then explains the characteristics of social enterprise, limitations due to social enterprise accreditation system, and response to overcome these by the government and civil society. In the next section, it analyzes civil society as a policy entrepreneur in the enactment process of the Framework Act on Cooperatives (FAC), which brought full-scale expansion of social economy discussions in South Korea. It then explains social economy ecosystem changes brought about by the development of cooperatives, and highlights the current state of social economy in South Korea. The final section is a conclusion.

AGENDA SETTING IN SOCIAL ENTERPRISE

Social enterprises have been established to provide welfare services, employment, and to contribute to the society, but may have different characteristics in different regions. Although social enterprises are closely related to welfare provision and employment, these issues have already been among the many social issues that South Korea had to deal with even before 1990s. South Korea was a typical developing country during the 1960s and 1970s. During the time, providing welfare services or solving unemployment problems was not within the political realm. It was only after the democratization in the early 1990s that these social issues became politicized and assigned under the government as their role.

Kingdon's "policy window" theory tried to systematically analyze which issues among numerous public affairs are selected as policy agenda. Policy windows can be described as a situation in which policy advocates try to draw attention to the issues of their interest, and an opportunity that opens in order for them to achieve their preferred methods. Policy windows open mainly from the political change among the three streams: problems, politics, and policy (Kingdon 1984). The typical approaches they take are changes in political power, parliamentary seats, or in public opinion. According to Cobb and Elder (1972), in order for a monopolistic decision-making system to transform, a change in public awareness of an issue is needed, after which the issue becomes active as an administrative issue, in other words, an institutional issue. In this sense, we can see that the dynamics concerning agenda setting policy play an important role in social enterprise. It is also likely that issues that concern or affects a large number of people will be of greater social importance, and as such will have a higher chance of being selected for policy agenda.

In case of South Korea, the 1997–1998 economic crisis heightened public awareness about unemployment and escalated popular demand for state action. The official unemployment rate was 8.6% in February 1999—the highest point since the 1980s. Before that crisis, South Korea had maintained near full employment for many years, and organized the welfare system under the implicit assumption that unemployment could be kept to a minimum (Kwon 2001). Traditionally, the welfare provision was within the family, in which unemployed people received help from their family or their savings. The economic crisis damaged this system, provoking demands for various welfare provisions that could simultaneously address the unemployment problem. The Kim Dae-jung administration established Productive Welfare as one of the three major state affairs (Presidential Committee on Social Inclusion 1999). The government amended the Living Security Act so it became the National Basic Living Security Act to realize productive welfare in order to guarantee basic living security for lower income bracket individuals and to help them to self-support and achieve self-reliance. One of the core concepts of this program was welfare-to-work. Public campaign by mass media proliferated, for example, the "Again Miracle of Han-river" campaign by the government emphasized a need to pull together to overcome the national crisis. Public opinion on many occasions set the tone of policy discussion in general while signifying policy image. A change in the tone indicates change in public awareness regarding a policy, while the level of the media coverage indicates the degree and extent of this change. These series of changes signify the weakening or collapsing of the monopolistic strength of the main decision-makers of a policy (Baumgartner and Jones 1991). As image changes concerning a policy, the position of the people involved in the policy decision lowers, and the lowered position increases more diverse actors' participation in the policy decision. The role of policy entrepreneur, involving properly synthesizing policy window streams, becomes important. Policy entrepreneurs can change social attention toward a certain issue in the government's agenda and act as crucial players in selecting and changing policy by proposing suitable measures for the issue (Kingdon 1984; Mintrom 1997). The wider the jurisdiction of a committee becomes, the better it can deal with the new issues, and the higher becomes the level of attention paid to the issue in question. The new issues are also closely related to the jurisdiction as well as the level of the committee. A wider jurisdiction expands both opportunities and possible places in which policy entrepreneur can perform, and this, in turn, closely interacts with the salience of the issue (Jones et al. 1993; Sheingate 2006).

Historically, South Korea had cooperatives and livelihood cooperative societies, but without linking social development with political involvement. The labor unions were likewise did not receive much attention. After 1990, however, these stood out as the main actor in the manufacturing community movement. These movements aimed at overcoming the financial disadvantages that residents from ghettos encountered, and hoped to establish an alternative economic community.[2] Efforts to expand cooperatives' activities in the third sector continued to receive attention after the 1990s. In 1995, the Kim Young-sam administration looked into cooperatives as potential producers within its poverty policy (Korea Institute for Health and Social Affairs 1999). Since then, Self Sufficiency Agencies have been established and the third sector's activities have been institutionally incorporated. In 1997, numerous civic groups emerged throughout the country to overcome the unemployment issue. Following the establishment of the "Overcoming Unemployment Movement Committee" (OUMC), which was established by the third sector and operated by public donations, the Public Service Employment Plan was implemented by this organization. The consumer cooperatives, received legal authority, with the enactment of the Consumer Cooperative Act in 1999, to act as public agents such as producers, producers' groups, cultural organizations, and also to participate in the government-commissioned businesses (Jang 2006; Eum 2008; Lee 2009). Attempting to resolve the financial crisis, the government absorbed the third sector, which at that time was providing little welfare service, into its institutional remit. The government recognized the effectiveness of linking to the third sector, which was attempting to expand during the Kim Dae-jung government. Productive welfare policy 2000 was realized through the government and the third sector's self-support as well as with the implementation of a social employment program created in 2003. The Ministry of Employment and Labor spent $6.77 million in the first year of the latter program and created 2,000 social jobs. Moreover, ten other ministries spent $1.25 billion in creating 20,000 social jobs. However, most of these initiatives relied on financial support from the government and were low income. The above factors instigated discussions about social enterprise initiatives that would reinvest their revenue in social schemes. The Ministry of Employment and Labor's Initial Plan to Promote Social Enterprise pointed out that "the discussion of adopting the system of European social enterprises went into a full swing as an alternative to the increase in demand of social services as well as the continuing development of the economy without new employment around 2000." The Social Enterprise Promotion Act (SEPA) was enacted to foster social enterprises systematically; these became institutionalized in 2007.

THE THIRD SECTOR AS A POLICY ENTREPRENEUR IN THE INSTITUTIONALIZATION OF SOCIAL ENTERPRISE

Policy entrepreneurs use various activities to promote their ideas, including identifying problems, shaping the terms of policy debates, networking in policy circles, and building coalitions (Mintrom and Vergari 1996). In

South Korea, discussion about social enterprise was raised by the third sector organizations in forums, seminars, and articles that highlighted the necessity of the institutionalization of social enterprises. By the late 1990s, however, the concept of social enterprise was still incomplete or distorted. The concept was popularized by Won-soon Park, who was an executive board member of The Hope Institute and Chul-young Lee who was president of the ARK Private Funds Investment Advisors in South Korea. As an executive board member, Park worked to spread the concept of social enterprise through numerous lectures and publications. He even referred to himself as a "Social Designer." In March 2002, Park managed to prove that a social enterprise could be successfully established in South Korea by establishing the "Beautiful Store." President Lee was the first person to initiate the U.S. concept of social enterprise into academic research in South Korea. He and two friends devoted private funds—$250,000—to promote research into social enterprise like that found at Columbia University into Korean national universities in 2004. Lee was also the first to organize a social venture contest in 2006, which is still continuing. This became popular among college students and contributed greatly to the establishment of new social enterprises in South Korea. With the casebook published by Jeong (2004) taking the lead, numerous other casebooks dealing with success stories of social enterprises in the United States were published, many with support from the OUMC. Following the success of project businesses from the SK Group and Kyobo as part of their Corporate Social Responsibility (CSR) activities in 2004, a model was created in which stable work creation and welfare services were provided by using the third sector, including nonprofit organizations and other associations.

The success of policy entrepreneurs influences others to emulate their success, and policy entrepreneurs serve to bring new policy ideas in good currency (Mintrom and Vergari 1996). In that sense, the success of the Beautiful Store and CSR projects became catalysts to promote social enterprise. The economic crisis and productive welfare policy led by the Kim Dae-jung administration were grounds for its further development. Since then, the adoption of social enterprises has been discussed in more depth. The Korean government officially certified social enterprise after 2007, but this belies the fact that there were social enterprises in South Korea before these government initiatives. When the first round of accreditation took place in 2007, Hamkke Ilhaneun Seasang, the name of a janitorial service company that translates to "A world working together" in English, was granted the status of social enterprise. Yet this company had already introduced itself as a "Social enterprise" since 2003. At least ten further companies existed in 2003 that called themselves social enterprises. There were also organizations that claimed to be social enterprises on the CSR level. The third sector argued that social enterprises existed before the establishment of the government policy and that the SEPA was in fact legislated in order to promote social enterprises at the governmental level, and subsequently acted as a catalyst to establish social enterprises.[3] The social enterprises increased in number, however, required the governmental support for sustainability. The Korean government organized the T/F, consisting of related departments, experts, and specialists in the third sector to discuss the direction of the related law. This met fourteen times, and ultimately the SEPA was enacted (Suk 2008).

CHARACTERISTICS, LIMITATIONS, AND ALTERNATIVES OF SOCIAL ENTERPRISE

The SEPA refers social enterprise "as an enterprise certified in accordance with Article 7," "that pursues a social objective, such as raising local residents' quality of life, etc., by providing vulnerable groups with social services or jobs while conducting business activities, such as the production and sale of goods and services, etc. (Article 2)." Based on this act, the Korean government initiated the "Social Enterprise Accreditation System" in 2007. Unless an organization is officially accredited by the government, it cannot call itself a "social enterprise," even if they believe that they pursue social values rather than maximization of profit. If they use the social enterprise title without earning this accreditation, they may be fined up to $8,300 based on SEPA.[4]

The Ministry accredits an organization as a social enterprise if it fulfills certain requirements.[5] When a company applies to be accredited, it first has to specify the objectives of the organization: (1) Job Provision; (2) Social Service Provision; (3) Mixed (Job Provision + Social Service Provision); (4) Local Community Social Contribution;[6] and (5) other purposes. It is precisely stipulated in Articles 5.2 of the SEPA that a local government has to promote social enterprise in their region. Public organizations should prioritize procuring goods or services from social enterprises (Article 12). Even after being certified, the Ministry of Employment and Labor monitors the social enterprises to see if they are operating their businesses according to the standards set by the Ministry as well as making profit. The accredited social enterprises may lose their certification, depending on the results of the monitoring (Article 18).

Characteristics: The characteristics of social enterprises have been affected by the system's accreditation prototype. According to a census taken in year 2009, there were about 320 social enterprises in South Korea, in which 238 had been converted from social job programs,[7] self-support organizations, and providers of vocational facilities for the disabled. In 2012, five years after the establishment of the SEPA, 603 of all 774 social enterprises were converted from these organizations. Social job programs, self-support organizations, and vocational facilities for the disabled had been voluntarily managed by the third sector and the government. When social job program was converted into a social enterprise, it still aimed for the employment of the vulnerable, but its remit was expanded to the whole nation. On the other hand, when self-support organization was converted into a social enterprise, it had to provide services to local vulnerable citizens. Thus, employment ratio of those with vulnerable status is around 50–60% of the total number of employees in social enterprises in South Korea (see figure 7.1).

European social enterprises tend to be regarded as a special form of organization for the employment of vulnerable groups. Work Integration Social Enterprise (WISE) refers to a general type of social enterprise in Europe. However, in the United States, companies run by social entrepreneurship and socially innovative ventures tend to be called as social enterprises. As for South Korea, since both cases of the United States and the UK were benchmarked and a social enterprise fostering policy was implemented, both types of socially innovative companies and WISE have appeared. However, as the requirements to get the certification as social enterprise were favorable for WISE, and it was overwhelmingly large during the first five years of policy implementation, Korean social enterprises were not branded as innovative enterprises, but were branded as enterprises for vulnerable people and small enterprises that does not make enough profits.

Limitations: Since the enactment of SEPA in 2007, existing organizations have been certified as social enterprises. However, as time proceeds, it becomes increasingly difficult to find organizations that can still be converted.

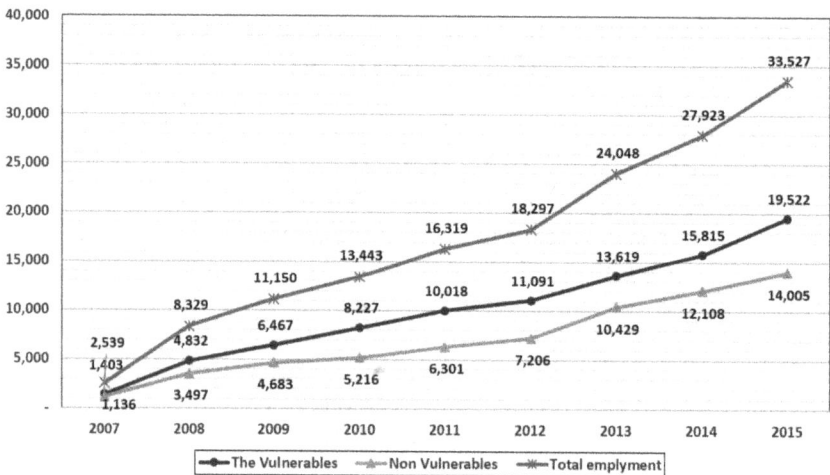

Figure 7.1 Vulnerable Status Employment in Social Enterprise, 2007–2015. *Source:* Calculated from the Korea Social Enterprise Promotion Agency database (2016).

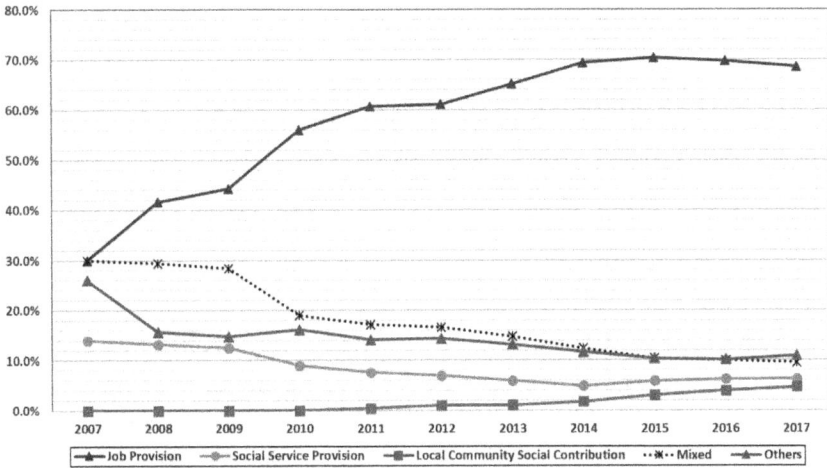

Figure 7.2 The Number of Accredited Social Enterprises by Accredited Type, 2007–2017. *Source*: Calculated from the Korea Social Enterprise Promotion Agency database (2018).

The unemployment problem, which has become more serious as time has gone by, especially in the case of youth unemployment, has emerged as a key issue in elections for the local governments. Local governments have thus begun to pay more attention to social enterprises in order to create jobs and foster more preliminary social enterprises. Starting with Seoul, supporting centers for social enterprises began to be established under local government organizations. Although existing civil servants had been responsible for this, field activists have gradually begun to get hired as civil servants to take over. As activists of the third sector were recruited as public officers, they began to implement the so-called social entrepreneurship education. The Social Entrepreneurship Education has been expanded as a way to increase the number of related programs and entrust regional centers so that the programs can be implement for local residents. Such "education" also holds "Idea Competitions," where winners receive some seed money and a small office in support to realize the winning idea. The organizations found through such competitions are collectively called social venture, and the government hoped to see them develop into social enterprises. Interview results point out that the people who started the social enterprise since 2011, especially the young people, received various supports from the government through winning such idea contests. However, social venture is in an unfavorable position in terms of its innovativeness to pass the government's certification review, and cases of them converting to general venture companies or foreign social enterprises have been increasing.[8] When SEPA was enacted, job creation, contribution to the local community, and the emergence of socially innovative companies were expected, but outstanding results were achieved only in job creation. Criticism has begun for social enterprises to rely on government funding. In addition, as the number of social enterprises increased, the need for dedicated agencies to support them continued to rise (see figure 7.2).

Alternatives: It is expressly stipulated in Articles 5.2 of the SEPA that a local government must promote social enterprise in their region. The head of a metropolitan city, a province, or a special self-governing province shall establish and implement a social enterprise support plan for his/her city and province under the conditions prescribed by the Presidential Decree, in order to promote social enterprise in the region under his/her jurisdiction and support them systematically (Article 13). Since the certification requirements are quite stringent, local governments have come up with the Preliminary Social Enterprise system. In 2011, the Korea Social Enterprise Promotion Agency (KoSEA) was established under the Ministry of Employment and Labor, and the agency had to have expertise in social enterprise and social economy because it was responsible for the "substantive" support needed for the field. The KoSEA launched various projects such as social entrepreneurship education, social venture idea contest, national network construction, and sales support business. In addition, the KoSEA designated local agencies in each region to have a consignment operating organization to carry out their projects. Mainly, third-party organizations were commissioned to operate institutions, and they served not only to help establish and operate social enterprises in the region, but also to promote social enterprises. These units have been referred to as Intermediary Organizations (IOs) in South Korea. In the government-centered support system, the third sector began to emerge as the main actor in the official delivery system. With the establishment of KoSEA and IOs, policies were implemented faster on site, and in the process, the voices of the sites that had been overlooked, especially the loopholes in policies, were collected and communicated to the central government. Various discussions have begun to flourish, such as the economic sustainability of organizations pursuing social purpose, the direction of government roles and policies, and the creation of an ecosystem to achieve both public interest and profitability.

THE THIRD SECTOR AS A POLICY ENTREPRENEUR IN THE INSTITUTIONALIZATION OF COOPERATIVES

Local governments sought ways to utilize resources from third sectors, including social enterprises, to create jobs and revitalize local communities. At that time, successful cases of regional establishments such as iCOOP cooperatives and Ansan Medical Cooperatives and activating communities led by local residents began to receive great attention. These cooperatives have been operating successfully for more than twenty years, but they have not come under the public spotlight or recognized by the government. This is deeply related to Korea's cooperatives history.

The beginning of South Korea's activities related on welfare and labor issues by the third sector was after the March First Independence Movement to fight against the Japanese colonial rule in 1919—this is when cooperative movement began (Jang 2006). After the independence in 1945, farmers formed agricultural cooperatives, but when its size and influence got bigger, the government started regulating them. As a result, management autonomy was damaged and turned into government-inspired agricultural cooperatives. Because it was so large in number it was difficult for the public to recognize that the cooperative was a private, voluntary, and independent production communal activity. However, from early 1960s, voluntary credit associations began emerging from metro regions and its vitalization led to consumer cooperative movement in the early 1980s and to the establishment of the Consumer Cooperative Federation in 1983. Before 1980s, the number of cooperatives, which included the Agricultural Cooperatives, Fisheries Cooperatives, and SME cooperatives, was established based on individual laws in keeping with government policies. In the third sector, there was a discussion that it was necessary to establish a framework act for the establishment and operation of a genuine cooperative without government control since the 1980s, but it was not materialized as a legislative activity. The cooperatives under the individual law have limited targets and areas of business feasibility and relatively difficult standards for establishment. Under the individual law system, sharing of individual cooperative values and their benefits was limited to a small number, and there was a problem that cooperation between cooperatives, promotion of a unified policy, and accurate survey were difficult (Jang 2017). This kind of social atmosphere began to change dramatically in 2008. When the global financial crisis in 2008 brought a slump in the employment rate, Mondragon Cooperatives Group in Spain received global attention by creating new jobs. Just as social enterprises in the early 2000s attracted attention with job creation and social innovative product and services, cooperatives gained global attention as an alternative to solving unemployment and revitalizing the local economy. Since the 2008 global financial crisis, consensus on the necessity of revitalizing cooperatives and the limitations of individual law systems have spread. This was a period when the government and the public were focused on creating jobs immediately after the enactment of the SEPA. In addition, the United Nations in 2009 designated 2012 as the year of cooperatives and encouraged member countries to develop a legal system for cooperative development, which opened a new policy window. According to Kingdon, the policy window opens in three streams: problems-political-policy. At this period, the policy window opened in all areas, from the problem stream that social enterprises cannot sufficiently respond to job creation and vitalization of the local economy, the political stream of the UN's recommendation, and the policy stream of the limitations of the existing individual cooperative laws. When the policy window opens like this, various policy entrepreneurs can appear, and they can set a new agenda and create a new flow of policy depending on how specific and professional alternatives are prepared and presented by them. In South Korea, activists who consistently insisted on the necessity of the FAC from the 1980s gathered together, and in October 2011, three parties each drafted the FAC and submitted it to the National Assembly. The Solidarity Association for the Enactment of the Framework Act on Cooperatives (SAEFAC) formed by twenty-nine CSOs in 2011, such as the existing Association of Consumer Cooperatives and YMCA,[9] played a key role as a policy entrepreneur in FAC enactment process. The SAEFAC not only participated in the drafting of legislation by submitting opinions directly to the legislators of the political parties,[10] but also actively participated in the public hearings of the National Assembly to present opinions. The SAEFAC persuaded domestic and foreign cases that cooperatives are an alternative to revitalizing the local economy and revitalizing the polarized market economy system, providing detailed policy content and alternatives, and allowing the government to adopt them. The third sector has played a role as a complete policy entrepreneur based on expertise and activity. Ultimately, FAC was enacted in December 2012 in South Korea. With the establishment of the FAC, the establishment of producer and consumer-oriented cooperatives that were not covered under the existing individual law system was guaranteed by law, and the establishment standards were also relaxed. In addition, the basis for establishing a comprehensive development plan for cooperatives and promoting consistent policies was prepared.

DEVELOPMENT OF COOPERATIVES AND CONSTRUCTION OF SE ECOSYSTEM

Since the establishment of the FAC, newly established cooperatives in South Korea have been based on this law. The law distinguishes two types: cooperatives and social cooperatives. The term "cooperative" means a business organization that intends to enhance its partners' rights and interests, thereby contributing to local communities by being engaged in the cooperative purchasing, production, sales, and provision of goods or services. And the term "social cooperative" means a cooperative that carries out business activities related to the enhancement of rights, interests, and welfare of local residents or provides social services or jobs to disadvantaged people, among cooperatives under subparagraph 1, but that is not run for profit (Article 2). When it

Table 7.1 The Number of Cooperatives Based on FAC in South Korea

	Cooperatives	Social Cooperatives	Federation	Total
Dec. 2014	5,938	262	35	6,235
Dec. 2016	9,954	604	57	10,615
Dec. 2018	13,267	1,185	74	14,526

Source: Ministry of Economy and Finance, Press Release (December 31, 2015; February 13, 2018; March 31, 2020).

is intended to establish a cooperative, five or more promoters qualified for membership shall prepare articles of association and shall report the articles of association to the competent Mayor/Do Governor having jurisdiction over its principal place of business (Article 15). And it can engage in any businesses except finance and insurance (Article 45). On the other hand, social cooperatives are the same as those formed by five or more members voluntarily, but they cannot be established without the approval of the Minister of Strategy and Finance as a nonprofit corporation (Articles 4 and 85). The principal business activities occupy not less than 40% of the entire business activities of a cooperative, and it is able to operate small loans to members and mutual aid programs (Articles 93 and 94). In addition, cooperatives and social cooperatives differ in compensation for losses and distribution of surplus and disposal of residual properties (Articles 51, 59, 98, and 104). Based on the FAC, which took effect on December 1, 2012, 52 new cooperatives were established a month, and the next year, more than 3,000 cooperatives were established, and since then, each year more than doubled from the previous year (see table 7.1).

With the explosive growth of traditional SEOs, cooperatives, local governments' interests expanded from fostering social enterprises to social economy itself. Accordingly, the existing social enterprise promotion ordinances were abolished or amended, and the ordinances for vitalizing the social economy began to be established. In addition, discussions on social finance began to take place as a way to cope with fragile financial access and financing for cooperatives. This atmosphere spread to discussions on the creation of an ecosystem where various SEOs can be developed, that is, the construction of a social economy ecosystem. The operation experience of IOs to support social enterprises contributes to the establishment of an integration support center that supports various SEOs such as self-sufficiency enterprises and village enterprises as well as cooperatives. Starting with Seoul, local governments put their own budgets to establish social economy support centers, and began to formally establish governance systems with local governments to revitalize local economy and the community. In particular, since the inauguration of the Moon Jae-in regime, social economy revitalization has emerged as a major national task, creating a stream of active cooperation with SEOs in the areas of social economy ecosystem creation, urban regeneration, and community care.

THE CURRENT STATE OF SOCIAL
ECONOMY IN SOUTH KOREA

Organizations: There are four representative organization types of SEOs in South Korea: Social Enterprises, (Social) Cooperatives, Village Enterprises, and Self-Sufficiency Enterprise (see table 7.2).

Self-sufficiency enterprise is an organization that operates self-supporting programs for the poor to escape from receiving pensions in the form of producer cooperatives or joint business by recipients of national basic living security and residents of low-income families. Village enterprise is a region-based organization established and operated by local residents or groups to solve common regional problems through profit projects that utilize local resources, and create income and jobs to effectively realize the benefits of the local community. This is aimed at revitalizing the local community. These four types of SEOs differ in terms of organizational requirements and operational principles, but what they have in common is that they use corporate elements to pursue public interest and social values. In particular, cooperatives and village enterprises have an important characteristic that local residents establish to create their own interests or community interests. What is striking in the increase of SEOs is that cooperatives have exploded since 2013 (see figure 7.3).

The Third Sector-Government-Private Firm Relations in Social Economy: Since 2000, a variety of SEOs have been active since the central government

Table 7.2   The Number of Detailed Organizational Forms within SEOs in South Korea

Year	Social Enterprises	Preliminary Social Enterprises	(Social) Cooperatives	Village Enterprises	Self-sufficiency Enterprise	Total
2007	55	—	—	—	—	55
2008	221	—	—	—	—	221
2009	298	—	—	—	—	298
2010	514	—	—	—	—	514
2011	669	436	—	550	—	1,655
2012	811	831	52	787	919	3,400
2013	1,080	743	3,114	1,119	1,112	7,168
2014	1,345	589	5,846	1,249	1,257	10,286
2015	1,640	492	8,188	1,342	1,421	13,083
2016	1,905	553	10,236	1,377	1,451	15,522
2017	2,161	731	12,170	1,442	1,092	17,596
2018	2,473	1,154	14,318	1,497	1,211	20,653
2019	2,865	1,767	16,795	1,592	1,176	24,195

Source: (Preliminary) Social Enterprise: Ministry of Employment and Labor Information Disclosure Request Data (May 13, 2020); (Social) Cooperatives: Korea Cooperatives (http://www.coop.go.kr, accessed April 18, 2020); Village Enterprise: Ministry of the Interior and Safety Information Disclosure Request Data (April 24, 2020); Self-Sufficiency Enterprise: Korea Development Institute for Self-sufficiency and Welfare (https://www.kdissw.or.kr, accessed June 28, 2020).

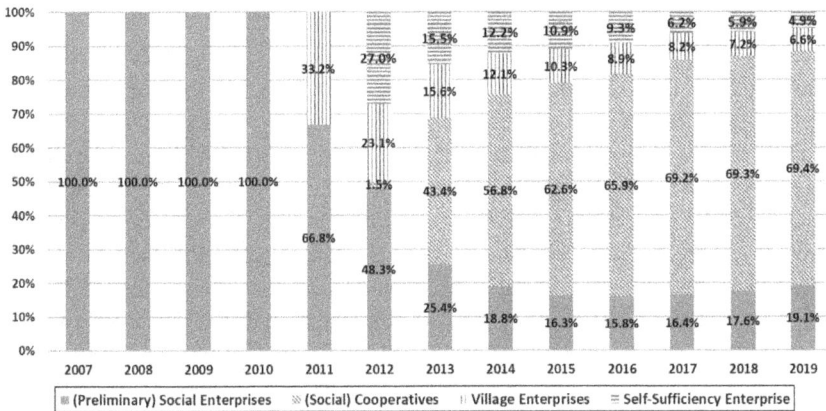

Figure 7.3 Proportion by Type of Detailed Organization within SEOs. *Source*: Calculated from the following databases—(Preliminary) Social Enterprise: Ministry of Employment and Labor Information Disclosure Request Data (May 13, 2020); (Social) Cooperatives: Korea Cooperatives (http://www.coop.go.kr, accessed April 18, 2020); Village Enterprise: Ministry of the Interior and Safety Information Disclosure Request Data (April 24, 2020); Self-Sufficiency Enterprise: Korea Development Institute for Self-sufficiency and Welfare (https://www.kdissw.or.kr, accessed June 28, 2020).

initiated policies for supporting social economy. Since the Moon Jae-in administration came into power, as one of the government's top 100 government tasks, "social economy revitalization" has been promoted for quantitative growth of SEOs, such as improving laws and institutions for fostering and supporting SEOs, conducting pilot projects, and spreading social awareness. As of 2018, a total of $255.6 million was executed as a policy to promote social economy by department at the central government level, and in 2019 it increased to $343.7 million. In addition, in the financial sector, a total loan of $36 million, a guarantee of $96.9 million, and $16.9 million were invested in 2018 to expand the financial accessibility of SEOs.[11] In addition to the establishment of local governments' social economy support and activation ordinances, official governance system among SEOs, councils and associations for social economy, and local governments began to operate. If local governments have focused on simply increasing the number of SEOs in the past, recently they have begun to discuss how the social economy can contribute to the projects of various local governments to revitalize the local economy and restore the local community.

In the social economy, the cooperation system among the third sector, private firms, and local governments began with social enterprises. The central and local governments had to financially support social enterprises based on SEPA. The links between social enterprises and private firms began when social enterprises were converted from CSR projects of the SK and Kyobo at the first round of accreditation in 2007. Excluding the cases of some large-scale companies post-2008, the business links to private enterprise were almost always one-time business projects, consulting services, or purchasing relationships. However, since 2010, as the support programs from the SK Group and Kyobo as well as from the local governments became known to the public through the media, investment and supports from the private firms grew considerably. Chairman Tae-won Chey of SK Group found a social enterprise while trying to evolve and develop existing CSR activities. At the symposium hosted by the central government in 2009, he announced SK's plans to promote social enterprises, and declared that it would foster social enterprises by raising funds of $41.5 million. After that, the Business Group for Social Enterprise was established within the Happiness Foundation which is the public interest foundation established by SK (Chey 2014). As of 2011, the SK Group established sixteen social enterprises directly and initiated a new social enterprise affiliated with the Ministry of Justice to create jobs, and turned the Maintenance, Repair, and Operation Korea, which generated $8.3 million in sales, into a social enterprise in 2012. The SK hosted the 2012 Social Enterprises International Forum and has been operating its own "Social Performance Incentive" system, which measures social values created by social enterprises and provides proportional incentives. It provided a total of $28.1 million incentives to 222 social enterprises for a total of five years from 2015 to 2019.[12] Another example, over the past eight years, the Hyundai Motor Group has provided subsidies to a total of 211 social enterprises through the H-On Dream Social Enterprise Start-up Audition, and achieved a total of 1,420 jobs through management mentoring, purchasing connections, and cooperation projects.[13] In addition, there are a number of cases where large companies have established and operated social enterprises as subsidiaries at the CSR level and are expanding the preferential purchase of SEOs' products in South Korea. The Moon Jae-in government declared not only revitalizing the social economy but also realizing the social value of public institutions as a major national task. As a result, public institutions in South Korea tried to realize social values that matched the purpose of establishment, and in this process, attention was paid to the role and performance of the social economy. A number of public enterprises have begun to prioritize the purchase of SEOs' products and have initiated cooperative projects with SEOs in the region. Korea Land and Housing Corporation (LH) held the 2018 Social Value Vision Declaration Ceremony as a public enterprise that made the most efforts to build a social economy ecosystem as well as to realize social values. The LH rented for less than the market price, nurtured about 600 SEOs, and purchased materials and services worth $112.1 million. In addition, LH, which participates in 124 urban regeneration projects among 265 nationwide, is cooperating proactively by encouraging local SEOs to participate in the urban regeneration process with local government.[14]

CONCLUSION

As Polanyi (1944) argued, after the establishment of the community, the social economy has existed even before the market was created. The voluntary economic activity of the private sector based on reciprocity and philanthropy has become more important as the crisis of the welfare state and the increase in unemployment after World War II. In South Korea, after the liberation from Japanese colonies in 1945, farmers' organizations voluntarily formed agricultural cooperatives, but they had a unique experience of being controlled by the dictatorship. Since the 1960s, voluntary credit cooperatives have been established around urban areas, and in the early 1980s it spread to consumer cooperative movements, spreading livelihood cooperative movements in various areas (Jang 2006; Eum 2008). The number was very small compared to the controlled Agricultural Cooperatives by the government, so there was a limit to inform the general public about the concept of genuine cooperatives. These various third sector production community activities have developed into self-sufficiency and social job programs since the 1998 economic crisis. At the time when social enterprises became a part of the government agenda, unemployment and welfare service provision were among the many social issues in South Korea. However, the economic crisis of 1997–1998 opened a policy window and the government changed its policy priorities. By the late 1990s, the concept of social enterprise was incomplete or distorted. However, CEOs of social enterprises that called themselves began organizing forums, seminars, and educational/training workshops since 1999. The concept of social enterprise was popularized by Won-soon Park and Chul-young Lee. They worked to spread the concept of social enterprise and successfully established the first social enterprise, "Beautiful Store," and hold a social venture contest from 2006. Although the academic discussion of established social programs was negative (Son 2005), a favorable image of social enterprises was established through the third sector's efforts, and the government recognized their efforts and capabilities. The success of the Beautiful Store and a number of CSR projects became the catalysts to promote social enterprise, and the enactment of the SEPA in 2007 was made possible. The Korean government officially certified social enterprise after 2007, but this belies the fact that there were social enterprises in South Korea before these government initiatives. Ultimately, the third sector played the crucial role of "policy entrepreneur" in agenda setting and policy implementation with regard to social enterprises in South Korea. However, by implementing the social enterprise accreditation system, the central government achieved results only in the creation of jobs for the vulnerable that were initially targeted, creation of socially innovative enterprises, and job creations and activation of the local economy. To overcome this, the government initiated a preliminary social enterprise system and began to discuss the construction of an ecosystem suitable for social enterprises. At the same time, the United Nations announced that 2012 would be the year of the cooperatives, and advised Member States to develop laws and systems to revitalize cooperatives. A new policy window was opened in three aspects: problems-political-policy streams. Cooperatives and third sector activists who have consistently raised the necessity of enacting the FAC since the 1980s formed the SAEFAC, and quickly and systematically made concrete alternatives based on theoretical and practical experience. The SAEFAC proposed this directly to politicians, including lawmakers, and actively participated in the enactment process of FAC. In this process, the genuine values, roles, and modes of operation of the cooperative began to be known to the general public, and naturally spread to discussions about the social economy itself. Subsequently, organizations beyond social enterprises and cooperatives that belonged to the social economy sector or pursued the public interest at least in a corporate manner began to be comprehensively discussed within the social economy sphere. Local governments have developed from ordinances to foster social enterprises to ordinances to revitalize the social economy, established a public-private governance system for revitalizing the social economy in the local government, and started to establish a dedicated support center for revitalizing the social economy. In particular, as the activation of the social economy was selected as a national task after the inauguration of the Moon Jae-in regime, local governments and public institutions are actively working to build a social economy ecosystem.

In South Korea, the term "social economy" itself is not a concept widely used in history, but a concept widely known to the public after being used in government policies. In addition, in the case of the first official social economy enterprise, social enterprise, it was accredited as a social enterprise and provided financial support by the government, so the development of social enterprises is also mentioned as an output of government policies. However, considering that social enterprises are not entirely dependent on government financial aid, and the period of financial support is limited to five years, and that there are many restrictions on the operation of the organization, it is difficult to consider it only as a result of government policy. In the case of cooperatives, there is no official financial support. The important thing is that any type of SEOs is difficult to operate without private resources and dedicated efforts. It is true that the government's fostering and supporting policies affect the proliferation of SEOs, but it requires voluntary efforts and enthusiasm from the third sector. In particular, in countries with insufficient public-private cooperation experience, such as South Korea, the third sector can also serve as a policy entrepreneur in order to recognize the necessity and role of SEOs to the government and the public, and to lead to the formation of government policies. The case of South Korea, which showcases successful development of social economy despite the absence of a welfare state or a well-developed third sector, should also hold numerous policy implications for other Asian countries.

NOTES

1. An earlier version of this chapter was published as an article titled, "Social Enterprise, Policy Entrepreneurs, and the Third Sector: The Case of South Korea" in the journal *Voluntas*, which gave the author permission to reprint.

2. And as of July 2000, approximately twenty-nine enterprises had been operating as cooperative (Lee 2001).

3. Seminar organized by a civil association, March 19, 2011; discussion forum organized by the third sector on the policies of social enterprise, September 22, 2011.

4. A dollar is equivalent to approximately 1,200 won in South Korean currency.

5. In order to become a SE in South Korea, an eligible organization must fulfill the following standard requirements: (1) it should take the form of an organization prescribed by the Presidential Decree, such as a corporation or an association under the Civil Law, a company under the Commercial Act, a nonprofit private organization, and so on; (2) it should employ paid workers and conduct business activities, such as the production and sale of goods and services, and so on; (3) its main purpose should be to realize a social objective, such as raising local residents' quality of life, and so on, by providing vulnerable groups with social services or jobs or contributing to local communities, in this case, detailed criteria for judgment shall be prescribed by the Presidential Decree; (4) it should have a decision-making structure in which interested persons, such as service beneficiaries and workers, and so on, can participate; (5) revenue from its business activities should meet or exceed the standards prescribed by the Presidential Decree; (6) it should have articles of incorporation, rules, and so on, in accordance with Article 9; (7) when it has distributable profits for each fiscal year, it should spend at least two-thirds of the profits for social objectives (applicable only to a company under the Commercial Law); and finally (8) it should satisfy the other matters prescribed by the Presidential Decree regarding operational guidelines.

6. The fourth type was added in 2011.

7. The jurisdiction of social job programs was operated under the Ministry of Employment and Labor and the OUMC.

8. Interview with the CEO Lee of social enterprise, March 16, 2015; Interview with the Assistant Director, Lee. March 13, 2015.

9. For detailed information, see Lee, Sun-young (n.d.).

10. For details, see National Assembly records on December 22, 2011, p.20, December 23, 2011, pp.5–6, and December 26, 2011, p.6 (National Assembly of Republic of Korea n.d. in Korean).

11. For details, see Korea Social Value and Solidarity Foundation (2019).

12. For detailed information, see the homepage of Center for Social Value Enhancement Studies.

13. For details, see Jin, Sang-hoon (2019).

14. For detailed information, see LH (2020) and Lee (n.d.).

REFERENCES

Aiken, Mike. 2006. "Towards Market or State? Tensions and Opportunities in the Evolutionary Path of Three UK Social Enterprises." In *Social Enterprise: At the Crossroads of Market, Public Policies and Civil Society*, edited by Marthe Nyssens, 259–271. London: Routledge.

Aiken, Mike, and Roger Spear. 2005. "Work Integration Social Enterprises in the United Kingdom." *EMES Working Papers* No. 05/01.

Auteri, Monica. 2003. "The Entrepreneurial Establishment of a Nonprofit Organization." *Public Organization Review* 3(2): 171–189.

Baumgartner, Frank R., and Bryan D. Jones. 1991. "Agenda Dynamics and Policy Subsystems." *The Journal of Politics* 53(4): 1044–1074.

Bornstein, David. 2007. *How to Change the World: Social Entrepreneurs and the Power of New Ideas.* Oxford: Oxford University Press.

Borzaga, Carlo, and Jacques Defourny (eds). 2004. *The Emergence of Social Enterprise*, Vol. 4. Hove: Psychology Press.

Campbell, Sandy. 1998. "Social Entrepreneurship: How to Develop New Social-Purpose Business Ventures." *Health Care Strategic Management* 16(5): 17–18.

Chey, Tae-won .2014. *A New Way: Social Enterprises and Social Progress Credit.* Seoul: The Story House (in Korean).

Christopher, et al. 2008. "Compumentor and the DiscounTech.org Service: Creating an Earned-Income Venture for a Nonprofit Organization." *Yale Case 08-013 January 15, 2008.* Accessed November 20, 2008. http://pse.som.yale.edu/casestudies.html.

Cobb, Roger W., and Charles D. Elder. 1972. *Participation in American Politics: The Dynamics of Agenda-Building.* Boston, MA: Allyn & Bacon.

Dees, J. Gregory. 1998. "Enterprising Nonprofits: What Do You Do When Traditional Sources of Funding Fall Short." *Harvard Business Review* 76(1): 55–67.

Defourny, J., and M. Nyssens. 2009. "Conceptions of Social Enterprise and Social Entrepreneurship in Europe and the United State: Convergences and Divergences." *Paper Presented at the Second EMES International Conference on Social Enterprise.* University of Toronto, Italy, July 1–4, 2009.

Defourny, Jacques. 2001. "From Third Sector to Social Enterprise." In *The Emergence of Social Enterprise*, edited by Carlo Borzaga and Jacques Defourny, 1–28. London: Routledge.

Eum, Hyungsik. 2008. "Social Economy in South Korea and Social Enterprise: Lessons from Europe and a Comparison." *The Institute for Policy Research Report No. 2*, Work Together Foundation. (in Korean)

Evers, Adalbert, and Jean-Louis Laville. 2004. "Defining the Third Sector in Europe." *The Third Sector in Europe* 11.

Jang, Jongick. 2017. "The Development of Social Economy in South Korea: Focusing on the Role of the State and Civil Society." *VOLUNTAS: International Journal of Voluntary and Nonprofit Organizations* 28(6): 2592–2613.

Jang, Wonbong. 2006. *Theory and Practice of Social Economy*. Seoul: Nanumuijip (in Korean).

Jeong, Sunhee. 2004. *Social Enterprise: Successful Social Enterprises in the U.S.* Seoul: Overcoming Unemployment Movement Committee (in Korean).

Jin, Sang-hoon. 2019. "Hyundai Motor Group Nurtured 211 Social Enterprises for 8 Years and Created 1,420 Jobs." *ChosunBiz*. Accessed June 29, 2020. https://biz .chosun.com/site/data/html_dir/2019/06/27/2019062701218.html (in Korean).

Jones, Bryan D., Frank R. Baumgartner, and Jeffery C. Talbert. 1993. "The Destruction of Issue Monopolies in Congress." *American Political Science Review* 87(3): 657–671.

Kerlin, Janelle A. 2006. "Social Enterprise in the United States and Europe: Understanding and Learning from the Differences." *Voluntas: International Journal of Voluntary and Nonprofit Organizations* 17(3): 246–262.

Kingdon, John W. 1984. *Agendas, Alternatives, and Public Policies*, Vol. 45. Boston: Little, Brown.

Korea Institute for Health and Social Affairs. 1999. *Health and Welfare Vision 2010: Realization of Productive Welfare Community*. Seoul: Korea Institute for Health and Social Affairs (in Korean).

Korea Social Value and Solidarity Foundation. 2019. *Social Economy Vision Forum Sourcebook*. Seoul: Korea Social Value and Solidarity Foundation (in Korean).

Kwon, Huck-ju. 2001. "Globalization, Unemployment and Policy Responses in Korea Repositioning the State?" *Global Social Policy* 1(2): 213–234.

Lee, Eun Sun. 2009. "A Comparative Analysis of the Characteristics of Social Enterprises in the United Kingdom, United States, and South Korea: An Institutional Approach." *Korean Journal of Public Administration* 47(4): 363–397 (in Korean).

Lee, Eun Sun. 2015. "Social Enterprise, Policy Entrepreneurs, and the Third Sector: The Case of South Korea." *VOLUNTAS: International Journal of Voluntary and Nonprofit Organizations* 26(4): 1084–1099.

Lee, Hyun Song. 2001. "A Comparison of Producer's Cooperatives in Korea." *Korean Journal of Sociology* 35(4): 95–127 (in Korean).

Lee, Jin-baek. n.d. "Once a Social Value Evangelist Is an Eternal Social Value Evangelist." *LIFEIN*. Accessed June 30, 2020. http://www.lifein.news/news/article View.html?idxno=5962 (in Korean).

Lee, Sun-young. n.d. "Let's Complement the Market Economy through Co-Operation." *Eroun Net*. Accessed June 15, 2020. http://Www.Eroun.Net/News/Articleview.Ht ml?Idxno=549 (In Korean).

LH. 2020. *Social Value Comprehensive Performance Infographic*, Seoul: LH. June 3, 2020.

Mintrom, Michael. 1997. "Policy Entrepreneurs and the Diffusion of Innovation." *American Journal of Political Science* 41(3): 738–770.

Mintrom, Michael, and Sandra Vergari. 1996. "Advocacy Coalitions, Policy Entrepreneurs, and Policy Change." *Policy Studies Journal* 24(3): 420–434.

National Assembly of Republic of Korea. n.d. "Personalized Legislative Contents Searching System." http://naph.assembly.go.kr.

OECD. 1999. *Social Enterprises*. Paris: Organisation for Economic Co-operation and Development.

Pearce, John, and Alan Kay. 2003. *Social Enterprise in Anytown*. London: Calouste Gulbenkian Foundation.

Polanyi, Karl. 1944. *The Great Transformation*, Vol. 2. Boston: Beacon Press.

Presidential Committee on Social Inclusion. 1999. *The Way of Productive Welfare to New Millennium*. Seoul: Presidential Committee on Social Inclusion (in Korean).

Salamon, Lester M., and S. Wojciech Sokolowski. 2006. "Employment in America's Charities: A Profile." *Nonprofit Employment Bulletin Number 26*, The Johns Hopkins Center for Civil Society Studies.

Sheingate, Adam D. 2006. "Structure and Opportunity: Committee Jurisdiction and Issue Attention in Congress." *American Journal of Political Science* 50(4): 844–859.

Social Enterprise London. 2004. "Social Enterprise London Business Plan 2004–2006." Accessed November 20, 2008. http://www.sel.org.uk.

Suk, Howon. 2008. *A Comparative Study on Work Integration Role of NGO and Social Enterprise*. Seoul: Seoul National University (in Korean).

Young, Dennis. 2003. "New Trends in the US Non-Profit Sector: Towards Market Integration." In *The Non-Profit Sector in a Changing Economy*, edited by OECD, 61–78. Paris: OECD.

HOMEPAGES FOR INFORMATION SOURCES

Center for Social Value Enhancement Studies. https://www.cses.re.kr.

Korea Cooperatives. http://www.coop.go.kr

Korea Development Institute for Self-sufficiency and Welfare. https://www.kdissw.or.kr

Korea Social Enterprise Promotion Agency. http://www.socialenterprise.or.kr/index.do

Ministry of Employment and Labor. http://www.moel.go.kr

Ministry of the Interior and Safety. https://www.mois.go.kr

Ministry of Economy and Finance. http://www.moef.go.kr

Chapter 8

How Is Social Economy Contributing to Achieving SDGs in Seoul?

Ilcheong Yi

INTRODUCTION

Actors[1] at the local or subnational level have a variety of competencies and often play unique roles in designing and implementing development policies and programs, ranging from territorial or urban planning to building safe, inclusive, and resilient infrastructure and the delivery of basic services. The 2030 Agenda for Sustainable Development particularly emphasizes the localization of the Sustainable Development Goals (SDGs) as key to the successful realization of its transformative vision, hence the importance of local actors to make development happen on the ground.

Localization of the SDGs begins with establishing local-level goals and targets that reflect place-specific economic, social, and environmental conditions. In all cases, national or subnational level development requires a hierarchy of objectives and goals. When local-level SDGs are established, the objectives or goals in this hierarchical structure may be incompatible or inconsistent with each other (ICSU and ISSC 2015).

These goals and objectives, however, may not be entirely irreconcilable since there are diverse ways to create institutional and policy complementarity to achieve multiple goals and objectives without sacrificing one goal or objective for another (Penouil 1981). It is indispensable, therefore, to identify and promote means of implementation of the SDGs which create synergies and minimize trade-offs between goals, targets, and policies in an integrated and balanced manner.

This chapter examines the potential of social economy (SE) in Seoul as a means of implementation of the Seoul's Sustainable Development Goals (S-SDGs), outlined in the policy document *The Seoul Sustainable Development Goals: Seventeen Ways to Change Seoul* (Seoul Metropolitan

Government 2017b). It focuses on how multiple values, concerns, and functions of SE in Seoul contribute to achieving the social, economic, and environmental dimensions of the S-SDGs in an integrated and balanced way. It will also identify tensions between goals and silo approaches which are the potential causes of synergy loss and trade-offs.

The scarcity of data on the functions and impacts of SE organizations and enterprises (SEOEs) remains a challenge for this kind of research. To address this challenge, this chapter employed a network analysis method to identify the interdependence and connections between SEOEs and S-SDGs. We used the mission statements and which explain the organizational goals and activities of 249 Certified Social Enterprises (CSEs) in Seoul (out of a total of 316) for the network analysis. Although the analysis does not show the actual impact of SEOEs and how this impact contributes to achieving the S-SDGs, it can shed light on the potential of SEOEs as a means of implementation and what limitations they have in this respect.

Given the importance for successful SDG implementation of policy coherence and policy alignment across different levels of governance (local, regional, national, global), this chapter also compares the local-level S-SDGs and the global-level SDGs in the 2030 Agenda. Given that national-level SDGs for the Republic of Korea had not been established at the time of writing, it is not possible to integrate the national level in this analysis.

The chapter is structured as follows. The first section explains the S-SDGs, their development and structure. It pays particular attention to the interdependence of goals and targets of the S-SDGs, and how they differ from the global SDGs. It is followed by an explanation of the contribution of Seoul's SEOEs based on the network analysis. Findings and lessons learned for Seoul and beyond are presented in the conclusion.

SEOUL'S SUSTAINABLE DEVELOPMENT GOALS

Sustainable Development before the 2030 Agenda

In the Republic of Korea, various activities for sustainable development, including public and CSOs working on sustainable development, were undertaken far earlier than the announcement of the 2030 Agenda. Influenced by the 1992 Earth Summit and its mechanism for local implementation known as Local Agenda 21, many CSOs and local governments started to collaborate with each other to establish local agendas and activities for sustainable development. Decentralization and local elected governments also had a positive impact on this public-civic partnership. As social movements diversified after the beginning of democratization in 1987, many CSOs working on issues related to the quality of life and the environment emerged to engage with policy processes in various ways. The activities undertaken by these environmental CSOs were further promoted by environmental protection and energy-related laws and associated regulations since 1992 (Lee et al. 2009).

By 2015, 210 out of 240 local governments in the Republic of Korea had established a Local Agenda 21 for Sustainable Development. Around 100 local governments, including the Seoul Metropolitan Government, created special organizations to implement their decisions.

The national government's organizational initiative to implement policies for sustainable development emerged later than those of local governments. In 2000, it established the national-level Presidential Council for Sustainable Development (PCSD) composed of government, civil society, and business representatives. The PCSD was mandated to set major policy directions and formulate plans to promote sustainable development (Pawar and Huh 2014). From 2000 to 2008, the PCSD adopted a multistakeholder participatory decision-making process that included government and nongovernment actors. Although the PCSD emphasized the integrated approach (across the economic, social, and environmental dimensions of sustainable development) that had been highlighted by the Earth Summit and follow-up activities, most of its policies were mainly environment focused (Pawar and Huh 2014).

The Framework Act on Sustainable Development (FASD) came into force in 2008, eight years after the PCSD was set up, with the Ministry of Environment assuming responsibility for implementation. The Act became the legal basis for the implementation of the 1992 Agenda 21 and the 2002 Plan of Implementation of the World Summit on Sustainable Development. The Act stipulated that national and local governments establish an implementation plan for sustainable development every five years. It also allowed delegates of the local Councils of Sustainable Development to participate in the PCSD. A system of coordination between national and local governments was also established (Kim et al. 2014).

The Lee government (2008–2013), however, shifted the policy focus from one centered on the concept of sustainable development to green growth, which significantly undermined the follow-up activities of the government within the framework of the FASD. Although the concept of green growth emphasized the harmonization of economic growth and environmental conservation, economic dimensions were more central to the policy framework while social concerns were residual to environmental and economic concerns. In fact, during this time market-based green economy solutions associated with the green growth initiatives of the Lee government dominated policy debates (Lee 2010).

This policy shift brought about a significant change in the government organizations and policies associated with sustainable development. First, declaring low-carbon green growth as a national vision, the government established a new Presidential Commission on Green Growth and the Framework Act on Low Carbon Green Growth in 2008 and 2010, respectively (Pawar and Huh 2014). The PCSD became the Ministerial Council for Sustainable Development, losing some of its previous influence. Government programs which highlighted the economic dimension of green growth were mostly top-down, albeit with token stakeholder consultation. Governments, particularly the national government and local governments whose leaders were from the same political party as the president, provided wide-ranging support for the institutions and organizations established for the market-friendly green growth approach. In the context of this national government drive for green growth policies, many NGOs, even those in the provinces and areas whose leaders sided with opposition parties, carried out programs funded by the government within the framework of green growth (Kim et al. 2014).

A particularly controversial green economy initiative was the Green New Deal. One of its flagship projects was the Four Major Rivers Restoration Project, which aimed to restore key rivers and to provide water security, flood control, and ecosystem vitality through 213 river-related infrastructure projects at a total cost of KRW 6.9 trillion (Cha et al. 2011). Even before the launch of these projects, many experts raised concerns about their negative impact on the environment. Opposition parties organized political protests against the projects and against the Lee government. The flagship project itself heightened the political rift between the government and opposition forces (Han 2015). In this context, green growth became a political symbol of the Lee government. Civil society and political opponents used the green growth concept as a focus of their criticism of the Lee government, preferring instead the more encompassing and integrated concept of sustainable development. This helped to strengthen initiatives and organizations associated with it, such as Local Agenda 21 (Pawar and Huh 2014).

SMG Initiatives for Sustainable Development before the 2030 Agenda

SMG initiatives for sustainable development began in the mid-2000s with the green growth concept led by Mayor Oh Se-hoon who was affiliated with President Lee's political party. His policies and programs were similar to those of the Lee government in that they emphasized the economic dimension and green economy. The SMG established a Green Growth Committee composed of SMG civil servants, experts, and representatives of business and civil society, which, however, rarely met. Most SMG programs at this time were designed and implemented in a top-down manner.

A different approach emerged after the opposition leader Park Won-soon assumed office in 2011. In order to highlight social and environmental dimensions of sustainable development, the SMG abolished the ineffective Green Growth Council, and passed an ordinance on the Seoul Council for Sustainable Development (the SCSD) and established the Council itself in 2013. Composed of nine representatives from the SMG, including the mayor, three members of the Seoul Metropolitan Council, and twenty-eight representatives from civil society and the business sector, the SCSD has three thematic working groups: Economy; Society and Culture; and Environment. Leaders of the SE sector, such as the head of the Seoul Social Economy Center and a representative of *Saenghyup* cooperatives take part in the working group on the economy.

The SMG had announced a Five Year Basic Plan for Sustainable Development (2015–2019) in 2015 even before the 2030 Agenda for Sustainable Development was launched. The Basic Plan identified thirty major targets related to economic, social, cultural, and environmental goals which are to be achieved by either 2020 or 2030, largely based on the SMG's policy priorities. They were selected from a pool of 725 indicators used to monitor and evaluate the performance of the SMG policies (Seoul Metropolitan Government 2015). SE, together with the sharing economy, became one of the major economic strategies to achieve sustainable development. SMG projects promoting special SE districts, area-based cooperatives, and SE as a means of providing social services were explicitly mentioned as means of implementation (Seoul Metropolitan Government 2015). The main purpose of the Five Year Plan, however, was to monitor and evaluate existing projects in the thirty policy areas associated with sustainable development rather than establish a new policy framework for sustainable development (see figure 8.1).

Establishing a 2030 Agenda and SDGs for Seoul

Since the 2030 Agenda was announced, progress in setting goals and targets at the national level in the Republic of Korea has been limited. The fragmented structure of ministries dealing with selected goals and targets and the absence of strong coordination have been some of the main causes for the relatively slow progress of the national government. Local governments such as the SMG, however, are making significant progress.

The SMG moved quickly to adopt the SDGs and adapt them to the local context. The SCSD started drafting SDGs for Seoul (S-SDGs) via a series of participatory processes, including expert meetings and public hearings in which CSOs from a wide range of sectors that were already actively involved in participatory governance mechanisms organized by the SMG also took part. In comparison with the national government, relatively few tensions have arisen over which bureau and departments of the SMG should be responsible for implementing the S-SDGs.

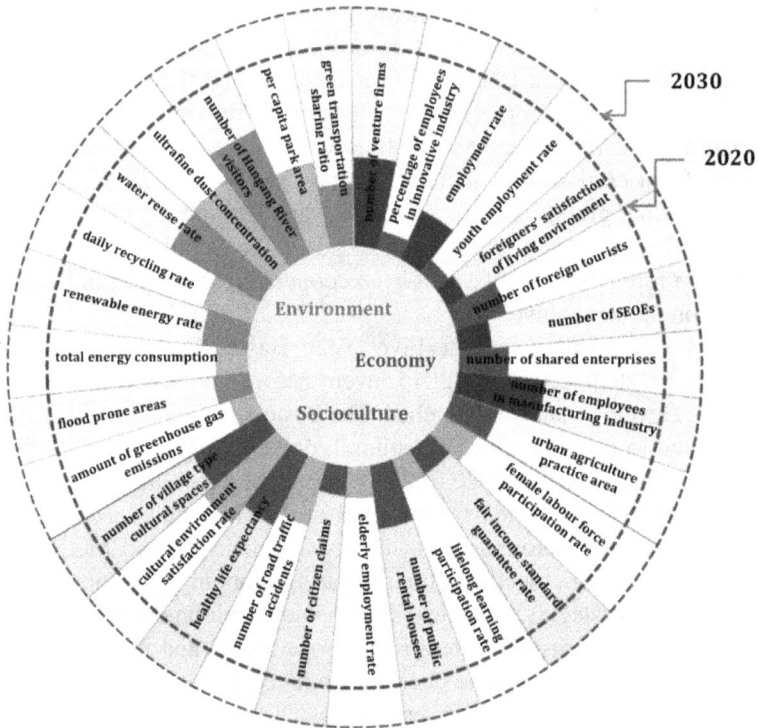

Figure 8.1   Five-Year Basic Plan for Sustainable Development (2015–2019). *Source:* Seoul Metropolitan Government (2015).

The SMG, however, faced two main challenges in establishing the S-SDGs. First, participatory governance processes required a lot of time to discuss the vast range of goals related to the economic, social, and environmental dimensions of sustainable development. The process was slow partly due to organizational difficulties, as the SDGs were not a priority issue for many CSOs. Second, there were no clear guidelines on how to establish S-SDGs. Many members of the SCSD had expertise on their sectors but lacked the rigorous, comprehensive knowledge and expertise needed to identify multiple linkages between goals and targets in a balanced and integrated manner.[2]

Establishing the S-SDGs was a process of learning by doing which took almost two years and was accomplished through a series of public hearings, discussions of commissioned research, and debate on which should be the priority goals and targets. The SMG announced the S-SDGs on November 22, 2017 (Seoul Metropolitan Government 2017a. See Appendix III for the list of targets and related policies).

The S-SDGs contain seventeen goals and ninety-six targets largely corresponding to the SDGs in the 2030 Agenda. Several features of the S-SDGs are notable in comparison with those of the 2030 Agenda.

- The S-SDGs have been designed to correspond to the seventeen SDGs in the 2030 Agenda in a way that reflects the specific conditions in Seoul. For instance, social development targets are set higher than the global targets. The Seoul target for under-five mortality is less than 2.5 per 1,000 live births, whereas the global target is set at less than 25 per 1,000; similarly the Seoul target for maternal mortality is more ambitious than the global target. Seoul aims to halve the 2016 rate of 8.4 per 100,000, whereas the global target is 70 per 100,000 live births.
- Regarding the role of the private sector, social enterprises are specifically mentioned in S-SDG 8.3: "Encourage small- and medium-sized enterprises to create decent jobs and provide active support to social enterprises." Similarly, social economic zones and integrated support systems for social economy at the district level are suggested as policy tools to achieve S-SDG 10 "Reduce all forms of inequality." Highlighting the role of SE for the reduction of inequality as well as economic growth and creation of jobs is notable in the S-SDGs, given that the 2030 Agenda mentions the role of cooperatives for productivity, inclusive economic growth, and job creation.
- Specific policy initiatives and projects of the SMG are suggested as a key means of implementation of the S-SDGs. Many of the projects focus on human rights, solidarity within and beyond Seoul, participation, and SE.
- The S-SDGs incorporate specific policy concerns of the SMG as targets. For instance, S-SDG 3 includes gambling in the addictions which should be addressed, while S-SDG 11 has a target of reducing the concentration of fine dust levels to 70% of the 2016 level. S-SDG 12 includes halving per capita food waste from the level of 2016. These are all specific environmental concerns of Seoul.
- Notable is the effort to localize global goals in an urban context. One example of this is the emphasis on building a food distribution system with local agricultural producers and urban agriculture defined as a practice of growing plants and raising animals for food, and processing and distributing them within the urban area (FAO 2007; UNESCAP 2012). Target 2.4 of the 2030 Agenda, "By 2030, ensure sustainable food production systems and implement resilient agricultural practices," corresponds to target 2.3 of the S-SDGs: "Establish a desirable distribution structure with the local agri-fishery producers, and support urban agriculture not only to encourage small-scale food production but also to cope with poverty and mental health."

- Some of the goals and targets do not express clearly enough the interdependence between economic, social, and environmental dimensions. For example, target 2.3 (see above) mentions poverty and health impacts but not environmental benefits which local small-scale food production could generate. Shifting food production to a location with high demand tends to reduce greenhouse gas emissions caused by transporting food over long distances, and a study estimated the available area for urban agriculture in Seoul is 51.17 square kilometers (Lee et al. 2015).
- Goals and targets in the 2030 Agenda which are less relevant to Seoul have been reinterpreted for the S-SDGS. The question of whether Seoul, as a land-locked city, had to have a goal corresponding to the 2030 Agenda's SDG 14 on life under water was a controversial issue in the process of deciding on the S-SDGs, for example. After a series of discussions including public hearings and SCSD meetings, it was decided to reinterpret SDG 14 as mainly concerning the protection and restoration of the natural quality of the Han River. This would serve as a means of implementation for the preservation of the ocean ecosystem into which the Han River flows. It is notable that S-SDG 14 suggests cooperation with neighboring provinces such as Gyeonggi and Incheon City to achieve this goal.[3]
- Some key values have been highlighted throughout the S-SDG document while others have not. For instance, the principle of leaving no one behind underpins most targets, and universal provision of social services is strongly emphasized where relevant. However, the transformative vision which aims to change structures and institutions generating injustice has not been intensively discussed and is not reflected throughout the document.
- Every goal and target is based on empirical evidence of the current situation in Seoul and is linked with existing SMG projects and policies to tackle issues.
- In cases where the problem a particular S-SDG aims to tackle would be more effectively addressed at a higher level of governance (such as the central government), the S-SDG indicates both targets and the need for coordination mechanisms. Infectious and noncommunicable disease-related targets 3.2, 3.3, and 3.4 are cases in point.
- All the goals and targets specifically focus on citizens of Seoul except for S-SDG 17 "Strengthening the cooperative relationships with foreign cities as a global leader in sustainable development."
- Financing development is the weakest part of the S-SDGs. The only target which is potentially linked with financing is S-SDG 16.4. "Significantly strengthen (i) the recovery and return of illicit assets and (ii) taxation of habitual tax delinquents and tax evaders." There is not a specific target associated with the role of the private sector in financing development, which is emphasized in the 2030 Agenda's SDGs.
- A system of indicators has yet to be established.

CONNECTING SUSTAINABLE DEVELOPMENT GOALS AND THEIR TARGETS

SDGs and Targets in the 2030 Agenda

Lack of integration across sectors when designing policies and implementing them has been one of the key problems of development interventions worldwide. Failures to create synergies, minimize trade-offs, and avoid coordination failures, or the so-called silo approach, have resulted in incoherent policies and adverse impacts on development (Le Blanc 2015).

Designing and implementing development goals in an integrated and balanced manner is one of the major concerns of the 2030 Agenda. Despite the emphasis on the triple bottom line that aims to strike a balance between economic, social, and environmental dimensions, the goals and targets have uneven connections with each other, partly due to the effects of political negotiations over priorities. Some goals are closely interconnected and mutually compatible, while others are less so.

Figures 8.2, 8.3, and 8.4 are based on a network analysis of the targets of sixteen of the SDGs (Le Blanc 2015). The analysis excludes SDG17, which relates primarily to the means of implementation for the other SDGs, as well as the specific means of implementation presented at the end of each SDG.

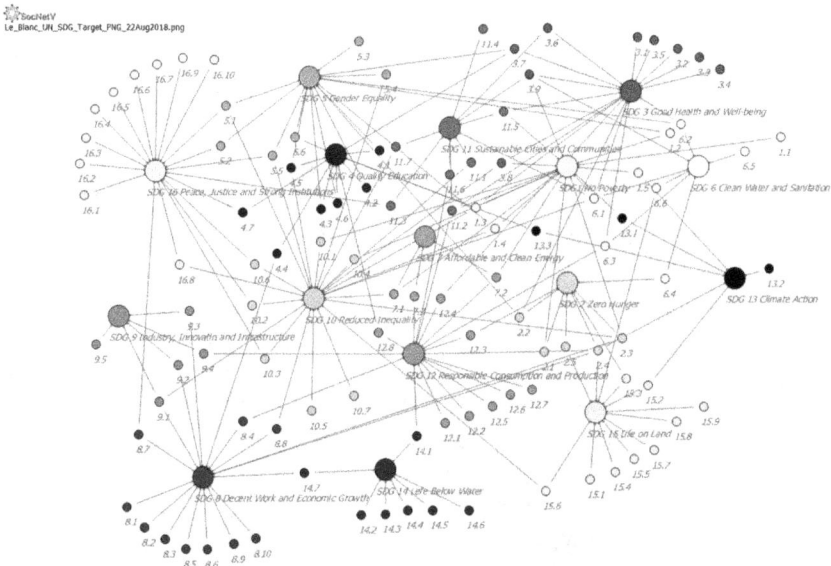

Figure 8.2   Connections between SDGs as Seen through Targets (2030 Agenda). *Source:* Le Blanc (2015). Reprinted with the permission of the United Nations.

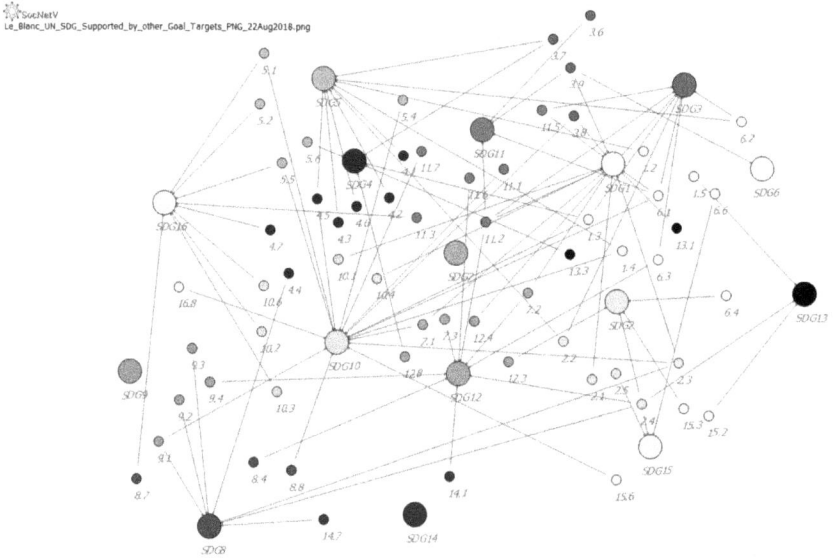

Figure 8.3   Interdependence between SDGs as Seen through Targets of Other SDGs (the 2030 Agenda). *Source*: Author's analysis of Le Blanc (2015).

This does not mean, however, that specific means of implementation do not have a potential to contribute to other goals.

Since this network analysis is a mapping of semantic relations between targets and goals as expressed in the wording of 2030 Agenda, the figures do not represent rigorous scientific analysis of the concrete linkages between goals and targets. This method runs the risk of analyzing buzzwords employed to dress up business as usual. However, statements of intent in development discourse do have a purpose. They not only lend legitimacy to justify developmental interventions but also provide a sense of direction regarding which development path policy makers might take (Cornwall and Brock 2005). The exercise can have a practical and political impact since the results help us to problematize dominant paradigms and explore alternative strategies and policy measures to maximize synergies and reduce trade-offs across sectors.

The bigger circles in figure 8.2 represent the sixteen SDGs, while the smaller circles are the targets. The targets are the same color as the goal to which they belong. Some targets are linked only to the one goal to which they belong, while others have lines linking with more than one goal, illustrating the interdependence between goals. For instance, target 16.1 "Significantly reduce all forms of violence and related death rates everywhere" is not associated with other goals, while 16.8 "Broaden and strengthen the participation of developing countries in the institutions of global governance" potentially

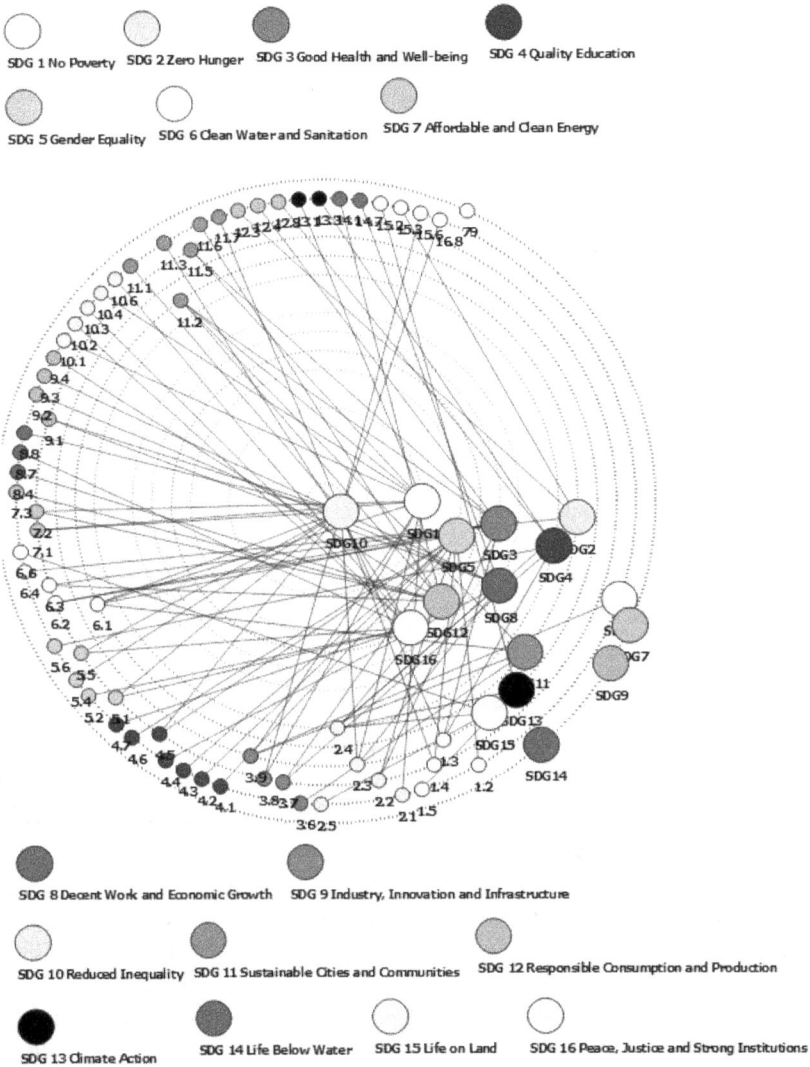

Figure 8.4   How SDGs Are Supported by Targets of Other SDGs. *Source*: Generated using software by S. P. Borgatti, M. G. Everett, and L. C. Freeman (2002).

also contributes to Goal 10 "Reduce inequality within and among countries," particularly target 10.6 "Ensure enhanced representation and voice for developing countries in decision-making in global international economic and financial institutions in order to deliver more effective, credible, accountable and legitimate institutions." Out of 107 targets examined, 62 are associated with more than one goal; 19 targets contribute to two or three goals other than the one to which they belong.

Table 8.1   **SDGs Connected with Targets of Other SDGs (the 2030 Agenda)**

Strength of Interconnections	SDGs	Number of Connections with Targets with Other SDGs	Percent of Total Connections
Weakest	SDG 7	0	0.0
	SDG 9	0	0.0
	SDG 14	0	0.0
Weak	SDG 6	1	1.1
	SDG 13	3	3.3
	SDG 15	3	3.3
	SDG 2	4	4.4
	SDG 11	4	4.4
Strong	SDG 4	5	5.5
	SDG 8	7	7.7
	SDG 3	8	8.8
	SDG 12	9	9.9
	SDG 16	9	9.9
Strongest	SDG 5	10	11.0
	SDG 1	12	13.2
	SDG 10	16	17.6
	Total	91	100.0

Source: Degree Prestige report of (Le Blanc 2015), Created by Social Network Visualizer v2.3: Sun, February 4, 2018.

Figures 8.3 and 8.4 illustrate how each SDG can be supported by the achievement of targets belonging to other SDGs. Figure 8.3 demonstrates how the individual SDGs are connected with the targets of other SDGs. Figure 8.4 illustrates how the connection of individual SDGs with the targets of other SDGs produces a hierarchical structure of SDGs composed of four clusters indicating degrees of interdependence: the closer to the center, the more connections the SDG has with the targets of other SDGs. SDG 10 (Reduced Inequalities), 1 (End poverty), and 5 (Gender equality) are the most densely connected goals while SDG 7 (Affordable and clean energy), 9 (Industry, innovation, and infrastructure), and 14 (Life below water) have no direct connections with the targets of other SDGs (see table 8.1).

The level of connection between each SDG with the targets of other SDGs indicates the opportunities to create synergies and minimize trade-offs between goals in the 2030 Agenda. It is understandable that SDGs 10, 1, and 5 are clustered as the most connected goals given the principle of leaving no one behind. It is disappointing, however, that despite obvious interdependence between SDGs 7, 9, and 14, there are fewer targets connecting these goals with each other (see figure 8.3). The lack of connections between certain goals points to the need to develop more innovative measures to create synergies between these goals.

S-SDGs and Targets

The S-SDGs also have connections between the goals and targets. Since the targets of S-SDG 17 include tasks which may be interpreted as an independent target rather than means of implementation for all other goals, such as the specific partnership with neighboring provinces to address the problems of Han River, they have been included in the analysis.

Compared to the 2030 Agenda, the S-SDGs have more connections between targets and goals. The nature of the connections between the targets and goals raises some unique features of the S-SDGs compared to those of the 2030 Agenda.

- First, compared to the 2030 Agenda, the S-SDGs have more targets addressing multiple goals. The proportion of targets contributing to the achievement of S-SDGs to which they do not belong is higher than that of the 2030 Agenda. In the S-SDGs, 72 out of 96 targets examined contribute to other S-SDGs, while in the 2030 Agenda 63 out of 107 targets examined

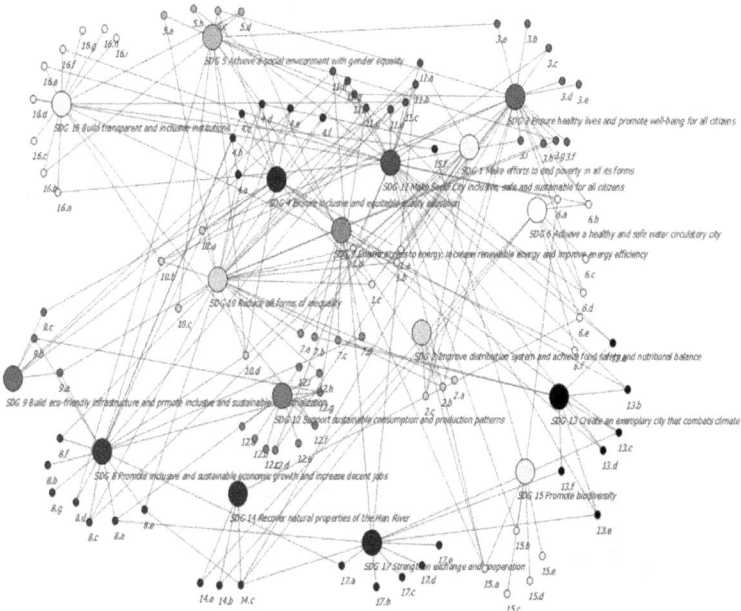

Figure 8.5   Connections between S-SDGs as Seen through Targets. *Source*: Author's analysis on the S-SDGs.

address other SDGs. This indicates that the targets of the S-SDGs have more multiple concerns and functions than those of the 2030 Agenda.

• Second, there is no S-SDG which does not have support from the targets of other SDGs. In the 2030 Agenda, SDGs 7, 9, and 14 do not have connections with targets of any other SDGs.

• Third, the 2030 Agenda and the S-SDGs have different degrees of connection between goals and targets. S-SDGs 10 (Reduce all forms of inequality), 5 (Achieve a social environment with gender equality and empower women), 3 (Ensure healthy lives and promote well-being for all citizens), and 8 (Promote inclusive and sustainable economic growth and decent work) are more supported by the targets of the other S-SDGs than the corresponding SDGs in the 2030 Agenda. On the other hand, the number of targets which contribute to S-SDG 1 (End poverty in all its forms) is smaller than the number of targets which contribute to SDG 1 in the 2030 Agenda. This partly reflects a greater policy concern about inequality and

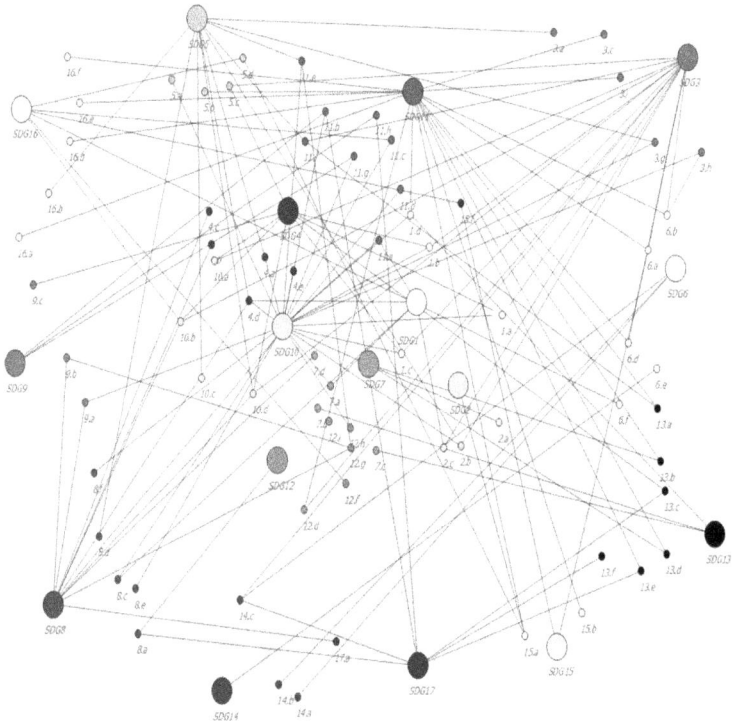

Figure 8.6 Interdependence between S-SDGs as Seen through Targets of Other S-SDGs. *Source*: Author's analysis on the S-SDGs.

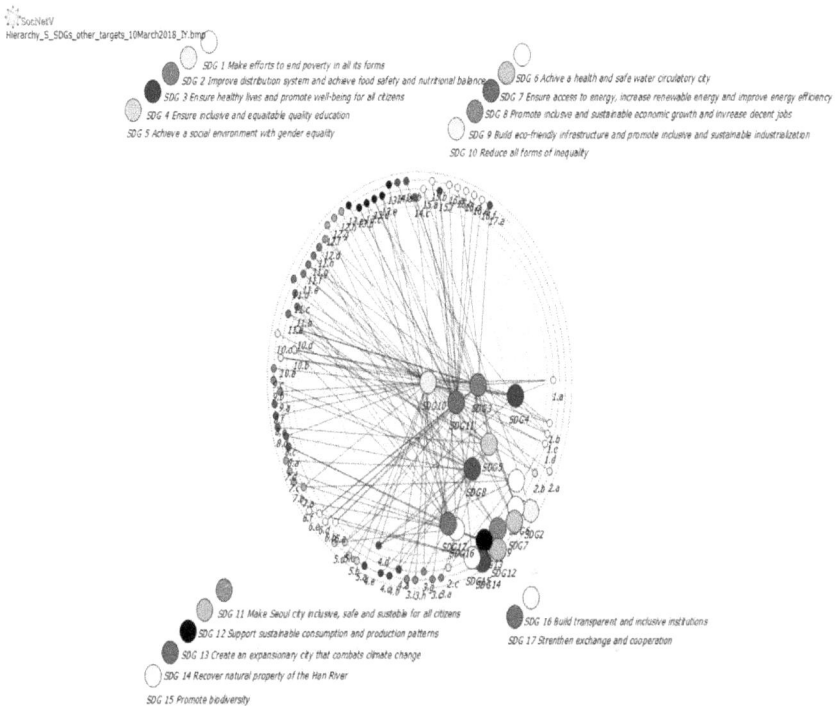

Figure 8.7 **How S-SDGs are Supported by Targets of Other S-SDGs.** *Source*: Author's analysis on the S-SDGs.

scarcity of jobs for youth (rather than poverty) in the case of the S-SDGs, due to the increasing political mobilization and influence of youth in the Republic of Korea (Park et al. 2013).

It is notable that the S-SDGs which have the strongest support from targets of other S-SDGs are directly associated with inequality, Seoul city and communities, health, economic growth and decent work, and gender equality. Compared with the 2030 Agenda, the S-SDGs have more support for the local context, health, and economic growth and decent work, while less for poverty.

The S-SDGs related to environmental objectives generally have weak support from the targets of other goals in S-SDGs; this is also the case of the 2030 Agenda. They are S-SDG 12 (Support sustainable consumption and production patterns); 14 (Conserve marine and coastal ecosystems through restoration of the Han River); 15 (Promote biodiversity through protecting and restoring natural ecosystems in the City); 7 (Ensure access to energy, increase the share of renewable energy and improve energy efficiency); and 13 (Create an exemplary city to combat climate change).

More innovative approaches need to be designed and implemented to create synergies and minimize trade-offs between environmental goals and other
goals, particularly economy-related goals such as S-SDG 8 which is strongly
integrated with goals other than environmental ones.

HOW SE CAN CONTRIBUTE TO
ACHIEVING THE S-SDGS

To successfully meet the goals and targets of the 2030 Agenda, policy makers
need to look for means of implementation which can avoid some of the limitations experienced while implementing the Millennium Development Goals
(2000–2015). SSE has the potential to meet this demand. It can mitigate the
bias toward global and national averages, which increase the risk of masking
deficits in achievement at the subnational level and diverting policy attention
and resources from marginalized and excluded groups (UN Inter-Agency Task
Force on Social and Solidarity Economy 2014). The way that SE in Seoul is
rooted in the local economy helps it to play a significant role in improving the
economic, social, and environmental conditions of poor and vulnerable people.

SSE is also a powerful means of implementation to address a hitherto
neglected aspect of development strategies, namely, the structures which generate social injustice such as exclusion and inequality in multiple dimensions.
The active citizenship and participatory democracy nurtured through SSE are
essential tools to address problems associated with structural determinants of
inequality and exclusion.

Integrated and Balanced Approach of SSE to the SDGs

One of the unique features of SSE as a means of implementation of the
SDGs in comparison with other development actors such as NGOs and private for-profit businesses is that it pursues explicit social and environmental
objectives through the production and exchange of goods and services and
relations with other economic entities. These multiple concerns and functions of SSE may be an answer to the key questions policy makers face when
implementing the SDGs: how to achieve sustainable development in its three
dimensions—economic, social, and environmental—in a balanced and integrated manner; and how to address the nexus between multiple policy tasks
and problems. Finding answers to these questions is particularly important
since policy makers have to deal with an overwhelming number of goals and
targets in the context of the 2030 Agenda (Boas et al. 2016). With its multiple
functions and concerns, SSE is well placed to address multiple goals and
targets in ways that maximize synergies and minimize trade-offs among the

goals. Its enhancement of democratic self-management and solidarity within and beyond SSEOEs can also enhance the people's ownership of the SDGs. Different SSE entities and actors, however, place differing emphasis on a variety of functions, values, and principles and engage in different economic activities and relations. Consequently, they may take differing paths toward contributing to achieving the SDGs.

The following section demonstrates the results of an analysis of the potential of SEOEs in Seoul to implement the S-SDGs taking into account the multiple goals and tasks they can address in a balanced and integrated manner.

The Contribution of CSEs to the S-SDGs

To understand how SEOEs can contribute to the S-SDGs, we analyzed public statements on their missions and activities using text mining and semantic network analysis methods. We retrieved relevant S-SDGs the SEOEs can potentially contribute to through qualitative semantic analysis, and visualized these functional connections using quantitative metrics and semantic network analysis software.

The focus was on CSEs, because they have several advantages for this analysis. First, since CSEs comprise diverse types of SEOEs, they are highly representative as a sample group of SE. Second, due to the rigorous screening and reviews undertaken by the KSEPA on the social functions and missions of these organizations, CSEs have less inclusion error and tend not to be for-profit enterprises claiming to be SE. Third, their management information and relatively well-systematized statistics are available to the public, which is crucial to an analysis of this kind.

Figure 8.9 illustrates the diverse ways in which CSEs in Seoul contribute to the S-SDGs. The size of the box indicates the number of SE functions and missions which support the S-SDG in question. The thickness of the line connecting the S-SDGs indicates to which extent the goals are supported simultaneously by the CSEs. For instance, because criteria for being recognized as a CSE require organizations to contribute to relieving poverty and to the economic empowerment of poor and vulnerable people, S-SDGs 1 and 10 have the largest boxes and the thickest connections.

Through the network analysis of 249 CSEs (out of 316 in Seoul) for which data were available (as of September 12, 2017), we divided the S-SDGs into five tiers, according to how many CSE statements contributed to them.

- Tier I—S-SDGs 10, 1, 11, and 8 (more than 100 CSEs);
- Tier II—S-SDGs 4, 12, 3, and 9 (30–99 CSEs);
- Tier III—S-SDGs 2, 5, 16, and 17 (10–29 CSEs);
- Tier IV—S-SDGs 15, 13, and 7 (1–9 CSEs); and
- Tier V—S-SDGs 6 and 14 (no CSEs).

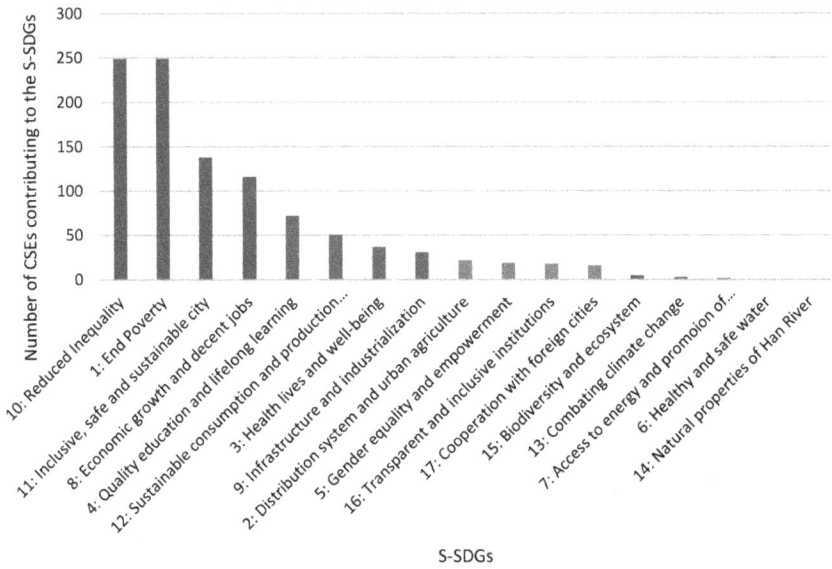

Figure 8.8 Number of CSEs Contributing to the S-SDGs. *Source*: Based on the data offered by Korea Social Enterprise Promotion Agency (KoSEA).

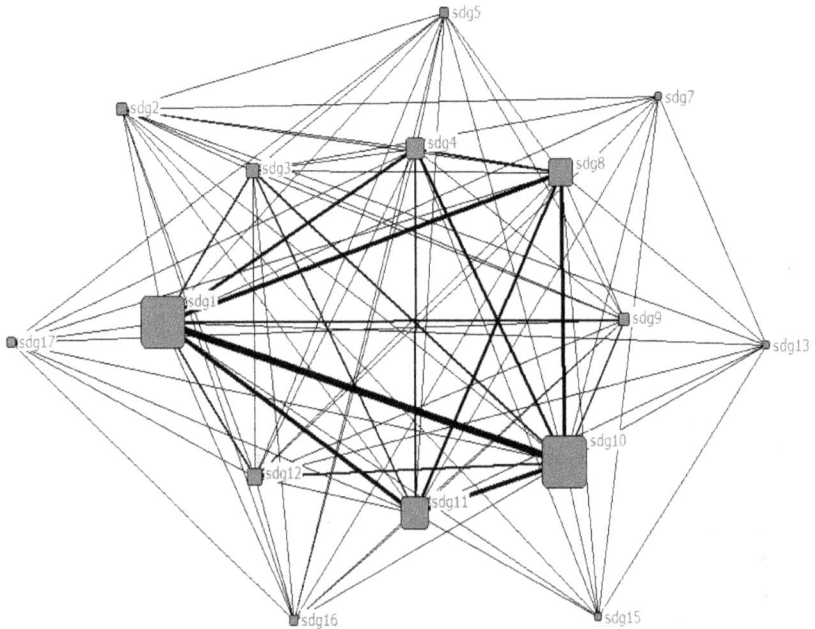

Figure 8.9 Number of CSEs Contributing to the S-SDGs. *Source*: Software: Borgatti, Everett, and Freeman (2002).

The following key findings can be drawn from this analysis.

- Since CSEs have to hire a certain number of people from vulnerable and poor groups in order to qualify as CSEs (Yi et al. 2018), all the CSEs highlight in their functions and missions achieving S-SDGs 1 and 10. Many of the CSEs which contribute to economic, social, and environmental improvement in Seoul (S-SDG 11) and to job creation (S-SDG 8) are also contributing to S-SDGs 1 and 10 by hiring poor and vulnerable people and improving living conditions in poor areas.
- Many CSEs contribute to Tier II S-SDGs. They often train and educate poor and vulnerable people to provide upcycled goods, IT infrastructure services, and care services. Given that many recipients of elderly care services are poor and vulnerable people (Yi et al. 2018), the provision of care services is an important channel by which CSEs link S-SDGs 3, 10, and 1.
- CSEs which contribute to S-SDG 10 are more likely to have missions and functions which address S-SDGs 1, 4, 8, and 11, creating a functional nexus between the following goals: Reduced inequality—End poverty—Inclusive and sustainable city—Economic growth and decent work—Quality education and lifelong learning. They also frequently engage with S-SDGs 3 and 9. For instance, one CSE studied was an NGO providing counseling services to foreign migrant workers and multicultural families. In addition to its counseling service, it became a social enterprise providing education and health care services for its clients, contributing to S-SDGs 3, 4, 10, and 11.
- Far fewer CSEs address S-SDGs 2, 5, 7, 13, 15, 16, and 17 (Tiers III and IV). It is, however, notable that the CSEs contributing S-SDG 2 (Urban-rural distribution system and urban agriculture), and S-SDG 5 (Gender equality) have diverse activities which potentially contribute to many other S-SDGs. In particular, the CSEs addressing SDG 5 (Gender equality) engage with a variety of activities associated with other S-SDGs. It indicates that although the number of CSEs addressing gender equality is small, they are trying to incorporate gender in a wide area of economic sectors. For instance, CSEs hiring women, particularly foreign women from multicultural families, were active in a variety of business sectors. They include environment, care, manufacturing of eco-friendly goods, cafeterias and restaurants, art, agriculture, and food distribution.
- The small number of CSEs contributing to S-SDG 17 seems to underestimate the contribution of SEOEs since it may be related to the selection criteria for CSEs which focus on poor and vulnerable people in the Republic of Korea. Many SEOEs working on fair trade supporting producers in developing countries are less likely to be selected because they primarily provide support for the poor and vulnerable in foreign countries.

• None of the CSEs' mission statements address Tier V S-SDGs 6 (Healthy and safe water) and 14 (Restoration of the Han River). Considering the variety of SMG projects associated with these goals, CSEs still have ample opportunities to explore economic activities associated with them, such as quality control of piped water, groundwater control, recycling of rainwater, environmentally friendly water purification plant, and controlling the quality and safety of the Han River and other rivers (Seoul Metropolitan Government 2017a).

• Not many CSEs engage with health (S-SDG 3) and education (S-SDG 4) at the same time. CSEs addressing S-SDG 11 (Inclusive and sustainable city), mostly through economic activities in the housing sector, do not address S-SDG 12 (Sustainable consumption and production). There are unexploited synergies for SEOEs to explore here.

• Many CSEs do not intend to address S-SDGs even though their activities are potentially highly relevant to addressing them. As a consequence, there are many sets of the S-SDGs which are not often simultaneously addressed. They are 2<>17; 5<>7; 7<>9; 9<>13; and 15<>16.

• It is notable that CSEs mostly involved in activities associated with industrialization and innovation pay less attention to energy and climate change, which is a sign that CSEs do not contribute much to minimizing the trade-off between industrialization on the one hand and energy consumption and climate change on the other hand.

As table 8.2 clearly demonstrates, there are many interlinkages between the targets for S-SDG 10 (Reduced Inequality), S-SDG 11 (Inclusive and sustainable city), S-SDG 3 (Healthy lives and well-being), S-SDG 8 (Economic growth and decent work), and S-SDG 5 (Gender equality). Our analysis shows that the missions and functions of CSEs contribute to further strengthening the synergies between these S-SDGs, except for S-SDG 5 (Gender equality). The small number of CSEs working on SDG 5 (Gender equality) is disappointing, in particular considering the ample opportunities for CSEs' activities to contribute to multiple goals including S-SDG 5.

CONCLUSION

Many local governments and CSOs in the Republic of Korea were active in establishing policies and organizations for sustainable development long before the announcement of the 2030 Agenda for Sustainable Development. Early engagement with the Local Agenda 21 process by local governments and CSOs, for example, played a significant role in spreading policies and practices for sustainable development. From 2008 to 2013, however, the

Table 8.2 S-SDGs Connected with Targets of Other S-SDGs

Strength of Interconnections	S-SDGs	Number of Connections with Targets with Other S-SDGs	Percent of Total Connections
Weak	S-SDG 12	1	0.8
	S-SDG 14	1	0.8
	S-SDG 2	1	0.8
	SDG 15	2	1.7
	S-SDG 7	2	1.7
	S-SDG 13	3	2.5
	S-SDG 6	3	2.5
	S-SDG 9	3	2.5
	S-SDG 1	5	4.1
Strong	S-SDG 16	6	5.0
	S-SDG 17	7	5.8
	S-SDG 4	9	7.4
Strongest	S-SDG 5	11	9.1
	S-SDG 8	11	9.1
	S-SDG 3	15	12.4
	S-SDG 11	18	14.9
	S-SDG 10	23	19.0
	Total	121	100

Source: Degree Prestige Report of S-SDGs, Created by Social Network Visualizer v2.3 (February 2018).

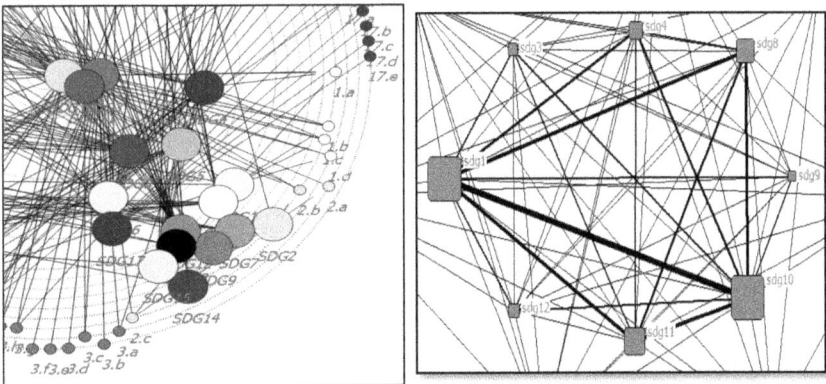

Figure 8.10 Juxtaposing Density of S-SDGs Interconnections and Pathways of CSE Contributions to the S-SDGs. *Source*: Software: Borgatti, Everett, and Freeman (2002).

national government emphasized the economic aspect of green economy, and this constrained the active movement of CSOs for sustainable development by diverting resources away from the integrated vision of sustainability toward a narrower focus on green growth. Resistance to this focus on the economic aspect served to position environmental initiatives as political symbols of the opposition parties. As a result, a sustainable development strategy was not put in place in Seoul until 2011 when the current mayor assumed power. Following a participatory process, the S-SDG framework of SDGs specifically for Seoul was announced in late 2017.

Reflecting the specific conditions of Seoul, the S-SDGs have a strong emphasis on the principle of leaving no one behind. They do not explicitly highlight the importance of realizing the 2030 Agenda's transformative vision, which is to change structures and institutions generating injustice. Our analysis finds that the S-SDGs are a well-integrated framework, with the targets for each S-SDG supporting other S-SDGs. The concern about how to address the nexus between the multiple problems that the goals aim to tackle has been reflected in the structure and contents of the S-SDGs and their targets. This points to a dense network of potential synergies.

In order to most effectively leverage these potential synergies, there should be more encouragement of social entrepreneurship, particularly in the sectors where the S-SDGs are closely interconnected. For example, more entrepreneurial efforts are needed to develop innovative models of SE. The practices of CSEs contributing to sustainable food distribution provide insightful lessons. Although small in number, they engage with diverse S-SDG areas, including S-SDG 2, S-SDG 12, and S-SDG 15.

Analysis of the missions and functions of CSEs demonstrates that Seoul's SEOEs engage with multiple concerns and activities that can potentially create a far greater number of synergistic impacts in relation to various S-SDGs. There are still many areas for SEOEs to engage in innovative approaches to achieving both their mission and the S-SDGs in an integrated and balanced manner. For instance, despite the close relationship between the goals, SEOEs engage less with the nexus between S-SDG 11 and 12, S-SDG 2 and 17, and S-SDG 5 and 7. In short, despite environmental activism having been one of the driving forces behind the current sustainability agenda, the environmental dimension of SE in Seoul appears to be the weakest. CSEs prioritizing economic and social objectives need to pay more attention to their potential to contribute to environmental S-SDGs. SE linkages with goals and targets associated with gender equality also need to be strengthened. Given that S-SDG 5 (Gender equality) is one of the goals supported by many targets of other S-SDGs, SEOEs working for gender equality need to be more innovative to link their economic activities to energy-related goals.

While the local-level impact of national policy, or the implications of policy coherence, have not been systematically analyzed in this chapter, it can be noted here that the weaker aspects of both the S-SDGs and SE in Seoul largely reflect policy preferences at the national level. Over several years, attention nationally has focused on employment creation, with SEOEs playing a significant role in this regard. An important avenue for employment creation has been the provision of social services within a context of welfare state or social policy expansion. As such, these economic and social dimensions of sustainable development are core features of national development policy. Furthermore, the criteria for certifying SEOEs as CSEs relate primarily to economic and social aspects, which create an incentive structure that promotes social enterprise activity in quite specific areas. A key question that remains open is whether the environmental dimension and gender equality can become stronger elements of SE at both national and local levels.

NOTES

1. Portions of this chapter earlier appeared in an internal policy report, "Social and Solidarity Economy for the Sustainable Development Goals: Spotlight on the Social Economy in Seoul, Geneva: UNRISD (2018)," which I had a privilege to work with colleagues and friends as a chief author. I would like to express my great appreciation to Professor Eun Sun Lee who provided me with a valuable advice and support on the network analysis. I would like to also offer my thanks to all the coauthors of the 2018 Report and Communication and Outreach team of UNRISD who provided valuable and constructive suggestions during the planning and development of this research.

2. Lee, Chang-Woo. Interview by Ilcheong Yi. Personal communication. Seoul. March 5, 2017; Lee, Eun Ae. Interview by Ilcheong Yi. Personal communication. Seoul. July 7, 2017.

3. It is notable in suggesting the need for collaboration with other cities and local areas for successful implementation (solidarity beyond subsidiarity).

REFERENCES

Boas, I., F. Biermann, and N. Kanie. 2016. "Cross-Sectoral Strategies in Global Sustainability Governance: Towards a Nexus Approach." *International Environmental Agreements* 16: 449–464.

Borgatti, S. P., M. G. Everett, and L. C. Freeman. 2002. *Ucinet for Windows: Software for Social Network Analysis.* Harvard: Analytic Technologies.

Cha, Yoon Jung, Myung-Pil Shim, and Seung Kyum Kim. 2011. "The Four Major Rivers Restoration Project." UN-Water International Conference: Water in the Green Economy in Practice: Towards Rio+20, Zaragoza, Spain.

Chang-Woo, Lee. 2017. personal communication with Ilcheog Yi, February 22, 2017 and July 6, 2017.

Cornwall, A., and K. Brock. 2005. "Beyond Buzzwords: 'Poverty Reduction', 'Participation' and 'Empowerment' in Development Policy." In *Overarching Concerns Programme Paper*, edited by UNRISD. Geneva: UNRISD.

FAO. 2007. "Profitability and Sustainability of Urban and Peri-urban Agriculture." In *Agricultural Management, Marketing and Finance Occasional Paper*, Vol. 19. Rome: Food and Agriculture Organization of the United Nations.

Han, Heejin. 2015. "Authoritarian Environmentalism under Democracy: Korea's River Restoration Project." *Environmental Politics* 24(5): 1–20.

ICSU and ISSC. 2015. *Review of the Sustainable Development Goals: The Science Perspective*. Paris: International Council for Science (ICSU).

Kim, Eun Jeong, Jeong Soon Kim, Min Seon Chang, Yoo Bong Lee, and Jong Hyeon Hong. 2014. *Research on the Legal Systems of Sustainable Development and Green Growth* (in Korean). Seoul: Korea Legislation Research Institute.

Le Blanc, D. 2015. "Towards Integration at Last? The Sustainable Development Goals as a Network of Targets." In *DESA Working Paper*. New York: UN DESA.

Lee, Gwan-Gye, Hyun-Woo Lee, and Jung-Hwan Lee. 2015. "Greenhouse Gas Emission Reduction Effect in the Transportation Sector by Urban Agriculture in Seoul, Korea." *Landscape and Urban Planning* 140: 1–7.

Lee, Wonhee, Hye Young Lee, Jong Hyuk Park, Kyeong Tae Joo, Young Jo Choi, and Hyuck Joon Kwon. 2009. *Review of Historical Trends of Environmental Regulations and Research on Improvement Measures* (in Korean). Seoul: Korea Association of Public Administration.

Lee, Yeon Ho. 2010. "The State-Market-Society Relationship Under the Lee Myong-bak Government: A Study of the Low Carbon Green Growth Policy" (in Korean). *Korean Journal of Legislative Studies* 30(3): 67–100.

Park, Won-ho, T. K. Ahn, and Kyu Hahn, S. 2013. "Framing the Issue of Economic Democracy during the 18th Presidential Election: A Survey Experiment" (in Korean). *Journal of Korean Politics* 22(1): 1–28.

Pawar, Manohar, and Taewook Huh. 2014. "Korean Response to Environmental Challenges: Origins, Drivers and Impacts of Green Growth on Development." In *Learning from the South Korean Developmental Success: Effective Developmental Cooperation and Synergies Institutions and Policies*, edited by Ilcheong Yi and Thandika Mkandawire. Basingstoke and New York: UNRISD and Palgrave Macmillan.

Penouil, M. 1981. "Looking Beyond Strategies of Polarized Development: Generalized Growth." In *Polarized Development and Regional Policies*, edited by A. Kulklinski. The Hague, Paris, and New York: UNRISD and the Mouton Publishers.

Seoul Metropolitan Government. 2015. *Basic Plan for Seoul's Sustainable Development*. Seoul: Seoul Metropolitan Government.

Seoul Metropolitan Government. 2017a. *2017 Seoul's Sustainable Development Reporting Conference* (in Korean). Seoul: Seoul Metropolitan Government.

Seoul Metropolitan Government. 2017b. "Seoul City Announces the 2030 Sustainable Development Goals." *Seoul Metropolitan Government*. Accessed November 26, 2017. http://english.seoul.go.kr/seoul-city-announces-2030-sustainable-devel opment-goals.

UNESCAP. 2012. "Urban Agriculture: Improving Food Security and Environmental Health of Cities." In *UNAPCAEM Policy Brief*.

UN Inter-Agency Task Force on Social and Solidarity Economy. 2014. *Social and Solidarity Economy and the Challenge of Sustainable Development*. Geneva: UNTFSSE.

Yi, I., H. Ahn, J. Jang, M. Jamillo, E. Lee, S. Lee, Y. Lee, P. Utting, and J. Yi. 2018. *Social and Solidarity Economy for the Sustainable Development Goals: Spotlight on the Social Economy in Seoul*. Geneva: UNRISD.

Chapter 9

Women on Wheels in New Delhi, India

Can Social Innovation Promote Gender Equality?

Bipasha Baruah

INTRODUCTION

The development sector's engagement with poverty alleviation and gender equality has evolved considerably over the past forty years. Significant efforts have been made to accommodate theoretical advancements in the broader field of gender and development. Programs designed to empower women— and men in some settings—have evolved from the welfare, efficiency, and equity-focused approaches of the 1970s and 1980s to the more recent empowerment, human rights, and capabilities-based approaches of the 1990s and the new millennium. Because of a broader structural understanding of the sources of women's poverty and disempowerment, today many more actors in development engage not just with employment and labor force participation as means to empower women but also with more politically sensitive issues (property rights, political participation, and the gendered division of household labor, to name a few) that they had previously been hesitant or unwilling to take on.

These progressive shifts have sometimes paradoxically occurred alongside changes that construct poverty alleviation and gender equality less as complex structural issues and more as technical-rational topics that can be addressed through a bureaucratic approach to development management and practice. There has been a gradual shift away from a political understanding of the causes of poverty and gender inequality to an apolitical and ahistorical management of its symptoms (Ramalingam 2013). The widespread use within donor agencies, government organizations, charities, and even NGOs of the language and logic of business management—through, for example, tools such as Results-Based Management and Logical Framework Analysis—has had a profound impact not just upon how development is conceptualized and operationalized but also upon the operational cultures and management styles of organizations working on the ground to alleviate poverty and promote gender equality. Consequently, these actors increasingly understand development more as a managerial issue that can be planned, carried out, and evaluated within short periods of time rather than as a messy, unpredictable process of social change.

Of course, it is important to remember that the technical-rational approach and the political approach are not entirely antithetical. Actors that understand development as a political process can nonetheless support a careful thinking through of the logical "theories of change," and recognize that in a context of scarce resources, a focus on efficient and effective use of resources is a serious responsibility for those supporting change. The two strategies do not have to be mutually exclusive.

This chapter is not in any way aimed at questioning the importance of careful marshaling of resources or of the need for accountability in development. Rather it seeks to emphasize that the depth of the impact upon people's lives must also be considered critical factors in promoting gender equality. Gender equality and poverty alleviation outcomes can be significant and valuable even when achieved at a relatively small scale. Quantity is not always more important than quality. Further, this research underlines the importance of addressing multiple barriers to women's employment and empowerment simultaneously to optimize outcomes. It demonstrates that providing skills and training—even in depth—is not sufficient when the barriers to women's employment go beyond knowledge and skills. The arguments presented in this chapter are based upon empirical research conducted in India with an initiative called Women on Wheels (WOW), which trains and employs poor urban women as chauffeurs and taxi drivers in the capital city of New Delhi. WOW's work is made possible by two organizations: a nonprofit organization (NPO) called Azad Foundation that provides professional driving training and organizes chauffeur placement services for women after they acquire their licenses; and a for-profit taxi company, Sakha Cabs, that employs drivers trained by its sister NGO.

To inform my research, I drew upon in-depth interviews conducted in New Delhi in 2012 and 2013 with all seven drivers employed at the time by Sakha Cabs as well as interviews with the founder, the chief operating officer, and two other staff members (a program officer and a program advisor) of the WOW initiative. My interviews with the drivers were open-ended, unstructured, and aimed at understanding how the training and employment provided by the WOW initiative had influenced their personal and professional lives.

My interviews with WOW staff were more structured and aimed at understanding programmatic challenges and opportunities.

I also relied upon secondary sources such as a publication called *Women with Wings: Stories about Women Drivers* about the lives of fifty women who trained as commercial taxi drivers and personal chauffeurs with Azad Foundation. Two journalists—Bharat Dogra and Reena Mehta—had produced this publication. To write it, they conducted a series of fifty semi-structured interviews in Hindi with trainees and drivers at the Azad Foundation's office in New Delhi in 2011. Interviewees were encouraged to tell their life stories in their own words and the publication was eventually produced in Hindi and English.

There is also a less formal participant-observation component to this research. I am currently working on several research projects in collaboration with New Delhi-based organizations and I use the Sakha cab service as often as possible. Extended conversations with the drivers I am assigned and my observations as we drive around New Delhi also inform this chapter. The WOW initiative has received a lot of attention in the past ten years in the mainstream media in India, North America, and Europe. *The Times of India, Indian Express, Asian Age, Guardian, Toronto Star, Globe and Mail, Business Standard,* and the *Seattle Globalist* are some newspapers that have written about Sakha Cabs recently (samples of media coverage can be found on Sakha's website: www.sakhaconsultingwings.com). I assembled and analyzed this coverage as secondary data along with other relevant scholarly and practitioner literature in gender and development.

The academic and practitioner literature on women's empowerment is extensive. However, research on the potential of innovations in skills and training to promote gender equality is rare. The International Centre for Research on Women (ICRW) is the only organization that has produced a scholarly assessment of how social and technological innovations might empower women and advance gender equality (ICRW 2009). This assessment identified three critical entry points for realizing women's empowerment: (1) technology use, (2) social norm change, and (3) economic resilience. Whereas this assessment expects that innovations that make a significant difference in women's lives may only fulfill one or two of the established criteria, I have found that women trained by the WOW initiative achieve all three. By putting women in charge of a technology to which they had no previous access, WOW not only creates dependable livelihood opportunities that enable women to permanently escape lives of poverty and indignity, but it also challenges deep-rooted gender and class stereotypes and barriers.

Writing about gender and technology, Hafkin and Huyer (2006) similarly identify three forms of capital that women need to be able to empower themselves: human capital, represented by training, skills, and knowledge;

financial capital represented by income, savings, assets, and resources obtained through credit-providing institutions; and social capital represented by access to networks and relationships based on trust, reciprocity, and camaraderie. Women trained and employed as commercial drivers through the WOW initiative appear to acquire all three forms of capital.

It is important to emphasize that although my research showed a range of significant benefits for women because of their participation in the WOW initiative, they simultaneously continued to face multiple challenges and inequalities linked to gender and socioeconomic background, underlining the need for comprehensive and sustained efforts. Since this research is modest in scope and exploratory in nature, its findings shed light upon problems that may well warrant more detailed investigation. I hope that the issues identified by my research will provide the grounding and detail against which other research, perhaps using very different methodologies, can be tested, verified, and advanced.

A BRIEF OVERVIEW OF THE WOW INITIATIVE

The World Economic Forum has consistently ranked India last among G20 countries for gender equality in the economic sphere. There are large numbers of highly educated and well-paid professional women in cities, but for poor women, both rural and urban, the opportunities for economic advancement are far more limited. Most find themselves in the informal sector doing poorly compensated, menial, and insecure work (Baruah 2004, 2007a). The numbers of urban poor have grown steadily in India. In some states and union territories—the National Capital Territory of Delhi is a good example—more than 50% of people below the poverty line reside in urban areas (Government of India 2009). Much greater attention is currently being paid to reducing urban poverty than in previous decades, but large-scale job training and livelihood programs still tend to be skewed in favor of men. The limited number of "income-generation" and skill development programs available to poor urban women in India tend to focus on stereotypically female occupations such as beautician training, tailoring, and embroidery (Vadera 2013). Organizations like the Self-Employed Women's Association (SEWA) and the Working Women's Forum that do offer more lucrative and innovative training opportunities for women tend to have a regional focus in cities like Ahmedabad and Chennai (Baruah 2010; Chen 2008). The lack of opportunities for training and skill development severely constrains the economic potential of poor urban women and compromises their and their dependents' overall well-being. There are virtually no opportunities for disadvantaged urban women with limited education and socioeconomic resources to acquire skills in more lucrative growing fields such as transportation, warehousing, and skilled construction work (ibid.).

An NGO called Azad Foundation was launched in New Delhi in 2008 to make a modest contribution toward addressing this gap. Its flagship initiative, WOW, recruits and prepares poor urban women to become professional and commercial drivers. Its motto "For Women, By Women" is seamless in its logic of dovetailing disadvantaged urban women's need for better paying economic opportunities with the transportation needs of the growing numbers of upper- and middle-class professional women and their families. Although New Delhi does not have a higher crime rate than cities of its size in other parts of the world, it does have the dubious distinction of being the city with the highest incidence of rape in India, and one of the least safe cities in the world for women, after Cairo (Egypt), Karachi (Pakistan), and Kinshasa (Democratic Republic of the Congo) (Goldsmith 2017). There is no empirical evidence to suggest that women-only taxi or bus services offer women a safer mode of transportation, but the logic that it might be a practical way to increase mobility and visibility for women in the city also made New Delhi a suitable location to launch the WOW initiative. The growth of similar initiatives in a range of different contexts—including with the support of donor organizations (see, e.g., UN Women 2016)—suggests that there is some confidence that the combination of employment and safety outcomes is attractive from both the demand and supply side.

Depending on individual circumstance and ability, it takes between eight and ten months for each learner to complete the training program developed by Azad Foundation. The first three months are a structured driving training program and the remaining time is used to provide actual city driving practice. Every trainee is required to log a minimum of 100 hours of training on the road. Driving skills, customer service, and English language training (a necessity for social mobility in the Indian context) are provided in-house by Azad Foundation's trainers and through a corporate social responsibility (CSR) collaboration with Maruti Suzuki, India's largest automobile manufacture company. Gender equality, legal rights, assertiveness training, and counseling services are provided by an NGO called *Jagori*, and self-defense skills are taught by the Women's Cell of the Delhi Police. The training costs about USD 85 per month. Since most women take between eight and ten months to complete the program and become skilled employable chauffeurs, the total cost of the program varies between USD 680 and 850. Many women are very interested in becoming professional drivers but cannot afford to give up their daily wages to join the training. Azad Foundation seeks out subsidies or fee waivers for such trainees through private donors and corporations. Additionally, it can provide trainees with a one-time interest-free subsistence loan of up to USD 200 that they can pay back upon completing the training and finding a placement.

Influencing government policies that are often apathetic and discriminatory toward the poor in general and women in particular is an important component of the Azad Foundation's work. As an example, procuring a driver's license requires a proof of residence in the name of the licensee. This requirement is difficult even for poor men to fulfill since they are much more likely to live in unlisted slums or other informal settlements than nonpoor applicants. It is much more difficult for women to procure a proof of residence since they are even less likely than the men in their households to have any documents such as electricity and water bills in their names. Completing the paperwork for something as seemingly simple as a learner's license can be extremely challenging. The Azad Foundation works with individual women to clear such hurdles and also advocates more broadly for pro-poor and pro-women policies at various levels of government.

The Azad Foundation has already enjoyed some success in this regard. As an example, in the aftermath of the 2012 Delhi Rape Case, which received global media attention, the city of New Delhi made a commitment to increase the number of female conductors in its public bus service. It has sought Azad Foundation's guidance on collaborating with an appropriate NGO for training and recruitment of female bus conductors. Public bus conductors in major cities in India are generally paid decent wages and receive government benefits such as health insurance and benefits. Although there are no explicit restrictions to prevent women from becoming bus conductors, the profession is almost exclusively male in cities in India. Azad Foundation's work may lead to the opening up of another male-dominated profession in India.

It became obvious soon after Azad was founded that it would not be enough to train and license women without also attempting to create employment for them. Azad's founder, Meenu Vadera, who had previously been a development professional in India and Uganda, arrived at this conclusion because there have been many attempts in the past, in both developed and developing countries, to create opportunities for women in nontraditional fields. Although there is no doubt that this can be done, much evidence suggests that it is easier for women to acquire the training than to subsequently find employment. Women face tremendous social and cultural barriers in entering traditionally male-dominated fields unless there is specific access to placement services (e.g., about women's employment in the construction industry, see Adubra 2005; Baruah 2010; Ness 2012; Watts 2009) as well as support for coping with broader social and economic constraints. Sakha Cabs, the for-profit taxi company, was established alongside Azad to provide employment to licensed women through its own radio taxi service and through chauffeur placement services with a range of employers, including individual women employers, families, NGOs, and corporations. Although the long-term viability of the initiative is difficult to predict, together Sakha

Cabs and Azad Foundation make up an innovative hybrid institutional model of entities that are independent but also interdependent for impact and financial sustainability. There are plans to introduce the WOW initiative in three other cities in India (Gurgaon, Jaipur, and Kolkata) using a similar model.

In its first year of operation (2008–2009), Azad Foundation trained nine women. Between 2008 and 2011, more than 100 women had registered, 80 had completed training and 35 had been employed as drivers with Sakha Cabs or placed as chauffeurs, and another 100 women were in various stages of the training (Vadera 2013). By October 2018, the WOW initiative had trained 1,500 women as drivers in cities across India: New Delhi, Jaipur, Indore, Kolkata, Bengaluru, Guwahati, and Ahmedabad (Narayanan 2018). The drivers trained by the WOW initiative are all working either for Sakha Cabs (or other for-profit taxi companies set up in different cities as part of the WOW model) or as chauffeurs for individuals, private firms, hotels, and NPOs. They continue to be mentored and supported by the NGO partner, Azad Foundation.

FINDINGS

In this section, I first elaborate upon the effects of the WOW program in the lives of drivers. Second, I discuss the opportunities and constraints facing Azad Foundation and Sakha Cabs. Finally, I describe the broader implications of the findings and identify why it is important for us to look beyond limited definitions of cost-effectiveness and scale to enable initiatives like WOW to succeed. I chose to organize findings this way because this is the order in which the research was conducted: I interviewed women about economic and social outcomes of becoming trained drivers; I interviewed program staff about institutional opportunities and constraints; and I finally used these findings to reflect on the wider implications of programs like WOW.

Economic and Social Outcomes for Female Drivers

In sharing findings about the effects of the WOW program in this section, I focus on the different levels (individual, family, community, and institutional) at which gender inequality is experienced and across which most definitions and conceptual frameworks of women's empowerment—including the ones I draw upon for this study (Hafkin and Huyer 2006; ICRW 2009) agree women must make sustained progress toward.

The economic benefits of employment as a personal chauffeur or as a commercial driver become clear when one understands that all women who sign up for training come from families living below the poverty line in urban slums and resettlement colonies in New Delhi with total monthly household incomes of USD 50–85. The average woman in the training program has only eight years of formal schooling. Many had never traveled alone outside their neighborhoods before they began their training. In addition to chronic poverty, many face violence, or the threat of violence, typically but not exclusively at the hands of male relatives. Ninety percent (45 out of 50) of the women in Dogra and Mehta's (2012) report indicated having experienced some form of physical or emotional violence in their lives. The fact that these women nonetheless aspire to complete a program that requires both long hours of training and challenging deep-seated social norms is evidence of their desire to make dramatic changes in their lives.

Depending on the employer, chauffeurs in large cities in India, including New Delhi, may negotiate monthly starting salaries between USD 85 and 168. Taxi drivers with Sakha Cabs earn a starting monthly salary of USD 100 with guaranteed 10% annual raises and a package of other benefits such as health care and contributions toward a national pension plan. The average monthly starting salary earned by a chauffeur or a taxi driver almost immediately makes her a co-breadwinner, if not the primary breadwinner in the family. All seven women currently employed as drivers by Sakha Cabs are either primary or sole breadwinners for their families. The other twenty-eight trained drivers are currently employed as chauffeurs by individuals, families, or businesses. With average incomes above USD 85 per month, they are also primary or co-breadwinners for their families. This would have been next to impossible for any of the women to accomplish had they remained in occupations such as domestic help, elder care, tailoring, embroidery, cooking, and meal services.

The women I interviewed spoke of significant changes in their ability to make important decisions about their lives and those of their children since they became involved in the WOW program. The higher incomes, job security, and social status derived from commercial driving have enabled women to make empowering decisions in their personal lives including leaving abusive marriages, reporting domestic and other abuse to police, filing for separation or divorce, assuming primary financial responsibility for children, enrolling or reenrolling (where children had previously been forced to leave due to financial reasons) children and younger siblings in school, providing financial support to aging parents, building new homes and upgrading old ones. Additionally, thirty-five of the fifty women interviewed by Dogra and Mehta (2012) indicated either having gone back to school, or wanting to go back, to complete formal education programs (usually high school) or other certificate and skills training programs that they had previously been forced to drop out of or unable to join for primarily financial reasons. An active process of what in development theory is called "adaptive preference" (Connell 1977) appears to be unfolding for all or most of the women who now want more from life than they had previously been able to expect.

Commercial driving has been and continues to be a completely male-dominated field in India. It is a livelihood option that is systematically denied to women. "We can quite easily count the total number of commercial women drivers in India. Imagine being able to confidently say that about a country of 1.2 billion people" exclaimed Meenu Vadera, the founder of Azad Foundation, during our interview in December 2012. Although large numbers of college-educated women from affluent and middle-class families drive cars in New Delhi and other metropolitan areas, it is virtually unheard of for a poor woman to be able to do so prior to the introduction of the WOW program. In its first two years of operation, Azad Foundation staff had struggled to convince young women and their families to join. The earning potential in commercial driving and the demonstration effect created by women who have already found work has made it relatively easier today to convince women and their families to try an unconventional occupation.

The increased mobility, visibility, and confidence that these women have enjoyed also enhanced their sense of belonging and entitlement to the services and benefits offered by the city. Prior to getting their licenses, none of the women would have been able to offer any proof of identity even though such documents are a prerequisite for accessing various rights and entitlements. As one driver impressed upon me "Before I got my license, if I had died on the street in an accident, no one would even have known who I was." Most nonpoor people in industrialized or emerging economies use driver's licenses as proofs of identity for everything from applying for utility connections to credit cards to passports. For people who have never possessed any proof of identity, a driver's license can represent a form of government-approved recognition of personhood that can then open other doors. This is perhaps best exemplified by the fact that even women who, for a variety of reasons described later in this chapter, ended up not working as commercial drivers after getting their licenses indicated that they regularly used their licenses as proofs of identity for purposes such as opening bank accounts and applying for documentation such as ration cards and voter registration cards. Additionally, all women who train as commercial drivers live in informal settlements with little or no tenure security. Several women indicated that because the driver's license must include residential address information, it can enable the women to access other utilities and services such as water connections and mobile phones. Such less-obvious social and economic benefits of possessing driver's licenses should not be underestimated.

Women who train as commercial drivers do simultaneously continue to face challenges on many fronts: skepticism or ridicule from family and friends, deep-rooted social prejudices against women drivers, balancing long working hours with family responsibilities, and lack of a sense of community beyond their peers in the program. Riding around New Delhi in a Sakha cab, it was difficult not to notice the challenges these women face while going about their jobs on a daily basis: the startled expressions from pedestrians and other drivers, the constant need to maneuver and defuse conflict when they are harassed or intimidated by aggressive male drivers, the condescending attitudes of parking attendants, and the absence of public toilet facilities for women. It is interesting to note, however, that none of the women I have spoken with for this research perceived these challenges as insurmountable or permanent. They were all very optimistic that social attitudes toward female drivers would change over time as more of them got behind the wheel. The blue uniforms worn by the women made their occupations as drivers more visible. The uniforms exposed drivers to increased hostility in some settings while simultaneously commanding respect in others. Nonetheless all the women I interviewed liked having to wear the uniform during working hours.

New Delhi has an extremely expensive real estate market by any standards in the world. Several NGOs I work with have unmarked offices in less expensive neighborhoods on the outskirts of the city and we have had to stop to ask for directions from other drivers on several occasions. Most people in New Delhi are accustomed to only seeing upper- and middle-class educated women drive cars. I noticed that even older men and women always used *"aap"*—the reverent version of "you" in Hindi, typically reserved for people of equal or higher social status—to address Sakha drivers. Two young women articulated my observations when they emphasized that no one had ever addressed them that way before they had started driving. In the context of a deeply (and very visibly) hierarchical and socially stratified city like New Delhi, it is not naïve to suggest that simply being seen driving a car elevates the social status of young women from disadvantaged backgrounds. The effects upon confidence and self-worth gained by the young drivers from such positive interactions with people from higher socioeconomic backgrounds cannot be ignored or trivialized.

All the drivers I spoke with also mentioned that attitudes within their families and communities had already shifted in the short time that they had started driving. Although they continued to shoulder much of the responsibility for childcare and household maintenance, they also emphasized that other family members had become more willing to share responsibility for domestic chores once the women started earning higher incomes from commercial driving. Other researchers working in India (see, e.g., Patel 2014 and other contributions to Nielsen and Waldrop 2014) have corroborated that gender roles tend to be malleable, that the intra-household division of labor is dynamic and negotiable, that economics often trumps "culture and tradition," and that oppression and agency can exist conterminously and hence are not mutually exclusive.

It is not surprising, then, to discover that mothers-in-law and husbands who had previously been unsupportive of women working as drivers became more willing to relieve them of some of their domestic chores as the women started to contribute a greater share of the household income. One driver described how her husband—who now not only cooks and cleans but also assumes the primary caregiver role for their toddler son—had been so incensed by her decision to learn to drive that he had traveled to the Azad Foundation office in 2010 to express his outrage. He had vowed that no woman in his family or in seven generations after him (a dramatic way of saying "forever" in Hindi) would ever drive a taxi. "How did he forget about seven generations of tradition within two years?" she wondered with wry amusement as we drove around the city.

Of course, it is important to remember that husbands and other family members allowing women to take on roles that benefit the household economically does not necessarily always lead to deep shifts in attitudes regarding women's status and rights. Other authors have emphasized that there may be less resistance to women taking part in income-generating activities because they are considered a "win-win" for the family (Agarwal 2003). While men may not challenge such activities at all, they are likely to be far more resistant to deeper economic and political demands from women—for independent land and property rights, for example—that challenge their traditional privileges and entitlement to resources.

How the women in the WOW program relate to one another is also instructive. Although Azad Foundation and Sakha Cabs do not in any formal way require trained women to provide emotional or financial support to other women, most women choose to do so. Of the fifty women interviewed by Dogra and Mehta (2012), forty-three identified the supportive institutional culture and the camaraderie they felt with other women in the program as being strong influences in their motivation to complete training. Evidence of women's willingness to support other women in the program may at least in part be attributed to their very small numbers and what Spivak (1996) has called "strategic essentialism." To put it simply, there are so few female commercial drivers that they must out of necessity present a unified front to gain visibility and status even though they may actually be a very diverse group in terms of their ideas, opinions, and preferences. Program staff at Azad Foundation and Sakha Cabs emphasized on several occasions that they often do not even get to hear about major problems in the lives of trainees and drivers until after the crises have been addressed because the women have built such a strong social support system. Accounts of drivers helping other drivers and trainees with money, emotional support, shelter, and childcare, for example, may certainly be explained by the logic that such solidarity is essentially a means to broader gains for a marginalized group. Whether such solidarity will endure as the group gets bigger remains to be seen.

It is important to emphasize that the increased access to income, familial support, and social networks enjoyed by women who work as commercial drivers does not in any way minimize the need for the state to create adequate social security floors to protect against vagaries in the job market, illness, maternity, old age, job losses, and other risks to people's well-being. There have been significant advancements in strengthening social protection floors in India recently, including unconditional cash transfer programs that enable poor women to make priority decisions for themselves and their dependents (Davala et al. 2015). Structural inequality constrains individual ability to exercise rights and demand entitlements. The benefits women derive from initiatives like WOW can only find optimal traction within the context of a wider and more comprehensive social security infrastructure.

Sakha Cabs' success has recently motivated at least two other cab companies in New Delhi, that had until now exclusively hired men, to also train and hire small numbers of women. These companies are simply aiming for a bigger share of the women-only niche market so their institutional cultures and structures remain mostly unchanged after they add a few women to their existing programs. There is little attempt to understand the social and economic factors that constrain women or to provide the type of holistic training and support services that Azad Foundation does. I called two Delhi-based companies that mentioned having female drivers on their websites to learn more about their cab services. Both told me that their female drivers were not allowed to pick up clients after 8 p.m. because it was not safe for women to be out late at night in New Delhi. Instead of building programs that make it possible for women to drive and be driven at all hours of day and night, as WOW has tried to do, the other cab companies had chosen to reinforce rather than challenge broader societal anxieties and taboos. That said, the sheer fact that other taxi companies have started hiring female drivers is cause for optimism that their institutional cultures and practices may also change over time.

It is important to emphasize that there have been very valid feminist criticisms that women's only taxi and bus services may very quickly become cosmetic technological fixes for broader concerns about women's safety in public spaces. In the aftermath of the widely publicized rape and murder of a medical student in New Delhi in December 2012, much of the mainstream media has described the WOW initiative as well as other women-only taxi and bus services as "solutions" for gang rape and sexual violence (see, e.g., Kapoor 2013). Azad Foundation and Sakha Cabs are quick to point out that they consider this to be a very simplistic association since it places the responsibility for preventing sexual violence on the victim rather than on the perpetrator. Violence against women, sexual or otherwise, is a structural global problem. Eliminating violence against women will require much deeper and more proactive engagement with the social structures and power relations that sustain and reproduce it. Researchers working in other contexts (see, e.g., Abdelnour and Saeed 2014) have noted how easily the quest to design, produce, promote, and deliver the most efficient technical panaceas can replace the need to understand complex structural problems.

The WOW initiative, on the other hand, does appreciate that reducing violence against women will require much more than women's only taxi services. It sees its services as a practical way to increase women's visibility and mobility within the city while simultaneously advocating for more proactive engagement with the social structures and institutions that maintain and perpetuate violence against women. Both Azad Foundation and Sakha Cabs participate actively in broader forums—such as those organized by feminist organizations and NGOs—that question and confront Indian society about its attitudes toward women. Other authors emphasize that organizations committed to transformative social change must necessarily strike a balance between the politics of the feasible and the politics of transformation (Rai 2002). As Molyneux (1998, 78) contends, "clearly practical interests can, at times should, be the basis for a political transformation."

Institutional Opportunities and Constraints

Since women rarely drive commercially in India, there appears, at least in theory, to be tremendous potential to create employment in this sector. The hybrid institutional model (nonprofit foundation and for-profit taxi company) was built purposively to ensure that Azad Foundation's work would not be completely dependent on grant or donor funding. The WOW initiative is not yet financially self-sustaining—largely because of the higher initial costs of setting up the physical infrastructure in the early years of operation—but it does expect to be in the future. As the initial costs of setting up the enterprise go down and level off over time, Sakha Cabs should become more profitable. This will allow the company not just to purchase more cars, hire more drivers, and offer better salaries and benefits but also to improve and expand Azad Foundation's training programs and support services.

Despite a promising start, deeply entrenched social barriers and prejudices continue to make it difficult for Azad Foundation to recruit women for the training program. The term "professional driver" is almost everywhere in the world, and certainly in India, associated with images of male drivers drinking, smoking, and generally living a rough and hardened life on the road. Like most stereotypes, this is an inaccurate and incomplete portrayal of the lives of male drivers but it is one that many young women and their families are familiar with and influenced by. Although there has been a limited demonstration effect due to the small numbers of women who are working as drivers, in a city of twenty-five million people there is currently not enough of a critical mass of female commercial drivers to ensure that women themselves as well as their families would consider it a viable livelihood option. The numbers of women who are interested in learning to drive have grown dramatically since the single-digit enrollment in 2009 but there are still far too few women who can see themselves driving professionally despite Azad's extensive outreach efforts in low-income neighborhoods throughout the city. It was beyond the scope of this research to understand why some families might be more supportive of professional driving as an occupation for women than others but research aimed at answering this question would certainly be useful.

Retention is also a challenge. Approximately 40% of women who enroll in the training program currently drop out (Vadera 2013). Large conventional skills training programs in India—with hundreds or thousands of trainees—have similar, if not higher, dropout rates, but the optics and effects upon morale for programs like WOW are more dramatic because they are much smaller to begin with (ibid.). The no-interest subsistence loans offered to trainees can ensure that women do not drop out of the training due to financial reasons but there are other reasons, including child and elder care responsibilities as well as lack of confidence, motivation, and family support, which often compel them to do so. The dropout rates for women in nontraditional occupations do tend to be high everywhere in the world (see, e.g., National Women's Law Centre 2014 for selected statistics about the United States).

Finding chauffeur placements for trainees after they have acquired their licenses can also be a challenge due to pervasive societal biases against women drivers. Very few individuals and companies are willing to consider hiring women as drivers. NGOs (both domestic and international) and other development or charitable organizations are more willing to do so because of their commitment to social justice but their support is not enough as the cohorts of licensed drivers grow larger every year. Taken together, these constraints may explain why Azad Foundation has in the last three years reached out to thousands of women, developed a list of 3,000 potential trainees, had conversations with almost a thousand women but convinced only 100 women to register with the program (Janardhan 2013).

It is important to emphasize that much like the Sakha drivers who are optimistic about the future, none of the program staff perceive these challenges as unsolvable or permanent. And they do have reason to be optimistic. A database of more than 150 clients—including NGOs, private companies, and individuals—was established to enable more successful placement. By June 2013, Azad Foundation had a waitlist of employers wanting to hire its graduates and each licensed driver had at least two interviews lined up upon completion of the program. The Chief Operating Officer stressed during an interview in mid-2013 that increasing the number of licensed drivers and reducing the time it takes the average trainee to complete training was proving to be a bigger challenge. Sakha Cabs also struggles to meet the demand for taxis, especially during holidays and festivals. I was compelled to hire taxis with a different company on Christmas and New Year's Day because all the Sakha Cabs had been booked well ahead of time.

Extensive media coverage and celebrity endorsements have helped give the two organizations visibility within and outside India. Popular Bollywood actor, Aamir Khan, featured the WOW initiative in an episode of his Hindi language TV talk show, *Satyamev Jayate*. Other celebrities and even heads of state (most recently British prime minister David Cameron) now hire Sakha Cabs when they visit New Delhi. The WOW initiative has also received several prestigious international awards for socially responsible innovation and business development. Although the media attention and awards have helped Sakha Cabs secure new clients, Azad Foundation staff members are quick to point out that they have not helped generate much funding for its work. Meenu Vadera, Azad's founder, explicitly identifies securing funding for WOW as one of the most frustrating and demotivating aspects of her work. As a unique and innovative program that helps break down boundaries for women and enables them to transform their living conditions, she had expected the rationale for the WOW initiative to be clear and compelling. She was surprised to discover otherwise.

Azad Foundation's work is currently supported by two UK-based charities, iPartner and Human Dignity Foundation. The WOW initiative also raises money through CSR initiatives, individual donors, and crowdfunding initiatives. Why have other—often better resourced entities with explicit commitments to gender equality and women's empowerment (including Indian and international development funding organizations, government agencies, and private sector organizations)—been unwilling or hesitant to support its work? I identify some of the reasons under the headings of "cost-effectiveness" and "replication and scale."

Cost-effectiveness

An entrenched but unquestioned preference for low-cost, high-volume interventions that can create a broad impact within a very short amount of time (typically less than three months) is one of the primary reasons for the hesitation—or outright refusal—to support WOW (Vadera 2013). The cost per trainee (approximately USD 850) and the training period (eight to ten months) for the WOW initiative seems very reasonable—especially considering that it turns women who have often never ridden in a private vehicle let alone driven one into commercial drivers—but it is much higher than the average costs for livelihood training programs for women. The founder of Azad Foundation emphasized that the maximum amount that potential funders she has approached were willing to provide was about USD 220 per person, which is obviously far too little for the type of well-rounded program the foundation offers.

There are also fundamental disagreements between Azad Foundation and potential funders about the social and cultural appropriateness of training women to be taxi drivers. "Wouldn't it be more appropriate for poor girls to learn to be beauticians or hotel maids?" is one question that Azad Foundation's staff find themselves answering frequently. Given the intellectual advancements in the field of gender and development that encourage us to challenge the social and political structures that sustain gender inequality, rather than just increase women's access to resources, it is surprising that professional staff within funding organizations, who typically have graduate degrees in development studies or related fields, do not appreciate that training women for low-wage feminized occupations reinforces rather than challenges social hierarchies and norms. The inability to appreciate what initiatives like WOW are trying to accomplish may be a result of the relatively low priority given to gender analysis by mainstream development actors as well as the inadequacy of teaching on gender and development in conventional development studies programs.

The fact that the WOW initiative requires women to be enrolled full time (six to eight hours a day) for eight to ten months is, according to Vadera (2013), also perceived as a "weakness" by some potential funders. During interviews Azad Foundation staff stressed that most livelihood programs require women to only commit to two or three hours of training a day, thereby perpetuating rather than challenging the entrenched patriarchal logic that women would (or should) only attempt to learn "income-generating skills" after they had completed all their household chores. The WOW initiative requires a very different level of time commitment from learners as well as tough negotiations with families and communities over gender roles and domestic responsibilities. The need to provide financial resources, counseling, assertiveness, and conflict-resolution training to enable women to negotiate optimal learning situations does significantly increase program costs for WOW but may also result in more transformative changes for women who complete the training. If we want to influence sustainable improvements in women's lives, we must be concerned with more than just enabling women to cope with the status quo and to perform their traditional roles better, since empowerment and coping are distinctly different. Elson (1995, 193) elaborates: "It is not a matter of wanting organizations that empower women as opposed to enabling them to cope, but of wanting organizations that seek to empower women as well as enabling them to cope—organizations that have the goal of transforming gender relations through practical action."

An insistence on low costs per trainee is problematic for other reasons. The idea that a maximum amount of USD 220 can enable a poor urban woman to pull herself out of poverty in a matter of months while her nonpoor counterparts in industrialized countries and emerging economies spend thousands of dollars to become employable is a double standard that is pervasive today in the development sector. That the tyranny of low costs reinforces existing global hierarchies based on gender and race is also patently obvious: Poor Third World women must be "empowered" as quickly and as cheaply as possible, and in very large numbers.

Even if we were to ignore our moral and philosophical discomfort with the emphasis on low costs, the perception that initiatives like WOW are not "cost-effective" is also untrue. From a purely economic standpoint, the total cost of the training (USD 850) is easily recovered by the trainees within a year of working as a chauffeur or taxi driver even if they also pay back the USD 200 subsistence loan in installments to Azad Foundation during the same time. There are very few existing livelihood programs that can make this claim. The return on investment for the learner is exceptionally high from a purely economic perspective. It is even higher if noneconomic gains for the women, their families, and communities are considered.

Given this preoccupation with quantity over quality, it is also easy to understand why the 40% dropout rate from Azad's training program may be perceived as proof of "failure" even though the corresponding dropout rates from large livelihood training programs, as described previously, may be even higher. Getting potential funders to appreciate the value of making a large difference in the lives of a small number of women while growing the program slowly to reach more women with all its depth and detail intact has been a persistent challenge for Azad Foundation's founder and staff.

Replication and Scale

Much like low costs, the words "replication and scale" have assumed the status of what Žižek (1989) would call "a sublime object of ideology" in contemporary development orthodoxy. They are perpetually invoked but seldom defined or analyzed. "Can it be replicated and scaled-up?" is a question that all development interventions and innovations are subjected to and the WOW initiative is no exception. The high program costs and the small numbers of women Azad has trained so far are easily invoked as impediments for "scaling up" the program.

The focus on large-scale interventions may seem reasonable in a country like India that has, depending on which measures and estimates we use, between 200 and 700 million poor people. However, it is important to unpack the two terms—"replicability" and "scalability"—instead of invoking them together unthinkingly to understand why criticisms that Azad Foundation's work can achieve neither are unfounded. Although initiatives based on public-private or private-NGO partnerships have their limitations (see, e.g., Baruah 2007b; Crawford 2003), the hybrid institutional model (nonprofit foundation and for-profit taxi company) that the WOW initiative is based upon is highly replicable and is indeed currently being replicated in three other Indian cities. The fact that the WOW initiative is designed to work with small numbers of women in each training cycle should be perceived as a strength and not a weakness of the program since it is precisely the focus on detail and depth of impact that makes the transformative differences in the lives of women and their families. Vadera (2013) explains: "In a livelihood intervention that is as socially disruptive as ours, each individual woman who chooses to complete her training and build a career as a professional chauffeur must be held within a carefully managed web of institutional systems that supports, advises, guides, counsels, and nurtures, that helps build on her strengths and launches her as a professional chauffeur" (152). The WOW initiative is committed to replication (and in doing so to "scaling-up" to reach more women) as long as the quality and nuance of its program are not compromised. By considering only numbers and not depth of impact in its conceptualization of "scale," potential funders ironically prevent WOW from "replicating and scaling up" its work. Emerging scholarship and practice that encourages us to move beyond "scaling up" to thinking about "scaling deep" to create more lasting social change (Coburn 2003; Koenig 2015) may encourage a different perspective about the work of organizations like Azad Foundation in the future. Other researchers have also pointed out some basic incongruities of the current "architecture of aid." De La Cruz (2009) notes, for example, that funders and organizations are often stuck in a vicious cycle where small women's groups are seen as not having the absorption capacity to grow. Consequently, funding is not increased, yet with increased funding organizational capacities would expand.

The pressure to scale-up interventions to reach millions of people without any real consideration for the depth of the impact has become so deeply entrenched that even organizations that exist to support and incubate social innovation now understand success and failure in solely numeric terms. As an example, the Ashoka Foundation, a global association dedicated to supporting the work of social innovators, turned down Meenu Vadera's application for a fellowship because the WOW initiative was deemed too expensive and time consuming to be scalable. Emerging research suggests that people innovate in different ways and that women may be more likely to perceive their effectiveness in terms of impact rather than scale (Segran 2010). The fact that only

40% of Ashoka fellows are women may not be surprising given the foundation's preoccupation with conventional notions of scale. Instead of questioning its tendency to privilege scale over impact, Ashoka ironically launched an initiative called WISE: Women's Initiatives for Social Entrepreneurship to enable women to scale up their ideas to reach larger numbers of people.

My criticisms of the obsession with cost-effectiveness and scale are not blind to the fact that there is indeed a great need for low-cost and high-volume technical and social innovations to improve the lives of poor people around the world. It is easy to appreciate the benefits that things like energy-efficient cook stoves, water purifiers, or solar lights can offer and the fact that they should probably be disseminated to large numbers of people to have a broad impact. The fact that such innovations, if combined with microcredit, for example, can also create livelihood opportunities for some women is also well established. My criticism has more to do with the assumption that such one-step simplistic interventions that make no effort to question entrenched inequitable social norms or structural global hierarchies will create lasting social change.

Funding organizations must also question the practice of working only with big institutions. It is easier and much cheaper to provide large amounts of money to a few institutions than providing smaller amounts to a larger number of institutions. However, the practice of privileging logistical convenience over effectiveness often results in smaller institutions working on new and innovative initiatives being denied the opportunity to create very meaningful differences in people's lives. There will always be a need for large-scale programs in development but instead of always spending millions of dollars in one place, going forward we must figure out how to spend 100K in ten different places. Writing about women's rights and gender equality in the context of the new aid environment, Collison et al. (2008) specifically emphasize that there is an urgent need to establish funding mechanisms that are accessible to a wide range of civil society organizations, not only the strongest and largest. Other scholars and practitioners are articulating similar perspectives. In an op-ed that was published in the *Toronto Star* on International Women's Day, the executive director of MATCH International Women's Fund, an Ottawa-based charitable foundation that funds women's rights organizations around the world, emphasized the need to fund small grassroots organizations that "do not fit into the tidy mold that donors are looking for" (Tomlin 2014).

CONCLUSION

The WOW initiative is an instructive example of how development impact can be broadened by linking up initiatives and creating pathways for women to use new skills and training. The transformative impact of this for very poor women in a context of highly constrained and stereotyped expectations for women should not be underestimated. Moving forward it is also important to appreciate that quantity is not always more important than quality. The depth of the impact and the detail of the intervention must also be considered critical factors in promoting gender equality and social change. Delivering quick, measurable results in large numbers is very different from delivering long-lasting development impact.

It would be unwise to conclude this chapter without locating the lessons learned from this initiative in New Delhi, India, within broader debates in the field of gender and development. The purpose of this chapter was certainly not to argue that initiatives like WOW, which adopt features typical of neoliberal development projects—such as corporate social responsibility contributions and a for-profit component, and that seek to empower smaller numbers of women individually as workers and entrepreneurs—are "better" in any way than organizations like the SEWA and Working Women's Forum that focus on unionization, establishment of cooperatives, and other grassroots mobilizing strategies in order to create solidarity among much larger groups of women. I have studied and written about such large membership organizations extensively and find them equally compelling. The important lesson that emerges from this research and other research conducted in the past on resource-poor women and paid labor in India and elsewhere seems to be that similar social and economic outcomes can be accomplished using both neoliberal and non-neoliberal strategies. The two may not be as different and diametrically opposed as they are often made out to be in the development literature, and they certainly do not have to be mutually exclusive. Therefore, we should also remain open to the possibility of promoting gender equality and progressive social change within the context of new and hybrid institutional arrangements such as the one presented in this chapter.

POSTSCRIPT

It is difficult to predict how sustainable the WOW model (and others like it) will be in the future. A couple of newer developments in the taxi industry may complicate matters. The first is the entry of rideshare companies like Uber into the Indian market. Uber has committed to enlisting one million female drivers worldwide by 2020; in India it has set a target for 50,000 drivers by 2020. Uber's major competitor in India is an Indian rideshare company called Ola Cabs, which has also committed to a target of 50,000 female drivers by 2020.

A female passenger was raped by an Uber driver in New Delhi in December 2014. Even before this happened, Uber had received a lot of criticism globally for not recruiting more women as drivers and for not being more responsive to concerns about the safety of female passengers. A combination of such pressures led Uber to briefly partner with UN Women in March 2015 to launch the one million women drivers' initiative (Uber Newsroom 2015). UN Women withdrew from this collaboration very shortly after (Alter 2015) over objections from the International Transport Federation (ITF) about Uber's safety record with women, the treatment of its drivers as well as broader concerns from ITF that the Uber rideshare business model creates precarious, poorly paid, part-time work that impoverishes the conventional taxi industry, and that stands to reinforce rather than subvert women's economic disempowerment and marginalization across the globe (ITF 2015). In its response to the announcement of the Uber-UN Women collaboration, ITF emphasizes: "The creation of one million precarious, informal jobs will not contribute to women's economic empowerment and represents exactly the type of structural inequality within the labour market that the women's movement has been fighting for decades. Uber's practices are defined by an aggressive informalisation of an industry that was already deregulated three decades ago" (ibid.). Despite UN Women's withdrawal from the initiative, Uber has remained committed to its goal of recruiting one million female drivers by 2020.

Uber's modus operandi is quite different from social enterprises like Sakha Cabs. Unlike companies like Sakha, Uber has access to significantly more capital. The Uber and Ola model is also different in that it offers loans and other financing as well as access to garages and second-hand car dealers to enable drivers to own their own cars. India is the first international market in which Uber offers financing—probably because it realized quite quickly that most people interested in driving for pay in India are not wealthy enough to own their own cars. Although women's taxi companies like Sakha also incorporate hybrid public-private components into its model, it still operates as a cooperative in which drivers are shareholders. The Uber model is much more explicitly and unapologetically individualistic and capitalistic.

Both Uber and Ola have approached Sakha Cabs and Azad Foundation with offers of various kinds. The basic thrust of these offers is that Uber would offer WOW access to extensive resources, which would enable WOW to dramatically scale up its operations. In turn, Azad and Sakha would train the taxi drivers that the rideshare companies would employ. What WOW stands to gain is obvious; what it stands to lose is less obvious. And whether it is possible to collaborate with entities like Uber while also retaining the depth and detail of its own program is presently a matter of conjecture.

REFERENCES

Abdelnour, Samer, and Akbar M. Saeed. 2014. "Technologizing Humanitarian Space: Darfur Advocacy and the Rape-Stove Panacea." *International Political Sociology* 8: 145–163.

Adubra, Ayele L. 2005. *Non-Traditional Occupations, Empowerment and Women: A Case of Togolese Women*. New York: Routledge.

Agarwal, Bina. 2003. "Gender and Land Rights Revisited: Exploring New Prospects Via the State, Family and Market." *Journal of Agrarian Change* 3(1/2): 184–224.

Alter, Charlotte. 2015 "UN Women Breaks Off Partnership with Uber." *Time*. Accessed June 7, 2017. http://time.com/3754537/un-women-breaks-off-partnership-with-uber.

Baruah, Bipasha. 2004. "Earning Their Keep and Keeping What They Earn: A Critique of Organizing Strategies of South Asian Women in the Informal Sector." *Gender, Work & Organization* 11: 605–626.

———. 2007a. "Women and Multiple Vulnerabilities: Opportunities and Constraints in Landed Property Ownership for Informal Sector Workers in Urban India." Paper presented at the Living on the Margins: Vulnerability, Social Exclusion and the State in the Informal Economy conference, Cape Town, South Africa (March 26–28, 2007).

———. 2007b. "Assessment of Public-Private-NGO Partnerships: Water and Sanitation Services in Slums." *Natural Resources Forum* 31: 226–237.

———. 2010. "Gender and Globalization: Opportunities and Constraints Faced by Women in the Construction Industry in India." *Labor Studies Journal* 35(2): 198–221.

Chen, Martha. 2008. "A Spreading Banyan Tree: The Self-Employed Women's Association, India." In *From Clients to Citizens: Communities Changing the Course of Their Own Development*, edited by A. Mathie and G. Cunningham, 181–206. Warwickshire, UK: Intermediate Technology Publications.

Coburn, Cynthia. 2003. "Rethinking Scale: Moving Beyond Numbers to Deep and Lasting Change." *Educational Researcher* 32(6): 3–12.

Collison, Helen, Helen Derbyshire, Brita Fernandez Schmidt, and Tina Wallace. 2008. *Women's Rights and Gender Equality: The New Aid Environment and Civil Society Organizations*. London: UK Gender and Development Network.

Connell, Raewyn. 1977. *Ruling Class, Ruling Culture*. Cambridge, UK: Cambridge University Press.

Crawford, Gordon. 2003. "Partnership or Power? Deconstructing the 'Partnership for Governance Reform' in Indonesia." *Third World Quarterly* 24(1): 139–159.

Davala, Sarath, Renana Jhabvala, Soumya Kapoor Mehta, and Guy Standing. 2015. *Basic Income: A Transformative Policy for India*. New Delhi: Bloomsbury.

De la Cruz, Carmen. 2009. *Financing for Development and Women's Rights: A Critical Review*. Madrid: WIDE, Globalising Gender Equality and Social Justice.

Dogra, Bharat, and Reena Mehta. 2012. *Women on Wings: Stories About Women Drivers*. New Delhi: Azad Foundation.

Elson, Diane. 1995. *Male Bias in the Development Process.* Manchester, UK: Manchester University Press.

Goldsmith, Belinda. 2017. "These Are the Most Dangerous Cities for Women." *Global Citizen.* October 16. Accessed June 25, 2020. https://www.globalcitizen .org/en/content/most-dangerous-best-cities-for-women-2.

Government of India. 2009. *India Urban Poverty Report.* New Delhi: Ministry of Housing and Urban Poverty Alleviation.

Hafkin, Nancy, and Sophia Huyer. 2006. *Cinderella or Cyberella? Empowering Women in the Knowledge Society.* Boulder: Kumarian Press.

ICRW. 2009. *Innovation for Women's Empowerment and Gender Equality.* Washington, DC: International Centre for Research on Women.

ITF. 2015. "UN Women + Uber = A Vision for Precarious Work." Accessed June 7, 2017. https://timedotcom.files.wordpress.com/2015/03/no-to-un-women-uber-par tnership.pdf.

Janardhan, Nayantara. 2013. Personal interview. New Delhi, India. June 15, 2013.

Kapoor, Desh. 2013. "Delhi Gangrape Solutions: Sakha Cabs for Women in Delhi; Cabs for Women Driven by Women." *Drishtikone.* Accessed December 22, 2015. http://www.patheos.com/blogs/drishtikone.

Koenig, Bonnie. 2015. "Scaling for Impact by Scaling." *Co-Creative Impact and Innovation Institute.* Accessed December 22, 2015. http://ci2iglobal.com/scaling-for-impact-by-scaling-deep.

Molyneux, Maxine. 1998. "Analyzing Women's Movements." In *Feminist Visions of Development: Gender Analysis and Policy,* edited by C. Jackson and R. Pearson, 65–88. London: Routledge.

Narayanan, Jayashree. 2018. "Celebrating Women on Wheels." *Delhi Post.* November 1. Accessed June 25, 2020. https://delhipostnews.com/celebrating-women-on-whe els.

National Women's Law Centre. 2014. *Women in Construction: Still Breaking Ground.* Washington, DC: National Women's Law Centre.

Ness, Kat. 2012. "Constructing Masculinity in the Building Trades: Most Jobs in the Construction Industry Can Be Done by Women." *Gender, Work & Organization* 19(6): 654–676.

Nielsen, Kenneth, and Anne Waldrop (eds). 2014. *Women, Gender and Everyday Social Transformation in India.* London and New York: Anthem Press.

Patel, Reena. 2014. "Today's 'Good Girl': The Women behind India's BPO Industry." In *Women, Gender and Everyday Social Transformation in India,* edited by K. Nielsen and A. Waldrop. London and New York: Anthem Press.

Rai, Shirin. 2002. *Gender and the Political Economy of Development.* Cambridge: Blackwell Publishers.

Ramalingam, Ben. 2013. *Aid on the Edge of Chaos: Rethinking International Cooperation in a Complex World.* London: Oxford University Press.

Segran, Grace. 2010. "Women Social Entrepreneurs Driven by Impact Rather than Scale." *INSEAD Knowledge.* Accessed December 22, 2015. http://knowledge.ins ead.edu/leadership-management/women-in-business.

Spivak, Gayatri. 1996. *The Spivak Reader: Selected Works of Gayatri Chakravorty Spivak.* New York: Routledge.

Tomlin, Jess. 2014. "Women and Girls Aren't Just Tools for Development." *The Toronto Star.* March 8.

Uber Newsroom. 2015. "UN Women + Uber = A Vision for Equality." Accessed June 7, 2017. https://newsroom.uber.com/un-women-uber-a-vision-for-equality-2.

UN Women. 2016. "Meri Safe Bus Launch." Accessed November 14, 2016. http://asi apacific.unwomen.org/en/news-and-events/stories/2016/02/meri-safe-bus-launch.

Vadera, Meenu. 2012. Personal interview. New Delhi, India. December 17.

———. 2013. "Women on Wheels." In *Aid, NGOs and the Realities of Women's Lives: A Perfect Storm,* edited by T. Wallace, F. Porter, and M. Ralph-Bowman, 143–154. Rugby: Practical Action Publishing.

Watts, Jacqueline. 2009. "'Allowed into a Man's World' Meanings of Work–Life Balance: Perspectives of Women Civil Engineers as "Minority" Workers in Construction." *Gender, Work & Organization* 16(1): 37–57.

Žižek, Slavo. 1989. *The Sublime Object of Ideology.* London: Verso.

Appendix I

Evaluation of the Major Legal Entities in Northeast Asia

China

Organizations		Democratic features		Economic features		Social features	
		Ownership	Establishment	Main activity	Profit distribution	Institutional mission	Target problem
Private nonenterprise units		—	A	A	B	B	A
Social organizations		—	B	—	B	A	B
Foundation	Public fundraising foundations	—	B	B	A	A	B
	Nonpublic fundraising foundations	—	B	B	A	A	B
Social service organizations		—	—	A	B	B	A
Labor unions		—	—	—	—	—	A
Cooperatives	Farmers' specialized cooperatives	A	A	A	B	B	A
	Supply and marketing cooperatives	B	B	A	—	B	B
	Industrial cooperatives	B	B	A	—	B	B
	Handicraft cooperatives	B	B	A	—	B	B
Rural credit cooperatives		—	—	A	—	B	A
Rural mutual financial cooperatives		B	B	A	—	B	A

(Continued)

Organizations		Democratic features		Economic features		Social features	
		Ownership	Establishment	Main activity	Profit distribution	Institutional mission	Target problem
Township enterprises	Rural township enterprises	B	B	A	—	B	—
	Urban township enterprises	B	B	A	—	B	—
Social welfare enterprises		—	A	A	—	B	A
Public institutions		—	—	B	—	A	B
Residents committees	Urban residents committees	A	—	B	—	B	B
	Villagers' committees	A	—	B	—	B	B
Companies	State-owned enterprises	—	—	B	—	A	B
	Joint stock limited companies	—	A	A	—	—	—
	Limited liability companies	—	A	A	—	—	—
	Shareholding cooperative enterprises	A	—	A	—	—	—

Japan

Organizations		Democratic Features		Economic features		Social features	
		Ownership	Establishment	Main activity	Profit distribution	Institutional mission	Target problem
Nonprofit organizations	Specified nonprofit corporations	A	A	B	A	A	A
	Approved specified nonprofit corporations	A	B	B	A	A	A
General incorporated organizations	General incorporated associations	A	A	—	B	—	—
	General incorporated foundations	A	A	—	B	—	—
Public interest organizations	Public interest incorporated associations	A	B	B	A	A	B
	Public interest incorporated foundations	A	B	B	A	A	B
Social welfare corporations		B	B	A	B	B	A
Medical corporation	Medical corporations	B	B	A	B	B	—
	Social medical care corporations	B	B	A	B	B	A
Incorporated education institutions		B	B	A	B	B	—
Religious corporations		B	A	—	—	B	—
Juridical persons for offenders rehabilitation		B	B	A	—	B	—
Labor unions		A	A	—	—	B	B

(Continued)

Organizations		Democratic Features		Economic features		Social features	
		Ownership	Establishment	Main activity	Profit distribution	Institutional mission	Target problem
Cooperatives	Consumers' cooperatives	A	B	A	B	B	A
	Producer cooperatives (agricultural, fisheries, forest, small-medium enterprises, etc.)	B	B	A	—	B	A
Shinkin banks		B	B	A	—	B	A
Mutual aid associations (various types)		B	B	A	—	B	B
Neighborhood associations	Neighborhood associations	—	—	—	—	—	B
	Authorized neighborhood associations	A	B	B	B	B	B
Independent administrative agencies		—	—	B	—	A	B
Special corporations		—	—	B	—	A	B
Special civil corporations		—	—	B	—	B	B
Third sector organizations		—	—	A	—	B	A
Town management organizations (TMO)		—	—	A	—	B	A
Councils for the revitalization of central urban districts		—	B	A	—	B	A
Companies	Stock companies	—	A	A	—	—	—
	Limited liability companies	B	A	A	—	—	—

South Korea

Organizations		Democratic features		Economic features		Social features	
		Ownership	Establishment	Main activity	Profit distribution	Institutional mission	Target problem
Nonprofit organizations	Incorporated associations	A	B	B	B	B	B
	Incorporated foundations	A	B	B	B	B	B
Public service corporations		B	B	B	A	A	—
Social welfare corporations		B	B	A	B	B	A
Medical corporations		B	B	A	B	B	—
School juridical persons		B	B	A	B	B	—
Confucian school foundations		B	—	B	B	—	—
Local credit guarantee foundations		B	—	B	A	A	A
Nonprofit, nongovernmental organizations		—	A	B	B	A	B
Labor unions		A	A	—	B	B	B
Cooperatives	Consumer cooperatives	A	B	A	B	B	A
	Producer cooperatives (agricultural, fisheries, forest, small–medium enterprises, etc.)	B	B	A	B	B	A
	Credit unions and community credit cooperatives	B	B	A	—	B	A

(Continued)

Organizations		Democratic features		Economic features		Social features	
		Ownership	Establishment	Main activity	Profit distribution	Institutional mission	Target problem
	General cooperatives	A	A	A	—	B	A
	Social cooperatives	A	B	A	A	A	A
Mutual aid associations (various types)		B	B	A	B	B	B
Self-support enterprises		—	A	A	B	B	A
Community business organizations		B	A	A	—	B	A
Rural community enterprises		—	—	A	—	A	A
Social enterprises	Certified social enterprises	—	A	A	A	B	A
	Precertification social enterprises	—	A	A	B	B	A
Residential autonomous committees		B	—	B	—	B	B
Public agencies	Public enterprises	—	—	B	—	A	B
	Public agencies	—	—	B	—	A	B
	Local public enterprises	—	—	B	—	B	B
Companies	Stock companies	—	A	A	—	—	—
	Limited companies	—	A	A	—	—	—
	Partnership companies	B	A	A	—	—	—
	Limited partnership companies	B	A	A	—	—	—
	Limited liability companies	B	A	A	—	—	—

Appendix II

List of governing laws and regulations of the major legal entities in Northeast Asia

CHINA

- Private nonenterprise units: *Interim Regulations on Registration Administration of Private Non-enterprise Unit*
- Social organizations: *Regulation on Registration and Administration of Social Organizations*
- Foundations: *Regulation on Foundation Administration*
- Labor unions: *Trade Union Law of the People's Republic of China*
- Farmers specialized cooperatives: *Law of the People's Republic of China on Farmers' Specialized Cooperatives*
- Rural credit cooperatives: *Interim Provisions on the Administration of Rural Credit Cooperatives*
- Rural mutual financial cooperatives: *Interim Provisions on the Administration of Rural Mutual Cooperatives*
- Township enterprises: *Law of the People's Republic of China on Township Enterprises*
- Social welfare enterprises: *Interim Law of the Administration of Social Welfare Enterprises*
- Public institutions: *Interim Regulation on the Registration of Public Institutions*
- Urban residents committees: *Organic Law of Urban Residents Committee of the Peoples' Republic of China*
- Villagers' committees: *Organic Law of the Villagers' Committees of the Peoples' Republic of China*
- Companies: *Company Law of the People's Republic of China*
- Shareholding cooperative enterprises: *Interim Regulations on Shareholding Cooperative Enterprises*

*Producer cooperatives and social service organizations are based on various regulations in the different levels or bodies of governments.

JAPAN

- Specified non-profit corporations: *Law to Promote Specified Nonprofit Activities*
- General corporations: *Act on General Incorporated Associations and General Incorporated Foundations*
- Public interest corporations: *Act on Authorization of Public Interest Incorporated Associations and Public Interest Incorporated Foundation*
- Social welfare corporations: *Social Welfare Act*
- Medical corporations: *Medical Care Act*
- Incorporated education institutions: *School Education Act*
- Religious corporations: *Religious Corporations Act*
- Juridical persons for offenders rehabilitation: *Offenders Rehabilitation Services Act*
- Labor unions: *Labor Union Act*
- Consumer cooperatives: *Consumer Co-operatives Act*
- Shinkin banks: *Shinkin Bank Act*
- Neighborhood associations: *Local Autonomy Act*
- Incorporated administrative agencies: *Act on General Rules for Incorporated Administrative Agency*
- Special corporations and special civil organizations: *National Government Organization Act*
- TMO and council for the revitalization of central urban districts: *Law for the Revitalization of Central Urban Districts*
- Companies: *Companies Act*
    *Producer cooperatives and mutual aid associations are based on various regulations in the different levels or bodies of governments.

SOUTH KOREA

- Nonprofit corporations: *Civil Act*
- Public service corporations: *Act on the Establishment and Operation of Public-service Corporations*
- Social welfare corporations: *Social Welfare Services Act*
- Medical corporations: *Medical Service Act*

- School juridical persons: *Private School Act*
- Confucian school foundations: *Property of Confucian Schools Act*
- Local credit guarantee foundations: *Local Credit Guarantee Foundations Act*
- Nonprofit, nongovernmental organizations: *Assistance for Non-Profit, Non-Governmental Organizations Act*
- Labor unions: *Trade Union and Labor Relations Adjustment Act*
- Consumers cooperatives: *Consumer Cooperatives Act*
- General and Social cooperatives: *Framework Act on Cooperatives*
- Credit unions: *Credit Unions Act*
- Community credit cooperatives: *Community Credit Cooperatives Act*
- Self-support enterprises: *National Basic Living Security Act*
- Rural community enterprises: *Special Act on Quality Improvement of Life of Farmers and Fishermen and Development Promotion of Agricultural and Fishing Villages*
- Social enterprises: *Social Enterprise Promotion Act*
- Residential autonomous committees: *Local Autonomy Act*
- Residential autonomous associations: *Special Act on the Promotion of Decentralization*
- Public enterprises and agencies: *Act on the Management of Public Institutions*
- Local public enterprises: *Local Public Enterprise Act*
- Companies: *Commercial Act*

 *Producer cooperatives, mutual aid associations, community business organizations, and precertification social enterprises are based on various regulations in the different levels or bodies of governments.

Appendix III

Seoul's Sustainable Development Goals (S-SDGs), Targets, and Related Policies

1. Devote efforts to end poverty in all its forms

   1.1 Make efforts so that no Seoul citizen lives below the national minimum through the national and Seoul social security system.
   1.2 Prepare and implement a social security system customized to Seoul to ensure the basic living of the vulnerable.
   1.3 Ensure rights to utilize economic resources and opportunities to receive basic public services and financial services for Seoul citizens, in particular, the vulnerable.
   1.4 Reduce exposure and vulnerability to economic, social, and environmental shocks and disasters for the vulnerable in Seoul.

   SMG's main projects: Seoul citizens' welfare standards, Seoul basic security system

2. Improve the distribution structure between urban and rural areas and support urban agriculture for food security and nutritional balance of the citizens

   2.1 Ensure safe, nutritious, and balanced food for all citizens.
   2.2 End all forms of malnutrition, and do utmost to manage the nutritional status of the biologically vulnerable class such as children under five, adolescent girls, expectant mothers, nursing mothers, and the elderly.
   2.3 Establish a desirable distribution structure with the local agri-fishery producers, and support urban agriculture not only to encourage small-scale food production but also to cope with poverty and mental health.

   SMG's main projects: Food master plan, public meal support project for urban–rural coexistence, Nutrition Plus project

3. Ensure healthy lives and promote well-being for all citizens

3.1 Halve maternal mortality ratio from the 2016 level.

3.2 End preventable deaths, aiming to reduce under-five mortality to less than 2.5 out of 1,000 live births.

3.3 Contain outbreaks of legal infectious diseases, and establish a comprehensive treatment system for infectious diseases for a swift management and treatment in case of outbreaks.

3.4 Reduce noncommunicable diseases through prevention and treatment, and significantly cut down number of suicides through mental health and well-being enhancement policies.

3.5 Strengthen the prevention and treatment of all types of addictions including drugs, alcohol, smoking, and gambling.

3.6 Halve the number of deaths and injuries from road traffic accidents from the 2015 level.

3.7 Provide professional nursing services and comprehensive health and medical consultation and information services for infants, expectant mothers, and seniors to prevent diseases and improve health.

3.8 Raise the proportion of public health and medical services to provide Seoul Universal Health Coverage (UHC).

3.9 Strengthen health care measures for the people and regions susceptible to hazardous substances.

SMG's main projects: Outreach Community Service Center, establishing safety net for public health and medical services, expanding the Citizen Health Management Centers, suicide prevention project

4. Ensure inclusive and equitable quality education and provide a lifelong learning opportunity for all

4.1 Ensure quality care and education for preschool children.

4.2 Ensure opportunity for all Seoul citizens to receive affordable and quality technical, vocational, and college education.

4.3 Increase more opportunities for youths and adults in Seoul to obtain skills and knowledge required for employment and entrepreneurship.

4.4 Eliminate gender disparities in education and ensure equal access to education and vocational training for the vulnerable including the disabled and the poor.

4.5 No Seoul citizen should have difficulties in life due to insufficient literacy, numeracy, and basic information and communication technology skills.

4.6 Expand education on sustainable development to Seoul citizens.

SMG's main policies: Expanding national and public child care centers, running the Seoul Free Citizen College, establishing the School for All

5. Create gender-equal social environment and improve capacity of women

    5.1 End all forms of discrimination against women and girls.
    5.2 Eliminate all forms of violence against women and girls.
    5.3 Recognize and value domestic work through the provision of public services, infrastructure, and social protection policies and the promotion of shared responsibility within the household.
    5.4 Ensure equal opportunities for women to participate in the decision-making process and exercise leadership.

SMG's main projects: Creating Safe and Happy Town for Women, operating the Community Solidarity for Protecting Children and Women, planning the Seoul Comprehensive Measures for Preventing Child Abuse

6. Create a healthy and safe water-cycle city

    6.1 Replace obsolete water supply pipes and strengthen water quality analysis, enabling all Seoul citizens to safely drink Arisu.
    6.2 Improve the water quality of the Han River system by conserving the river ecosystem, managing the total water pollution load, improving the quality of discharged water, and replacing outdated sewer pipes.
    6.3 Expand rainwater management facility, and manage groundwater in a sustainable way.
    6.4 Manage the quality, quantity, and aquatic ecosystem of the Han River system in an integrated manner.
    6.5 Create Han River forests, riverside wetlands, and naturally protected shore to recover the natural properties of the Han River system.
    6.6 Support the participation of the local community to improve water management.

SMG's main projects Arisu (tap water) quality management, creating a water-cycle city (managing groundwater, reusing rainwater, etc.), creating an eco-friendly water purification plant, ensuring the safety of water quality for Han River and its tributaries

7. Ensure basic energy rights, increase share of renewable energy, and raise energy efficiency

    7.1 Ensure basic energy rights to the energy vulnerable.
    7.2 Reach 20% share of renewable energy.
    7.3 Increase energy efficiency in building and transportation sectors.

7.4 Expand support for green technology R&D including renewable energy technology sector, and promote the seven major green industries (renewable energy, LED, green cars, green buildings, green services, green IT, urban resource circulation).

SMG's main projects: Distributing one solar panel per household, promoting the Building Retrofit Program (BRP), Phase 2 of One Less Nuclear Power Plant project

8. Promote inclusive and sustainable economic growth, and increase decent jobs

8.1 Pursue a sustainable gross domestic product and gross regional domestic product growth based on win-win relationship with other regions.

8.2 Support restructuring into a high value-added industry and bolster industry diversification through creativity and innovation to continuously improve productivity.

8.3 Induce small and medium-sized enterprises to create decent jobs and actively support social enterprises.

8.4 Reduce unemployment rate, create decent jobs, and achieve equal pay for work of equal value.

8.5 Substantially reduce the proportion of unemployed youth who do not participate in education and training.

8.6 Protect labor rights for all workers including migrant workers, and promote safe and secure working environments.

8.7 Devise sustainable tourism policies that actively promote Seoul city's unique culture and products, and foster a high-quality tourism industry to contribute to more jobs.

SMG's main projects: Adoption of the worker-director system, creating the Changdong and Sangye New Economic Center, expanding the Seoul Living Wage system, Labor-valuing Seoul, creating the Seoul Start-up Hub, building the G-Valley Workers Culture and Welfare Center

9. Build eco-friendly and useful infrastructure, and encourage inclusive and sustainable industrialization

9.1 Expand quality and environmentally friendly infrastructure available for all citizens for economic activities and a happy life.

9.2 Bolster support for future technology-based manufacturing and high value-added businesses.

9.3 Increase workforce and investment on research and development, and raise the competitiveness of science and technology-based industries.

SMG's main projects: Formulating a public transportation plan focusing on railways, creating innovation cluster

10. Devote Efforts to reduce all forms of inequality

10.1 No Seoul citizen should live below the 40th percentile of the median income through national and Seoul's social security system.
10.2 Empower and promote the social, economic, and political inclusion of all.
10.3 Improve discriminatory laws, policies, and practices to ensure equal opportunity.
10.4 Achieve high level of equality through fiscal, wage, and social protection policies.

SMG's main projects: Fostering Special Social Economic Zones, establishing an integrated support system for social economy at autonomous Gu districts

11. Make cities inclusive, safe, and sustainable for all citizens

11.1 Come up with a minimum living standard for Seoul citizens to improve the environment in low-income neighborhoods and obsolete residential areas, and ensure housing rights to all citizens by providing more affordable housing.
11.2 Establish safe, convenient, and sustainable transportation systems for all citizens by linking with the capital region transportation system.
11.3 Formulate and implement socially integrative urban planning that expands citizen participation, includes the socially disadvantaged, and ensures diversity.
11.4 Protect the history and culture, and natural heritage of Seoul, create a city in which nature, history, culture, and the future coexist, and promote cultural diversity.
11.5 Strengthen disaster relief system for citizens who are vulnerable to disasters, such as the poor, children, women, seniors, and the disabled to create a safe city Seoul responding to large-scale disasters.
11.6 Reduce fine dust concentrations by 70% from the 2016 level.
11.7 Minimize areas that do not have access to parks and green areas, and ensure universal access to public green spaces for women, children, seniors, and the disabled.

11.8 Strengthen economic, social, and environmental links between Seoul and metropolitan areas for a balanced development in the capital region.

SMG's main projects: Expanding public rental housing, bike-sharing system, carrying out traditional culture discovery support project, establishing an integrated preservation and management system for designated cultural properties of Seoul, planning fine dust reduction measures by emission sources.

12. Support sustainable consumption and production patterns to become a way of life

12.1 Achieve a virtuous cycle of economic growth through environmental improvement, and devise a comprehensive measure for sustainable consumption and production.

12.2 Achieve the sustainable management and efficient use of natural resources.

12.3 Halve per capita food waste from the 2016 level.

12.4 Reduce the use of hazardous chemical substances and manage hazardous waste in a scientific and environmentally friendly manner to minimize the negative impact on the health of the citizens and the environment.

12.5 Substantially reduce waste generation through prevention, reduction, recycling, and reuse.

12.6 Urge and support companies within Seoul to publish sustainable management reports.

12.7 Promote citizens' purchase of eco-friendly products, and promote sustainable public procurement practices such as purchasing eco-friendly products by government agencies.

12.8 Ensure that all citizens have the relevant information and awareness for sustainable development and lifestyles in harmony with nature.

12.9 Review taxation and subsidy schemes that encourage environmentally unfriendly consumption and production, and improve them continuously and gradually

SMG's main projects: Strengthening cooperation and networking in and outside Korea on shared economy, establishing the Seoul Upcycling Plaza, pursuing zero direct landfilling of domestic waste

13. Create an exemplary city in coping with climate change

13.1 Identify risks related to climate change early on and come up with measures, and strengthen ability to swiftly recover in case of natural disasters.

13.2 Integrate climate change measures into SMG's policies, strategies, and planning.

13.3 Raise awareness on climate change response by expanding the scope of people subject to climate change education, and strengthen local capacity by expanding autonomous districts cooperation and community support programs.

13.4 Integrate climate change measures into SMG's policies, strategies, and planning.

13.5 Reduce greenhouse gas emissions by 40% from the 2005 level and integrate greenhouse gas mitigation and adaptation policies.

13.6 Participate in international organizations' climate change mechanism, form partnerships to run climate change-related programs, and strengthen international cooperation

SMG's main projects: Phase 2 of One Less Nuclear Power Plant-Seoul Sustainable Energy Action Plan, promoting the Energy Dream Center, strengthening international cooperation on climate change

14. Conserve the marine ecosystem through recovering natural properties of the Han River

14.1 Prevent and drastically reduce pollution from waste and green algae in the Han River system.

14.2 Strengthen Han River's ecological health to improve the resilience of the marine ecosystem including that of the West Sea.

14.3 Cooperate with Gyeonggi-do and Incheon to raise the research capacity and scientific knowledge on the impacts of Han River on the marine ecosystem.

SMG's main projects: Implementing the green algae alert system, recovering the Han River ecosystem, creating the Han River forests

15. Promote biodiversity through conserving and recovering the natural ecosystem within the city

15.1 Manage forests, mountains, wetlands, and streams in Seoul in a healthy manner and ensure sustainable use of the ecosystem service.

15.2 Sustainably manage mountains and forests in Seoul by planting native tree species in damaged parts of the forest, and strengthening forest fire prevention to protect trees.

15.3 Increase the nature and ecological protection areas such as the Ecological Landscape Conservation Area, Wildlife Protection Area, and Migratory Bird Protection Area by 17% from the 2014 level.

15.4 Improve biodiversity by creating small-scale biotops, restoring species, and expanding habitats.

15.5 Strengthen the management of the influx of exotic species and illegal releases, and control the cause of the spread of invasive alien species.

15.6 Integrate the values of biotops and biodiversity into SMG's planning and development process.

SMG's main projects: Strategies to improve biodiversity

16. Build transparent and inclusive institutions for a just Seoul

16.1 Significantly reduce all forms of violence and violent crimes stemming from it.

16.2 Significantly reduce all forms of crimes against children including abuse and exploitation.

16.3 Set up social, cultural, and physical environments that ensure the human rights of the citizens, and pursue all municipal administration from a human rights perspective.

16.4 Significantly strengthen the recovery of stolen assets and the taxation on habitual tax delinquents and tax evaders.

16.5 Eradicate all forms of corruption and bribery.

16.6 Expand transparent and accountable administration and institutions.

16.7 Realize resident participatory administration to strengthen citizen participation in the whole policy process.

16.8 Enhance all citizens' information accessibility and ensure access to information for the information vulnerable.

16.9 Actively support each autonomous district of Seoul to realize sustainable development.

SMG's main projects: Expanding resident participatory budgeting, pursuing the Human Rights City, Seoul, planning Seoul's Comprehensive Measures on Preventing Child Abuse, establishing citizen-focused platform for utilizing big data, promoting town communities

17. Strengthen exchange and cooperation with foreign cities as a global leader of sustainable development

17.1 Bolster exchange and cooperation on science, technology, and innovation with foreign cities and strengthen knowledge and policy sharing based on mutual agreement.

17.2 Spread the achievements of the S-SDGs to developing countries and support them to implement the SDGs.

17.3 Share the achievements of the S-SDG with Korean and foreign cities and strengthen global leadership for a sustainable development.

17.4 Promote partnerships among Seoul Metropolitan Government, civil societies, and companies to implement sustainable development.

17.5 Devise and support ODA programs for the sustainable development of cities in developing countries

SMG's main projects: Introducing outstanding policies to foreign cities, pursuing a sustainable and shared city, inviting international organizations and carrying out exchange and cooperation

Source: Seoul Metropolitan Government brochure "Seoul Sustainable Development Goals (SDGs) 2030: 17 Ways to Change Seoul". January 2018. http://gov.seoul.go.kr/archives/98727

S-SDGS, TARGETS, AND RELATED POLICIES

1. Devote efforts to end poverty in all its forms

1.1 Make efforts so that no Seoul citizen lives below the national minimum through the national and Seoul social security system.

1.2 Prepare and implement a social security system customized to Seoul to ensure the basic living of the vulnerable.

1.3 Ensure rights to utilize economic resources and opportunities to receive basic public services and financial services for Seoul citizens, in particular, the vulnerable.

1.4 Reduce exposure and vulnerability to economic, social, and environmental shocks and disasters for the vulnerable in Seoul.

SMG's main projects: Seoul citizens' welfare standards, Seoul basic security system

2. Improve the distribution structure between urban and rural areas and support urban agriculture for food security and nutritional balance of the citizens

2.1 Ensure safe, nutritious, and balanced food for all citizens.

2.2 End all forms of malnutrition, and do utmost to manage the nutritional status of the biologically vulnerable class such as children under five, adolescent girls, expectant mothers, nursing mothers, and the elderly.

2.3 Establish a desirable distribution structure with the local agri-fishery producers, and support urban agriculture not only to encourage small-scale food production but also to cope with poverty and mental health.

SMG's main projects: Food master plan, public meal support project for urban-rural coexistence, Nutrition Plus project

3. Ensure healthy lives and promote well-being for all citizens

3.1 Halve maternal mortality ratio from the 2016 level.

3.2 End preventable deaths, aiming to reduce under-five mortality to less than 2.5 out of 1,000 live births.

3.3 Contain outbreaks of legal infectious diseases, and establish a comprehensive treatment system for infectious diseases for a swift management and treatment in case of outbreaks.

3.4 Reduce noncommunicable diseases through prevention and treatment, and significantly cut down number of suicides through mental health and well-being enhancement policies.

3.5 Strengthen the prevention and treatment of all types of addictions including drugs, alcohol, smoking, and gambling.

3.6 Halve the number of deaths and injuries from road traffic accidents from the 2015 level.

3.7 Provide professional nursing services and comprehensive health and medical consultation and information services for infants, expectant mothers, and seniors to prevent diseases and improve health.

3.8 Raise the proportion of public health and medical services to provide Seoul UHC.

3.9 Strengthen health care measures for the people and regions susceptible to hazardous substances.

SMG's main projects: Outreach Community Service Center, establishing safety net for public health and medical services, expanding the Citizen Health Management Centers, suicide prevention project

4. Ensure inclusive and equitable quality education and provide a lifelong learning opportunity for all

4.1 Ensure quality care and education for preschool children.

4.2 Ensure opportunity for all Seoul citizens to receive affordable and quality technical, vocational, and college education.

4.3 Increase more opportunities for youths and adults in Seoul to obtain skills and knowledge required for employment and entrepreneurship.

4.4 Eliminate gender disparities in education and ensure equal access to education and vocational training for the vulnerable including the disabled and the poor.

4.5 No Seoul citizen should have difficulties in life due to insufficient literacy, numeracy, and basic information and communication technology skills.

4.6 Expand education on sustainable development to Seoul citizens.

SMG's main policies: Expanding national and public child care centers, running the Seoul Free Citizen College, establishing the School for All

5. Create gender-equal social environment and improve capacity of women

5.1 End all forms of discrimination against women and girls.

5.2 Eliminate all forms of violence against women and girls.

5.3 Recognize and value domestic work through the provision of public services, infrastructure, and social protection policies and the promotion of shared responsibility within the household.

5.4 Ensure equal opportunities for women to participate in the decision-making process and exercise leadership.

SMG's main projects: Creating Safe and Happy Town for Women, operating the Community Solidarity for Protecting Children and Women, planning the Seoul Comprehensive Measures for Preventing Child Abuse

6. Create a healthy and safe water-cycle city

6.1 Replace obsolete water supply pipes and strengthen water quality analysis, enabling all Seoul citizens to safely drink Arisu.

6.2 Improve the water quality of the Han River system by conserving the river ecosystem, managing the total water pollution load, improving the quality of discharged water, and replacing outdated sewer pipes.

6.3 Expand rainwater management facility, and manage groundwater in a sustainable way.

6.4 Manage the quality, quantity, and aquatic ecosystem of the Han River system in an integrated manner.

6.5 Create Han River forests, riverside wetlands, and naturally protected shore to recover the natural properties of the Han River system.

6.6 Support the participation of the local community to improve water management.

SMG's main projects Arisu (tap water) quality management, creating a water-cycle city (managing groundwater, reusing rainwater, etc.), creating an eco-friendly water purification plant, ensuring the safety of water quality for Han River and its tributaries

7. Ensure basic energy rights, increase share of renewable energy, and raise energy efficiency

7.1 Ensure basic energy rights to the energy vulnerable.

7.2 Reach 20% share of renewable energy.

7.3 Increase energy efficiency in building and transportation sectors.

7.4 Expand support for green technology R&D including renewable energy technology sector, and promote the seven major green industries (renewable energy, LED, green cars, green buildings, green services, green IT, urban resource circulation).

SMG's main projects: Distributing one solar panel per household, promoting the Building Retrofit Program (BRP), Phase 2 of One Less Nuclear Power Plant project

8. Promote inclusive and sustainable economic growth, and increase decent jobs

8.1 Pursue a sustainable gross domestic product and gross regional domestic product growth based on win-win relationship with other regions.

8.2 Support restructuring into a high value-added industry and bolster industry diversification through creativity and innovation to continuously improve productivity.

8.3 Induce small- and medium-sized enterprises to create decent jobs and actively support social enterprises.

8.4 Reduce unemployment rate, create decent jobs, and achieve equal pay for work of equal value.

8.5 Substantially reduce the proportion of unemployed youth who do not participate in education and training.

8.6 Protect labor rights for all workers including migrant workers, and promote safe and secure working environments.

8.7 Devise sustainable tourism policies that actively promote Seoul city's unique culture and products, and foster a high-quality tourism industry to contribute to more jobs.

SMG's main projects: Adoption of the worker-director system, creating the Changdong and Sangye New Economic Center, expanding the Seoul Living Wage system, Labor-valuing Seoul, creating the Seoul Start-up Hub, building the G-Valley Workers Culture and Welfare Center

9. Build eco-friendly and useful infrastructure, and encourage inclusive and sustainable industrialization

9.1 Expand quality and environmentally friendly infrastructure available for all citizens for economic activities and a happy life.

9.2 Bolster support for future technology-based manufacturing and high value-added businesses.

9.3 Increase workforce and investment on research and development, and raise the competitiveness of science and technology-based industries.

SMG's main projects: Formulating a public transportation plan focusing on railways, creating innovation cluster

10. Devote efforts to reduce all forms of inequality

10.1 No Seoul citizen should live below the 40th percentile of the median income through national and Seoul's social security system.

10.2 Empower and promote the social, economic, and political inclusion of all.

10.3 Improve discriminatory laws, policies, and practices to ensure equal opportunity.

10.4 Achieve high level of equality through fiscal, wage, and social protection policies.

SMG's main projects: Fostering Special Social Economic Zones, establishing an integrated support system for SE at autonomous Gu districts

11. Make cities inclusive, safe, and sustainable for all citizens

11.1 Come up with a minimum living standard for Seoul citizens to improve the environment in low-income neighborhoods and obsolete residential areas, and ensure housing rights to all citizens by providing more afford-able housing.

11.2 Establish safe, convenient, and sustainable transportation systems for all citizens by linking with the capital region transportation system.

11.3 Formulate and implement socially integrative urban planning that expands citizen participation, includes the socially disadvantaged, and ensures diversity.

11.4 Protect the history and culture, and natural heritage of Seoul, create a city in which nature, history, culture, and the future coexist, and promote cultural diversity.

11.5 Strengthen disaster relief system for citizens who are vulnerable to disasters, such as the poor, children, women, seniors, and the disabled to create a safe city Seoul responding to large-scale disasters.

11.6 Reduce fine dust concentrations by 70% from the 2016 level.

11.7 Minimize areas that do not have access to parks and green areas, and ensure universal access to public green spaces for women, children, seniors, and the disabled.

11.8 Strengthen economic, social, and environmental links between Seoul and metropolitan areas for a balanced development in the capital region.

SMG's main projects: Expanding public rental housing, bike-sharing system, carrying out traditional culture discovery support project, establishing an integrated preservation and management system for designated cultural prop-erties of Seoul, planning fine dust reduction measures by emission sources.

12. Support sustainable consumption and production patterns to become a way of life

12.1 Achieve a virtuous cycle of economic growth through environmental improvement, and devise a comprehensive measure for sustainable con-sumption and production.

12.2 Achieve the sustainable management and efficient use of natural resources.

12.3 Halve per capita food waste from the 2016 level.

12.4 Reduce the use of hazardous chemical substances and manage hazardous waste in a scientific and environmentally friendly manner to minimize the negative impact on the health of the citizens and the environment.

12.5 Substantially reduce waste generation through prevention, reduction, recycling, and reuse.

12.6 Urge and support companies within Seoul to publish sustainable man-agement reports.

12.7 Promote citizens' purchase of eco-friendly products, and promote sus-tainable public procurement practices such as purchasing eco-friendly products by government agencies.

12.8 Ensure that all citizens have the relevant information and awareness for sustainable development and lifestyles in harmony with nature.

12.9 Review taxation and subsidy schemes that encourage environmentally unfriendly consumption and production, and improve them continuously and gradually.

SMG's main projects: Strengthening cooperation and networking in and outside Korea on shared economy, establishing the Seoul Upcycling Plaza, pursuing zero direct landfilling of domestic waste

13. Create an exemplary city in coping with climate change

13.1 Identify risks related to climate change early on and come up with measures, and strengthen ability to swiftly recover in case of natural disasters.

13.2 Integrate climate change measures into SMG's policies, strategies, and planning.

13.3 Raise awareness on climate change response by expanding the scope of people subject to climate change education, and strengthen local capacity by expanding autonomous districts cooperation and community support programs.

13.4 Integrate climate change measures into SMG's policies, strategies, and planning.

13.5 Reduce greenhouse gas emissions by 40% from the 2005 level and integrate greenhouse gas mitigation and adaptation policies.

13.6 Participate in international organizations' climate change mechanism, form partnerships to run climate change-related programs, and strengthen international cooperation

SMG's main projects: Phase 2 of One Less Nuclear Power Plant-Seoul Sustainable Energy Action Plan, promoting the Energy Dream Center, strengthening international cooperation on climate change

14. Conserve the marine ecosystem through recovering natural properties of the Han River

14.1 Prevent and drastically reduce pollution from waste and green algae in the Han River system.

14.2 Strengthen Han River's ecological health to improve the resilience of the marine ecosystem including that of the West Sea.

14.3 Cooperate with Gyeonggi-do and Incheon to raise the research capacity and scientific knowledge on the impacts of Han River on the marine ecosystem.

SMG's main projects: Implementing the green algae alert system, recovering the Han River ecosystem, creating the Han River forests

15. Promote biodiversity through conserving and recovering the natural ecosystem within the city

15.1 Manage forests, mountains, wetlands, and streams in Seoul in a healthy manner and ensure sustainable use of the ecosystem service.

15.2 Sustainably manage mountains and forests in Seoul by planting native tree species in damaged parts of the forest, and strengthening forest fire prevention to protect trees.

15.3 Increase the nature and ecological protection areas such as the Ecological Landscape Conservation Area, Wildlife Protection Area, and Migratory Bird Protection Area by 17% from the 2014 level.

15.4 Improve biodiversity by creating small-scale biotops, restoring species, and expanding habitats.

15.5 Strengthen the management of the influx of exotic species and illegal releases, and control the cause of the spread of invasive alien species.

15.6 Integrate the values of biotops and biodiversity into SMG's planning and development process.

SMG's main projects: Strategies to improve biodiversity

16. Build transparent and inclusive institutions for a just Seoul

16.1 Significantly reduce all forms of violence and violent crimes stemming from it.

16.2 Significantly reduce all forms of crimes against children including abuse and exploitation.

16.3 Set up social, cultural, and physical environments that ensure the human rights of the citizens, and pursue all municipal administration from a human rights perspective.

16.4 Significantly strengthen the recovery of stolen assets and the taxation on habitual tax delinquents and tax evaders.

16.5 Eradicate all forms of corruption and bribery.

16.6 Expand transparent and accountable administration and institutions.

16.7 Realize resident participatory administration to strengthen citizen participation in the whole policy process.

16.8 Enhance all citizens' information accessibility and ensure access to information for the information vulnerable.

16.9 Actively support each autonomous District of Seoul to realize sustainable development.

SMG's main projects: Expanding resident participatory budgeting, pursuing the Human Rights City, Seoul, planning Seoul's Comprehensive Measures on Preventing Child Abuse, establishing citizen-focused platform for utilizing big data, promoting town communities

17. Strengthen exchange and cooperation with foreign cities as a global leader of sustainable development

17.1 Bolster exchange and cooperation on science, technology, and innovation with foreign cities and strengthen knowledge and policy sharing based on mutual agreement.

17.2 Spread the achievements of the S-SDGs to developing countries and support them to implement the SDGs.

17.3 Share the achievements of the S-SDG with Korean and foreign cities and strengthen global leadership for a sustainable development.

17.4 Promote partnerships among Seoul Metropolitan Government, civil societies, and companies to implement sustainable development.

17.5 Devise and support ODA programs for the sustainable development of cities in developing countries

SMG's main projects: Introducing outstanding policies to foreign cities, pursuing a sustainable and shared city, inviting international organizations, and carrying out exchange and cooperation

Source: Seoul Metropolitan Government brochure "Seoul Sustainable Development Goals (SDGs) 2030: 17 Ways to Change Seoul." January 2018. http://gov.seoul.go.kr/archives/98727

Index

About the Editors and Contributors

Euiyoung Kim is a professor of political science and international relations at Seoul National University (SNU). He is also the director of the Center for Social Innovation Education and Research at SNU and serves as a commissioner of Seoul Democracy Commission. He received his Bachelor of Political Science degree from Seoul National University in 1984 and his MA and PhD in political science from University of Michigan, Ann Arbor in 1997. His research concentrates on Korean politics, particularly focusing on citizen politics and governance issues. Professor Kim was the president of Korean Political Science Association in 2018. He was also the secretary general of World Civic Forum, a joint initiative of UN DESA and Kyung Hee University.

Hiroki Miura is a senior researcher of the Center for Social Innovation Education and Research and Education, Seoul National University, South Korea. He received his PhD in political science from Kyung Hee University in 2009. His PhD dissertation won the Excellent Dissertation Award from the Korean Political Science Association. His research topics include democratic governance and civic empowerment, social resilience and ecosystem, and political economy of coevolution. As an academic expert, he has engaged in policy formation process of national and various local governments in South Korea on these issues. He is also teaching NGO and citizen politics at Kyung Hee University and Civil Society and Global Governance at Kyung Hee Cyber University.

* * *

Bipasha Baruah is a tenured full professor and the Canada Research Chair in Global Women's Issues at Western University. She earned a PhD in environmental studies from York University, Toronto, in 2005. She conducts interdisciplinary research on gender, economy, environment and development; and social, political, and economic inequality. Dr. Baruah serves frequently as an expert reviewer, consultant, and advisor to international development and environmental protection organizations. The Royal Society of Canada named Dr. Baruah to The College of New Scholars, Artists and Scientists in 2015. "The College" is Canada's only national system of multi-disciplinary recognition for the emerging generation of Canadian intellectual leadership. Every year, it names individuals who have made exceptional professional contributions to Canada and the world within fifteen years of completing their doctorates.

Siqi Chen received her BA in sociology and math from Skidmore College. She is currently pursuing her MA in statistics at Columbia University.

Gibin Hong is a political economist working on the institutions and policies of alternative socio-economic system, focusing on P2P/Commons, psybernetics, and social and solidarity economy. He has translated Karl Polanyi's *The Great Transformation* into Korean.

Xiaoshuo Hou is an associate professor of sociology and Asian studies at Skidmore College. She is the inaugural holder of the Frances Young Tang '61 Chair in Chinese studies. She received her PhD in sociology from Boston University. Her research interests include development sociology and economic sociology with a particular focus on China. She is the author of *Community Capitalism in China: The State, The Market, and Collectivism* (2013) and one of the co-editors of the *Wiley-Blackwell Encyclopedia of Race, Ethnicity, and Nationalism* (2016). She is currently working on a project on the informal economy and the emerging precariat in two Chinese migrant communities.

Denison Jayasooria is an associate fellow and former Practice Professor for Public Advocacy at the Institute of Ethnic Studies (KITA), National University of Malaysia (UKM). He holds a PhD in sociology from Oxford Brookes University, UK. He is the chair of the Asian Solidarity Economy Council and a board member of Intercontinental Network for the Promotion of Social Solidarity Economy (RIPESS) which is a global grassroots movement of social and solidarity economy (SSE) practitioners and researchers. RIPESS has consultative status with ECOSOC and is an active observer member of the UN Task Force on SSE. He is also a member of the editorial committee on the SSE Encyclopedia under United Nations Research Institute for Social Development (UNRISD).

Taekyoon Kim is a professor of international development and vice-dean for academic affairs of the Graduate School of International Studies at Seoul National University. He has BA in sociology from Seoul National University, MA in international relations from the University of Oxford, and DPhil in social policy from the University of Oxford and another PhD in international relations from Johns Hopkins School of Advanced International Studies. He was a Fulbright Wilson Fellow at the Woodrow Wilson International Center for Scholars and visiting professor at the University of Tübingen, Lingnan University, and the University of Paris IV. His research interests focus on international development, international political sociology, global governance, Global South studies, and South-South and triangular cooperation. His main research publications appear at *Oxford Development Studies*, *Journal of Democracy*, *Global Governance*, *International Relations of the Asia-Pacific*, *International Sociology*, and so on.

Eun Sun Lee is an assistant professor in Department of Economics at Gyeongnam National University of Science and Technology (GNTECH), where she teaches courses on social economy. She received BA in economics from Kyung Hee University, and MA and PhD degrees in public administration from Korea University. Both of her master's and doctoral dissertations are on social enterprise. Before joining GNTECH, she was a postdoctoral researcher at the Community Wellbeing Research Center, Seoul National University, and in Graduate School of Governance at Sungkyunkwan University. Her research interests focus on social economy, civil society, and governance.

Marguerite Mendell is distinguished professor emerita, School of Community and Public Affairs, and director of the Karl Polanyi Institute of Political Economy, Concordia University, Montreal. Her research interests and publications include the social and solidarity economy, processes of economic democratization, social finance, and the life and work of Karl Polanyi.

Masanari Sakurai is currently a professor at the Faculty of Policy Science at Ritsumeikan University in Japan. He received his PhD in policy science from the Ritsumeikan University in 2003. During 2013–2014 he was a visiting professor at Geography Department of the University of Toronto. He is an author of the book *Globalizing Welfare: An Evolving Asian-European Dialogue* (2019). He is a board member of Japan NPO research association between 2008 and 2010 and from 2016. He was the organizing committee chief of the International Conference on Social Enterprise in Asia (ICSEA) 5th conference in 2018.

Hyuk-Sang Sohn is a professor of Graduate School of Public Governance and Civic Engagement and the director of Center for International Development Cooperation at Kyung Hee University. He received BA, MA, and PhD in political Science from Seoul National University, University of Pennsylvania, and Kyung Hee University, respectively. His research interests are the political economy of development, international development cooperation, development NGOs, and development evaluation. He was awarded *the Outstanding Academic Achievement* for publishing "Do Different Implementing Partnerships Lead to Different Project Outcomes? Evidence from the World Bank Project-Level Evaluation Data," in *World Development* by Korean Political Science Association in 2017.

Ilcheong Yi is a senior research coordinator at UNRISD. He is in charge of Social and Solidarity Programme and UNTFSSE Knowledge Hub. He is currently supervising several projects directly related to SSE, such as Sustainable Development Performance Indicators, SSE Statistics, and Guidelines on public policy for SSE at the city and provincial levels. He joined UNRISD in October 2008. Born in the Republic of Korea, he was trained as a political scientist (BA and MA from the Department of Political Science, Seoul National University) and as a social policy analyst (DPhil from Oxford University). His specialization is in the issues of poverty, social policy, labor policy, social economy, and historical analysis of the economic and social development process. Prior to joining UNRISD, Ilcheong Yi was an associate professor at Kyushu University, Japan (2004–2008), Korea Foundation visiting professor in the Department of East Asian Studies, University of Malaya, Malaysia (2003–2004), and visiting research fellow at the Stein Rokkan Centre, University of Bergen, Norway (2002–2003). He has fulfilled a number of consultant, field researcher, and project development roles for international and national organizations, including the ILO, UNRISD, JBIC, and KOICA.

www.ingramcontent.com/pod-product-compliance
Lightning Source LLC
Chambersburg PA
CBHW050640280326
41932CB00015B/2722